Visual Insight
Paint Shop Pro 6 Keyboard Shortcuts

File Menu	Alt+F
New	Ctrl+N
Open	Ctrl+O
Browse	Ctrl+B
Save	Ctrl+S
Save As	F12
Save Copy As	Ctrl+F12
Delete	Ctrl+Delete
Print	Ctrl+P

Edit Menu	Alt+E
Undo	Ctrl+Z
Redo	Ctrl+Alt+Z
Command History	Shift+Ctrl+Z
Cut	Ctrl+X
Copy	Ctrl+C
Copy Merged	Shift+Ctrl+C
Paste:	
As New Image	Ctrl+V
As New Layer	Ctrl+L
As New Selection	Ctrl+E
As Transparent Selection	Shift+Ctrl+E
Into Selection	Shift+Ctrl+L
Clear	Delete

View Menu	Alt+V
Full Screen Edit	Shift+A
Full Screen Preview	Shift+Ctrl+A
Normal Viewing	Ctrl+Alt+N
Image Info	Shift+I
Grid	Ctrl+Alt+G

Image Menu	Alt+I
Flip	Ctrl+I
Mirror	Ctrl+M
Rotate	Ctrl+R
Crop To Selection	Shift+R
Resize	Shift+S

Colors Menu	Alt+C
Adjust:	
Brightness/Contrast	Shift+B
Gamma Correction	Shift+G
Highlight/Midtone/Shadow	Shift+M
Hue/Saturation/Lightness	Shift+H
Red/Green/Blue	Shift+U

Colors Menu (continued)	Alt+C
Colorize	Shift+L
Histogram:	
Equalize	Shift+E
Stretch	Shift+T
Posterize	Shift+Z
Edit Palette	Shift+P
Load Palette	Shift+O
Set Palette Transparency	Shift+Ctrl+V
View Palette Transparency	Shift+V
Decrease Color Depth:	
2 colors (1-bit)	Shift+Ctrl+1
16 colors (4-bit)	Shift+Ctrl+2
256 colors (8-bit)	Shift+Ctrl+3
32K colors (24-bit)	Shift+Ctrl+4
64K colors (24-bit)	Shift+Ctrl+5
X colors (4/8 bit)	Shift+Ctrl+6
Increase Color Depth:	
16 colors (4-bit)	Shift+Ctrl+8
256 colors (8-bit)	Shift+Ctrl+9
16.7M colors (24-bit)	Shift+Ctrl+0

Layers Menu	Alt+L
Select Current Layer	Ctrl+layer number

Selections Menu	Alt+S
Select All	Ctrl+A
Select None	Ctrl+D
From Mask	Shift+Ctrl+S
Invert	Shift+Ctrl+I
Modify:	
Feather	Ctrl+H
Transparent Color	Ctrl+T
Hide Selection Marquee	Shift+Ctrl+M
Promote To Layer	Shift+Ctrl+P
Float	Ctrl+F
Defloat	Shift+Ctrl+F

Mask Menu	Alt+M
Hide All	Shift+Y
Invert	Shift+K
Edit	Ctrl+K
View Mask	Ctrl+Alt+V

Capture Menu	Alt+A
Start	Shift+C

Window Menu	**Alt+W**
New Window	Shift+W
Duplicate	Shift+D
Fit To Window	Ctrl+W

Palette, Window, Or Bar *(display or hide)*

Tools Options Palette	o
Color Palette	c
Layer Palette	l
Tool Palette	p
Histogram Window	h
Toolbar	t
View All Tools And Windows	Shift+Ctrl+T
Minimize PSP To Start Bar	Shift+C

Tools And Brushes

Zoom (Magnify)	g
Deform	d
Crop	r
Mover	v
Selection	s
Freehand Selection	a
Magic Wand Selection	m
Eye Dropper	y
Paintbrush	b
Clone	n
Color Replacer	, (comma)
Retouch	z
Eraser	e
Picture Tube	. (period)
Airbrush	u
Flood Fill	f
Text	x
Line	i
Shape	/
Vector Object Selection	q

Node Commands

Alternate Edit and Drawing Modes	Ctrl+E

Edit Submenu:

Undo	Ctrl+Z
Redo	Ctrl+Alt+Z
Copy	Ctrl+C
Paste	Ctrl+V
Delete	Delete
Select All	Ctrl+A
Select None	Ctrl+D
Join Select	Ctrl+J
Break	Ctrl+K

Node Commands *(continued)*

Close	Shift+Ctrl+C
Reverse	Ctrl+R
Reverse Path	Shift+Ctrl+R

Node Type Submenu:

Asymmetric	Shift+Ctrl+S
Symmetric	Ctrl+S
Cusp	Ctrl+X
Smooth/Tangent	Ctrl+T
Convert To Line	Ctrl+L
Line Before	Ctrl+B
Line After	Ctrl+F
Curve Before	Ctrl+1
Curve After	Ctrl+2
Refresh	F5
Quit	Ctrl+Q

Browser

File|Browse (When Browser Is Not Open)	Ctrl+B
File|New Folder (When Browser Is Opened)	Ctrl+B
File|Update Thumbnails	F5
File|Print	Ctrl+P
Edit|Select All	Ctrl+A
Edit|Select None	Ctrl+D
View|Refresh Tree	Ctrl+F5
Find|File Name	Alt+F3 or Ctrl+F
Find|Repeat Find	F3
ImageFile|Copy To	Ctrl+Y
ImageFile|Delete	Ctrl+Delete
ImageFile|Move To	Ctrl+M
ImageFile|Rename	Ctrl+R
ImageFile|Information	Shift+I or Alt+Enter
ImageFile|Open	Enter
Window|Fit To Thumbnails	Ctrl+W
Next Pane	F6 or Shift+Tab
Previous Pane	Shift+F6

PAINT SHOP PRO 6
Visual Insight

Ramona Pruitt

Joshua Pruitt

Paint Shop Pro 6 Visual Insight
© 2000 The Coriolis Group. All Rights Reserved.

The Coriolis Group, LLC
14455 North Hayden Road, Suite 220
Scottsdale, Arizona 85260

480/483-0192
FAX: 480/483-0193
http://www.coriolis.com

Library of Congress Cataloging-In-Publication Data
Pruit, Ramona.
Paint Shop Pro 6 visual insight/ by Ramona Pruitt and Joshua Pruitt.
    p. cm
ISBN 1-57610-525-3
    1. Computer graphics. 2. Paint shop pro.
I. Pruitt, Joshua. II. Title.
T385.P875 2000
006.6'869--dc21   99-049157
                                    CIP

President, CEO
Keith Weiskamp

Publisher
Steve Sayre

Marketing Specialist
Beth Kohler

Project Editor
Melissa D. Olson

Technical Reviewer
Joyce Evans

Production Coordinator
Meg E. Turecek

Cover Designer
Jody Winkler

Layout Designer
April Nielsen

Printed in the United States of America
10 9 8 7 6 5 4 3

CORIOLIS

We graciously dedicate this book to you, our readers, whether you are aspiring or already accomplished graphic artists. It is our fondest wish that this book will help to bring you closer to your artistic goals and make your digital graphics experiences productive and enjoyable.

❧

About The Authors

A writer and digital graphic artist, **Ramona Pruitt** resides in Nashville, Tennessee. She is co-owner of Mid-TN Network, a Web hosting firm that provides hosting and graphic design services to people and businesses in the Nashville area. She has enjoyed a multifaceted career history, but once she had her first glimpse into the realm of computer graphics, she knew that it was something she wanted to pursue, and her hobby soon became her business. Her other interests include reading, sewing and fashion design, hiking, classic and blues rock music, and spending quality time with a beautiful German shepherd. She welcomes email addressed to **wildflower@mid-tn.com**.

Also living in Nashville, Tennessee, **Joshua Pruitt** is a systems administrator and instructor at a local college, where he teaches Unix essentials and other computer classes. He is co-owner and an integral part of the Web design team at Mid-TN Network and also does freelance networking and consulting for small businesses. With business partner, Ramona, he has written one other computer graphics book, *Teach Yourself GIMP in 24 Hours* (Sams). His interests include following the politics of the tech industry and tinkering with computers old and new. You can email him at **joshua@mid-tn.com**.

Acknowledgments

It's mind-boggling when you realize just how many people are involved in bringing a project such as this one to fruition. We'd like to thank, first of all, the creators of Paint Shop Pro, and all the folks at JASC, for providing such a wonderful, inspiring, and truly amazing program. Next we'd like to thank David Fugate, our agent at Waterside Productions, for getting us the gig and for always being so courteous and helpful. A special thanks goes to the two editors at The Coriolis Group who were very involved in the project, Mariann Barsolo and Melissa Olson, and of course, to all the rest of the people at Coriolis who worked behind the scenes to help bring the book to completion, including Meg Turecek, April Nielsen, and Jody Winkler.

Contents At A Glance

Table Of Contents

Introduction

When learning to use any application, especially one as robust as Paint Shop Pro 6, sometimes the best thing to do is to dive right in, push every button, and try out new things. This book was written to help you do just that—by taking you through the program step-by-step in a visually oriented, interactive fashion. We are confident that, as you make your way through the book, you will not only gain a basic feel for the software, but with a little practice and effort, you may just find yourself becoming a true Paint Shop Pro guru.

The Book's Structure

This book is divided into two sections. The first section, which contains Chapters 1 through 8, focuses primarily on the basics of the program. These chapters introduce the fundamental tools and procedures used in the graphics-creation process, beginning with the essentials and moving on to introduce increasingly advanced topics and material, including specialty features exclusive to the program.

The second section, which encompasses Chapters 9 through 14, includes hands-on projects through which you will be lead fully and systematically. By performing the steps as outlined, you will be able to examine firsthand the steps and concepts required to create a particular effect or look.

The books in the Visual Insight series are formatted in such a way as to lead you visually through the software program, with the added benefit of enabling you to flip through the pages and see at a glance the tasks that can be accomplished and how to accomplish them in a quick and easy fashion.

How To Use This Book

The book can be approached in several different ways, according to your skill level:

- If you are new to the world of digital graphics, you'll probably get the most out of this book by taking the progressive path—start on page 1 and follow diligently through the chapters in order from the beginning to the end.

- If you already have a base knowledge of graphics but you're not familiar with Paint Shop Pro, you may wish to merely skim the first couple of chapters to acquaint yourself with the location and functions of the essential tools and then move on to the more advanced stuff.

- For those of you who have used Paint Shop Pro, this book can serve to introduce and explain the many features new to version 6 of the program; it will also provide you with new ideas and techniques that you may not have been exposed to before—a creative shot in the arm, so to speak. Feel free to jump around to the topics that interest you.

Whatever your level, we encourage you to experiment with the many different aspects of the program. In any graphics program, there are usually a number of methods that can be used to execute any one given task, and by adding your own creative modifications to the techniques and projects in this book, you may come up with something truly spectacular.

About Paint Shop Pro 6

Paint Shop Pro started out as a small shareware application in 1991. As it worked it's way into bulletin board systems and FTP archives around the world, it began to earn a reputation for itself as being affordable, easy to use, and a considerably good bargain.

Over the course of subsequent releases, PSP has evolved and developed into something significantly greater than its humble beginnings. Over time, many advanced features were added, such as enhanced layering and masking capabilities, plug-in support, many built-in effects, sophisticated vector design tools, and so forth. Nowadays, thanks in great measure to the success of the World Wide Web (and user desire to create stunning Web sites and graphics), Paint Shop Pro is considered to be an outstanding graphic design application available for the Windows platform. It not only possesses a well-organized, easy-to-learn user interface that is streamlined, powerful, and laden with features, it also still retains a modest price tag. It is indeed one of the best values available today for digital design. You can download a fully functional 30-day trial version of the program at **www.jasc.com/**.

Paint Shop Pro Update

Paint Shop Pro 6 Visual Insight was written to complement version 6 of the Paint Shop Pro program. Shortly after this book's first printing, a downloadable program update patch was released, and it was subsequently incorporated into the program. For the most part, the update addressed minor bugs and improved the program's operation. However, one of the feature enhancements enabled the Picture Frame Wizard to offer the choice of adding a new frame to either the inside or the outside borders of an image. Therefore, the instructions in the framing projects in Chapters 8 and 9, which deal with enlarging canvas sizes to accommodate frames, can be disregarded if you're using Paint Shop Pro 6.01 or greater. Several other feature enhancements don't affect the contents of this book. If you have version 6 and would like to acquire the update patch, you can find it at **www.jasc.com/patches.html**.

Part I
Techniques And Tasks

Chapter 1
Basic Tools

- Learn to navigate the Paint Shop Pro interface

- Open, create, and save images

- Become familiar with the basic tools and functions

- Learn to set program preferences

By Joshua Pruitt

Your First Paint Shop Pro Session

To begin using Paint Shop Pro effectively, familiarity with the basic design tools, dialog boxes, settings, and the work environment is a must. The most basic of functions, although they may seem simple, will become the workhorse of your digital design endeavors. Learning them well can ensure that the bulk of tasks, from the simple to the somewhat complex, can be taken care of with relative ease. Once you know how the interface operates and where to find things, the more advanced techniques fall into place and are not as difficult to learn as they might seem.

In this chapter, you will begin with an introduction to the application interface; learn how to use the palettes, menus, and buttons; touch on the topic of customizing the most commonly used Paint Shop Pro settings; and start learning how to work with and save images.

Opening Paint Shop Pro

When you open Paint Shop Pro for the first time, you will be greeted with the splash screen, and then the Tip Of The Day dialog box appears. After you close the tip dialog box, the application will be ready for you to use, explore, and customize.

Tip Of The Day

If you don't like the Tip Of The Day dialog box popping up every time you start the application, you can easily disable it by unchecking the Show Tips On Startup option. However, you might want to leave it enabled for a while—the people at JASC have included some useful information.

It's handy to use the Next Tip button to go through all the tips in one session—to get a feel for the most helpful topics and use them as a type of reference. If you disable the dialog box, you can bring it back up anytime by choosing Tip Of The Day from the Help menu.

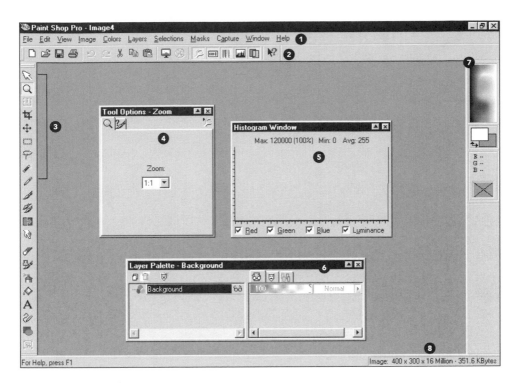

Exploring The Interface

After Paint Shop Pro has finished loading, you're ready to begin working with and manipulating images. Among the major components of the Paint Shop Pro work environment are the image window(s), toolbars, palette dialog boxes, and menu items. They all function in a fairly consistent manner, so working with them is easy once you understand the basics. Note the following components:

1. Menu bar

2. Toolbar

3. Tool palette

4. Tool Options window

5. Histogram window

6. Layer palette

7. Color palette

8. Status bar

The Toolbar

The first user interface component you'll want to familiarize yourself with is the toolbar. The toolbar is the collection of icons at the top of your Paint Shop Pro window. The icons represent essential control functions of the application:

1. Create New Image

2. Open Image

3. Save Image

4. Print Image

5. Undo

6. Redo

7. Cut

8. Copy

9. Paste

10. Full Screen Preview

11. Normal Viewing

12. Toggle Tool Palette

13. Toggle Tool Options Window

14. Toggle Color Palette

15. Toggle Histogram Window

16. Toggle Layer Palette

17. Help

Tooltips

Hold the mouse cursor over any of the icons for a few seconds. A tooltip message pops up to name the icon, and some explanatory text appears in the status bar. Tooltips are helpful when you forget what a particular icon does, or when you're searching for the right function.

Enabling Toolbars

To enable or disable any of the Paint Shop Pro toolbars and dialog boxes, right-click on the toolbar space. This brings up a menu where you can click on any item to disable it; click again to bring it back. Enabled elements are marked with a depressed border around the icon.

Preferences

You can easily define which buttons you want to appear on your toolbar by opening the Customize Toolbar dialog box. You can get to it either by right-clicking on the toolbar and selecting Customize from the pop-up menu, or by choosing Preferences directly from the File menu.

Customizing Toolbars

In the Customize Toolbar dialog box, the left side lists available functions that are not present on the toolbar, and the right side lists buttons that are, by default, on the toolbar. Use the Add and Remove buttons to shift toolbar functions between the right and left. Use the Move Up and Move Down buttons to alter the position of the new icon on the toolbar. Click on Close to save your customized toolbar, and click on Reset to set the buttons back to the Paint Shop Pro default.

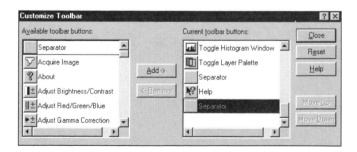

Opening And Creating Images

Because Paint Shop Pro is an image manipulation application, opening, altering, creating, and saving images are the most basic functions. To open an image stored on your hard drive, click on the Open Image icon, which looks like a yellow folder (or use the File|Open menu item).

The Open Dialog Box

Paint Shop Pro will bring up the Open dialog box after you click on the Open Image icon. From this dialog box, you can navigate around the Windows directories (folders) until you find the graphics file you are looking for (provided that the file is in a supported graphics format). Select it and click on the Open button (or simply double-click on it), and your image will appear in its own editing window.

If you check the Show Preview checkbox, the Open dialog box shows a preview of the image before you open it. Click on the Details button to view other useful information, such as file dimensions and color depth.

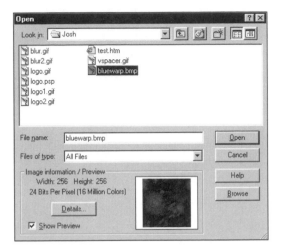

Browsing In Paint Shop Pro

The Paint Shop Pro Browse feature is perhaps one of the coolest and most useful features of this program. It lets you look through a listing of your images in the form of thumbnails (small representations) so that you can easily select the desired image. This is particularly helpful when you have a lot of files and cannot seem to remember just where you stored that important image.

Thumbnails

To use the Browse feature, simply click on the Browse button in the Open dialog box, or use the File|Browse menu item. Once the dialog box is open, you can navigate your file system tree in the window on the left and preview all your images on the right. Opening the images is a simple as double-clicking the thumbnails.

Creating A New Image

To create a new blank image, click on the New Image button on the toolbar (the blank file icon) or use the File|New menu item. This brings up the New Image dialog box.

The New Image Dialog Box

The New Image dialog box enables you to set the width, height, and resolution for the file dimensions. By default, measurements are in pixels (a pixel is one on-screen dot), although inches and centimeters also are available from the drop-down menus on the right. In the New Image dialog box, you'll find the following:

- *Resolution*—Refers to how many pixels per inch (or centimeters) are represented. A higher number represents a higher-quality, and therefore larger, image.

- *Background Color*—Determines the background color of your new blank image. White or black is used most often, obviously.

- *Image Type*—Refers to the amount of colors your image is capable of representing. It is almost always best to start with the highest possible color count and reduce color depth later as needed.

PC monitors cannot display more than 72 dots per inch (dpi) on screen, so when you're creating images for use on Web sites or in other digital documents, remember that a resolution of no greater than 72 dpi is needed (this is the reason 72 dpi is the Paint Shop Pro default). Anything greater than 72 dpi will use memory and disk resources needlessly. Resolutions greater than 72 dpi are necessary only for high-quality print work.

- *Memory Required*—Represents how much space in RAM the image resides in upon creation. It doesn't represent how much space on the hard drive the image will take up, because some types of data used in the editing process are not saved on disk in the image file itself.

Displaying Your New Image

Once the options for your new image are set, the new blank image appears in its own editing window.

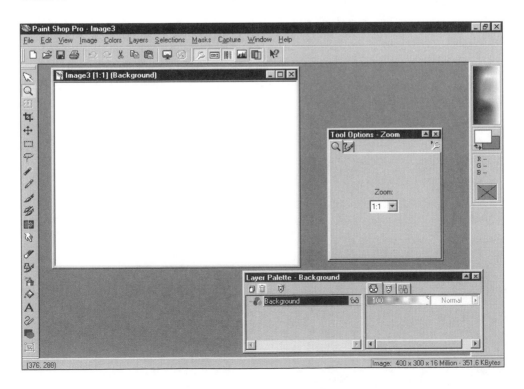

Saving Your Images

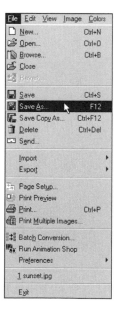

The procedure for saving images is about as straightforward as opening and creating them. When your image is just the way you want it, simply use the Save icon (which looks like a floppy disk) or the File|Save menu item.

You should save often during the editing process. Nothing is more frustrating than losing changes and hours of work due to a system crash or simple human error. JASC's native PSP format is well-suited for saving your changes while the image is still a work in progress.

The Save As Dialog Box

If this is the first time an image has been saved, the Save As dialog box will appear. Now you need only find the location in which you would like to store the image, give it a name, select a file format from the Save As Type drop-down menu, and click on Save. Nothing to it. If the image parameters are incorrect for the file format you've chosen, Paint Shop Pro will alert you and present you with options.

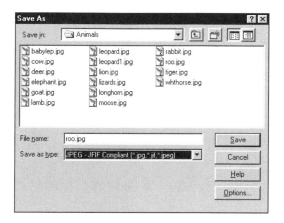

Saving From The File Menu

If your image has been saved before, the Save As dialog box may not appear; Paint Shop Pro will instead promptly save the changes to your image on disk without your input. If for any reason you would like to override this behavior (to save your image in a different location, for example), simply select File|Save As.

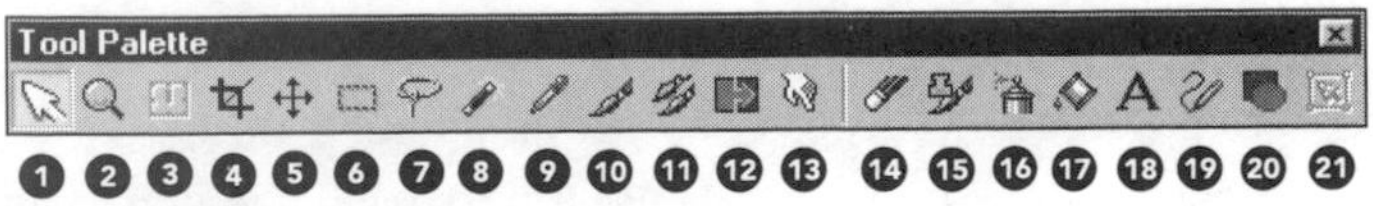

Tool Palette

The Tool Interface

As a Paint Shop Pro user, you will have at your disposal a large variety of effects, plug-ins, picture tubes (for painting with objects), and other such things with which you can drastically enhance your images (and create some pretty eye-catching stuff). Despite all that, Paint Shop Pro's 21 basic tools will undoubtedly become the things you rely on most for your artistic tasks:

1. Arrow

2. Zoom

3. Deformation

4. Crop

5. Mover

6. Selection

7. Freehand

8. Magic Wand

9. Dropper

10. Paintbrush

11. Clone Brush

12. Color Replacer

13. Retouch

14. Eraser

15. Picture Tube

16. Airbrush

17. Flood Fill

18. Text

19. Draw

20. Preset Shapes

21. Vector Object Selection

Positioning The Tool Palette

The Tool palette can usually be found occupying either the left or top of the application work space. You can easily change its position by simply clicking and dragging on the "grabber" portion of the toolbar (the raised bars located at the top or left). Move the palette to the edge of the screen to redock it into the application border. This also applies to the toolbar.

Toggle Tool Palette

In addition to using the right-click menu to show and hide the Tool palette, you can also use the Toggle Tool Palette button on the toolbar.

Using A Tool

To use a particular tool, simply click on the tool icon to activate it. Your cursor will change shape accordingly to match the tool (for example, the cursor becomes a magnifying glass when the Zoom tool is used and a brush when the Paintbrush tool is used).

The Color Palette

In the Color palette, you can easily select colors by moving your cursor over the multicolor palette (where it turns into an eyedropper icon). The color over which your cursor hovers is reflected inside the color information box at the bottom of the Color palette (the color information box gives you useful information about the color at hand as well, such as the RGB—or Red, Green, Blue—represented with numeric values ranging from 0 to 255). Click on the color with the left mouse button to set it as the foreground color and with the right mouse button to set it as the background color. The two colored boxes in the Color palette represent the foreground and background colors, respectively. You can click on the double-arrow icon to switch these two colors.

The Color Dialog Box

If you find that selecting the color via the multicolor palette is too imprecise, you can use the Color dialog box. Simply click the foreground or background boxes to bring up this dialog box. It gives you exacting control over the color-picking process and lets you enter in the desired values by RGB, HSL (Hue, Saturation, Lightness), and hexadecimal (which is *very* useful when creating graphics for the Web).

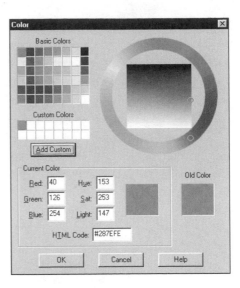

The Tool Options Window

Every Paint Shop Pro tool has variable options that you can set and customize. These options are contained within the Tool Options window. The contents of this window change with each different tool, so it's a good idea to keep it open nearly all the time so the options are always available.

Toggle Tool Options Window

If you don't see the Tool Options window, you can easily bring it back by selecting the Toggle Tool Options Window icon on the toolbar. As you begin working with the basic PSP tools, it would be a good idea to keep your eye on the Tool Options window to familiarize yourself with the kind of alterations certain tools can accept. You'll find that many of these tools work in a similar, consistent manner.

The Automatic Rollup Feature

One interface feature that is new to Paint Shop Pro 6 is the Automatic Rollup feature, which helps keep certain palettes "out of the way" when they're not being used. Essentially, if the cursor moves to another window (such as the image window) and selects it into the foreground, the palettes with this feature will "roll up" to consume less space.

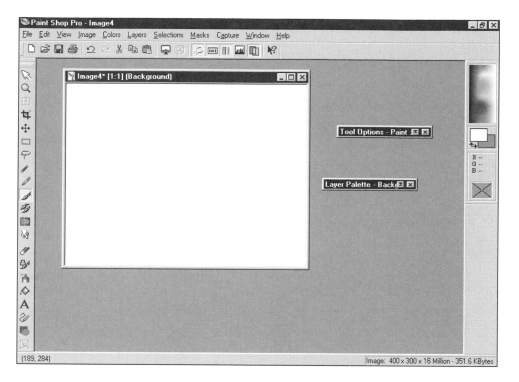

Disabling Automatic Rollups

Only certain palette windows have this feature (Tool Options, Layers, and Histogram), and they are identified as having a Lock Window Open button, just to the left of the standard Close button. To temporarily disable the Automatic Rollup feature, click on the Lock Window Open button; click the button again to unlock the window. In the locked position, it will appear as a standard triangle; in the unlocked position, it will appear as an upside-down triangle with a small line underneath.

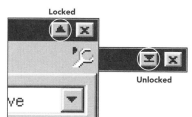

Drawing Tools

The first types of tools I'll talk about are the
drawing and painting tools. They enable you
to "draw" and "paint" into your image with
colors and patterns much as you would a normal painting. In fact, they resemble the kinds
of tools a painter or sketcher might have—
brushes, airbrushes, erasers, and so on.

The Paintbrush

The simplest of tools is also the simplest to use.
Just open or create an image, activate the
Paintbrush tool, and paint over your image
with the mouse. The rest of the drawing tools
work in the same fashion according to their
respective tasks.

Using Brush Options

A look at the Tool Options window shows the
available brush options—and there are many
to choose from. The first tab gives you options
for brush size, shape, opacity, density, hardness, and step.

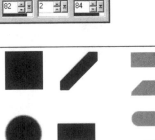

Shape

Paint Shop Pro lets you use different shapes
for your brushes, ranging from squares and
circles to lines and slashes (for more calli-
graphic strokes).

Size

Size simply refers to the diameter of the brush
in pixels.

Hardness

Hardness refers to the degree of *antialiasing* effect; in other words, the smoothness of the brush stroke itself. A "harder" brush stroke will have a crisper edge.

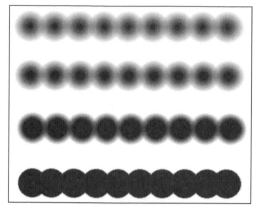

Opacity

Opacity defines how richly the "paint" is applied. A lower opacity will result in a softer, more transparent color.

Density

Density simulates the bristles on a paintbrush. Lowering this value will lower the amount of bristles with which the paint is applied, resulting in a dry, speckled stroke.

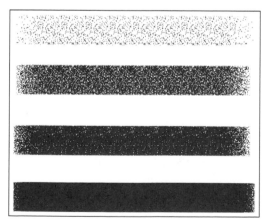

Step

Step refers to the frequency of contact between the brush and the painting surface. Decreasing this value will result in a smoother, more refined stroke.

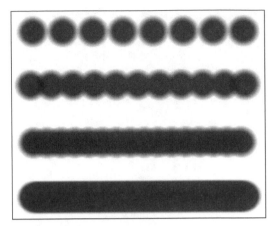

Setting The Brush Type

By using the Brush Options button, to the right of the Shape menu, you can also choose from a selection of brush styles simulating real drawing utensils, each with its own look and feel.

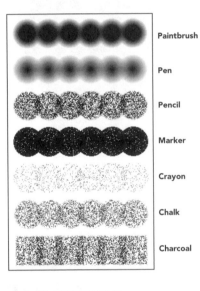

Paintbrush

Pen

Pencil

Marker

Crayon

Chalk

Charcoal

Custom Brush Options

Additionally, you can select Custom from the Brush Options menu to use, and even create, a set of custom brushes.

Choosing A Custom Brush

Choosing a custom brush is easy: Simply select the brush and click OK. The Edit button lets you adjust parameters (that is, Step parameters) for the brush. Delete removes the brush from your system.

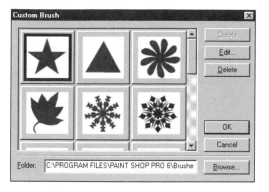

Paper Textures

One of the neatest things about Paint Shop Pro's brush tools is that they give you the ability to use custom paper textures. Custom paper textures allow you to alter the way in which the paint is applied to the surface, resulting in a soft, textured surface.

Texture Options

Paper textures are good for adding depth to two-dimensional objects; you can also use them for tileable backgrounds. You can find the list of available textures by clicking on the second tab in the Tool Options window.

The Build Up Brush option forces the patterned brush to behave more like an airbrush, in that continued application of paint will result in a darker texture. Without this option, the color is always applied evenly.

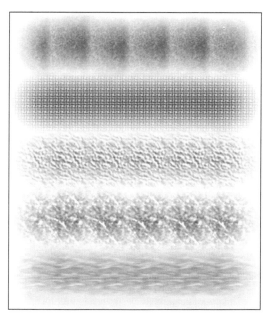

Eraser

 The Eraser tool functions exactly opposite of the Paintbrush—it enables you to correct mistakes by erasing previously painted areas—just like a real eraser.

Using the Eraser tool in combination with the texture papers can make for some interesting effects in the right situation.

Airbrush

The Airbrush tool behaves a little differently than the Paintbrush tool. It tries to emulate the look and feel of an airbrush or spray paint can. In fact, it almost feels like the color is being sprayed on when you use this tool. The resulting strokes look a little less refined, and a little more hand-painted, than the standard Paintbrush strokes.

Retouch

The Retouch tool, as its name suggests, is great for retouching images. It can act as a smudger, pushing and softening the paint in much the same way you might use your finger on a pencil or charcoal drawing to soften the edges or add a little texture and shading. Unlike your finger, however, this tool has a few more options available to play with, such as Sharpen, Emboss, Lighten RGB, and so on. With these options, you can manipulate lighting, color, and even odder properties. Don't you wish you could do that with your finger?

Flood Fill

The Flood Fill tool takes a more hard-lined approach to using color—it fills a predefined section of your image entirely with color in one stroke. This makes it easy to work with large areas of color.

Flood Fill Options

The Flood Fill tool can do much more, however. Paint Shop Pro's Flood Fill lets you not only use paper textures (as with the brushes) and patterns, but also Gradient Fill styles. Gradient fills add a completely new dimension to filling color and is an exciting feature.

Gradient Fill

Gradient fill essentially blends different colors into a smooth pattern. You can use Gradient Fill styles by selecting your gradient from the Fill Style menu in the Tool Options window. There are different styles listed to give you different styles of gradation, such as Linear (side to side), Sunburst (from the center out), and so on. To fill your image or selection with a gradient fill, select a type of gradient from the Fill Style menu, then click on the second tab in the Tool Options window. From this tab, you can preview and manipulate your gradient.

Gradient Options

The default color scheme for gradients is to fill from your foreground color to the background color—but this isn't your only option. A look in the Gradient pull-down menu will give you a list of preset color choices to play with (including more than one color) and even transparencies for creating unusual and realistic effects. Within this tab, you can also change the settings of your gradient, such as position, center, direction, and so on. Of course, the available options depend on the type of gradient you are using. Any changes made to the gradient are immediately reflected in the preview window.

Gradient Editor

Once you've set the properties for your gradient, you can click on the Edit button. Here in the Gradient Editor dialog box, you can load the preset gradients, alter them, save your own custom gradients, and even import and export them to other machines with Paint Shop Pro in the form of GRD files.

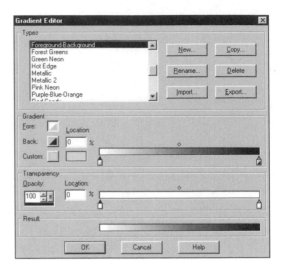

The lower half of the dialog box is where you make your big changes. The gradient edit area is where most of the editing occurs. You can position the center of the color transition by using the diamond-shaped control points above the edit area (the bar). You can add a new color by clicking on an area directly below the edit area where you want the new color to appear. This will create a small bucket icon. You can move this icon to adjust the position of the color or select it to change the color.

Gradient Color Control

You can change the color for the position you have enabled by using one of three color control buttons. The top button sets the color as foreground, the middle button sets the color as background, and the bottom button sets the user-defined color. To set a user-defined, or custom, color, click on the color edit box to the right to bring up the Color dialog box (just as with the Color palette). You can also set color and control point position as a percentage by using the Location text box. After you have set your parameters, simply close the Edit dialog box, click the Flood Fill cursor over the part of your image you want to fill, and let it do its thing.

The Shape Tools

 Whereas the drawing tools behave like real-life drawing and painting implementations, the shape tools act more like drafting tools, allowing you to create exact geometric shapes.

The Line Tool

The Line tool draws lines. But not just straight ones; it is capable of so much more. When you activate the Line tool, the Tool Options window adjusts to let you customize your line. You can simply draw a perfectly straight line or use Line Type options, such as Freehand, to draw wavy or curved lines. The Line Width option controls the thickness of your line.

To draw a straight line, just click the image area where you want the line to start, drag (you will see a line preview outline), and release when your line is the way you like it.

Shapes

The Shape Tool lets you draw exact and accurate shapes, such as ellipses, circles, rectangles, stars, triangles, and so forth. Simply select a shape from the Shape Type menu, choose the style and line width, place the cursor in the image window, hold down the left mouse button, and drag your cursor to create the shape.

If you hold down the Shift key while drawing your shapes, they will stay exactly proportionate on every side. For example, this lets you create isosceles triangles and other shapes that are perfectly symmetrical.

The View Tools And Other Tools

 The view tools can be used to help you gain a different perspective on your image during the creation and editing process.

The Arrow

The arrow is almost the neutral tool. It doesn't really do that much unless your image is zoomed or is simply too large to fit inside the image window (in which case scrollbars will be present on the sides of your window). In either of these situations, your cursor will change into a hand icon, which you can use to move the image around inside the windows simply by clicking on and dragging the image.

The Zoom Tool

The Zoom tool makes it easy to view an image from "afar" or really close up (which is great for detail editing and clean-up work). To use it, simply activate the tool and click the left mouse button to zoom in or the right mouse button to zoom out. You can also adjust the distance at which you view an image by using the View menu.

Normal Viewing

 You can also easily restore the image to its natural size by using the Normal Viewing button on the toolbar.

The Dropper

 You can use the Dropper to select any color in your image. Simply activate the tool, place the cursor over the color you want to select, and click the left or right mouse button (for foreground or background color). The selection will then be reflected in the Color palette. This is a great tool for color matching.

The Text Tool

The Text tool lets you express yourself with words in your graphics. The obvious application for this is creating headers and logos.

The Text Entry Dialog Box

To insert text into your image, simply activate the Text tool and click anywhere on your image. This will bring up the Text Entry dialog box. You can change your font and font size and apply bold, italics, underline, and justification much in the same way you would in any other Windows application.

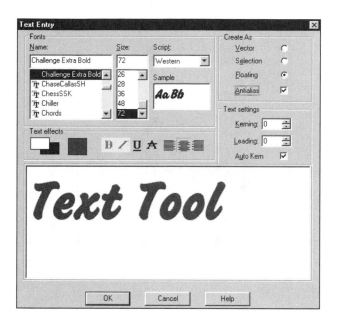

Positioning Text

Once you've finished customizing your text, simply click OK and your text will appear in the image. Position your cursor over the text selection until it appears as a double-arrow icon, then click and drag your text into its proper position. A right-click will seat the selection into the image.

A Word About Antialiasing

Antialiasing is an option that has appeared with the Shape tools and the Text tool, among others, so I'll offer a short explanation as to what exactly antialiasing is. Antialiasing, for the most part, is a process by which an image object is made to appear smoother by softly blending the pixels along the edges with the adjacent colors. In other words, it gets rid of the jaggies, which overall is a very good thing, especially at large sizes. By using the antialias option with your tools (especially the Text tool), your objects will appear much cleaner.

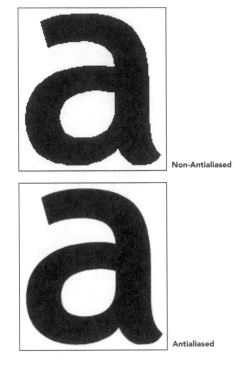

Non-Antialiased

Antialiased

Sometimes antialiasing can make very small text more difficult to read. In this case, fonts designed to be legible at small sizes, such as Courier New, Verdana, Andale Mono, and so on, without the antialiasing option, may be best. My general rule is to turn antialiasing off when using anything under 10 or 12 points.

Customizing Your Work Environment

Paint Shop Pro is a robust, adjustable application. In addition to altering the look and feel of the toolbar, you can also make subtler, internal alterations to personalize your work space to make for a more enjoyable experience. In the following sections, I'll cover the most common alterations, optimizations, and tweaks (the preferences with which it is good to be familiar from the beginning).

General Program Preferences

The File|Preferences menu gives you a wide range of options for customizing Paint Shop Pro. The first item, called General Program Preferences, brings up the Paint Shop Pro Preferences dialog box, which controls the bulk of Paint Shop Pro's application options. This dialog box covers a lot of customizations; I'll cover the most common ones here.

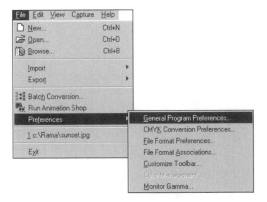

Undo Settings

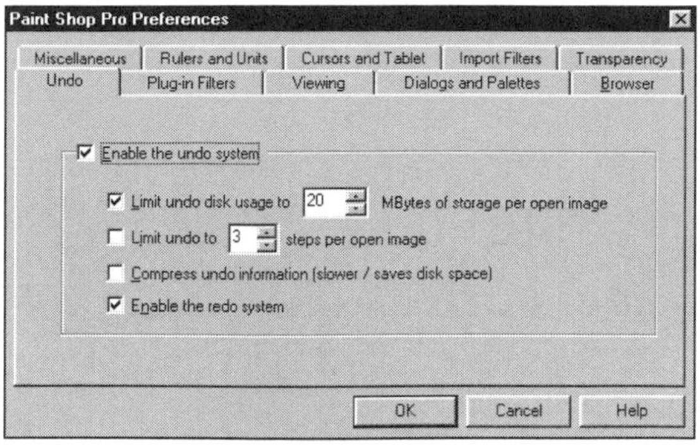

The first tab you will encounter deals with the Undo system. Paint Shop Pro, of course, lets you undo and redo a number of operations using the Undo and Redo buttons in the toolbar. However, the Undo system takes up hard drive space, so you may want to limit it if space is running tight. You can limit the undo functions by limiting the disk space used (making the number of undos variable according to image size) or by simply limiting the number of undos used (to three undos, for example).

Undo And Redo Buttons

The Undo and Redo buttons in the toolbar are fairly simple to use. Undo reverts your image back one step before your most recent action, and Redo returns your image to the latest state. You can go back and forward this way any number of times. This helps you correct mistakes easily without losing any work.

Even if you are running low on disk space, I suggest leaving yourself, at the very least, one undo available. There is nothing worse than throwing away an entire hour's worth of work just because you cannot undo one simple mistake.

Plug-In Preferences

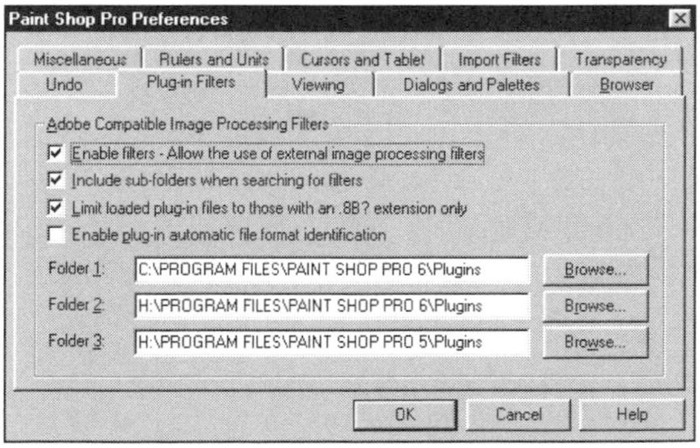

The next set of preferences in the Paint Shop Pro Preferences dialog box deal with Photoshop-compatible plug-ins, most of which work quite well with Paint Shop Pro. Click the Plug-In Filters tab to bring up this next screen. To use these plug-ins, Paint Shop Pro has to know where to find them. This area is where you give PSP the directories in which your favorite plug-ins are stored.

The first option simply allows you to enable or disable the use of plug-in filters (if you know you aren't going to be using them, there is little point in leaving this option enabled).

The second option, Include Sub-Folders When Searching For Files, enables you to better organize your (if you're like me) hundreds of plug-ins into a filing system that is somewhat more orderly. This simply means that if you define a folder as containing plug-ins, Paint Shop Pro will also search any subfolders within the directory for more plug-ins.

The Limit Loaded Plug-In Files To Those With An .8B? Extension Only option simply forces PSP to load only those plug-ins that end with the .8b extension (such as .8bf), which is common with Photoshop-compatible plug-ins.

Browse For Folder

And finally, the three text boxes beneath store the paths to the plug-ins themselves (the names of the folders on your hard drive in which the plug-ins are stored). You can use the Browse button beside each one to find the folders by using a simple Windows dialog box.

Viewing Preferences

The Viewing tab leads to options that affect the behavior of the Zoom tool and other viewing tools.

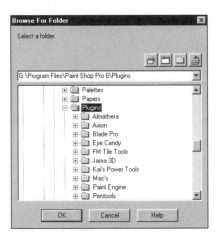

Dialogs And Palettes

The Dialogs And Palettes tab includes options that affect the way in which the Paint Shop Pro interface behaves in general. Worthy of noting here is the Enable Automatic Rollups For Floating Palette option, which lets you enable and disable the Automatic Rollup feature.

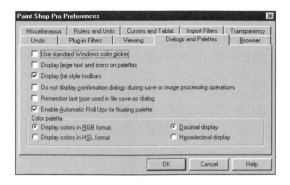

Browser

The Browser tab sets preferences for the Paint Shop Pro Browse feature, such as the thumbnail size and selection color. The Save Browser File option refers to the fact that the browser saves an index file (JBF) in every directory browsed. This way, the browser doesn't have to rescan the same images every time a directory is browsed, but it can, instead, pick up the information from the index file. This is a great time-saver because only new images need be scanned. It's especially useful for frequently browsed directories with many large images. You may want to disable this option, if you browse network drives and don't want to leave mysterious (to other users) JBF files all over the place, or if you browse a lot of read-only media, such as CD-ROMs.

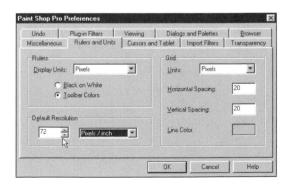

Rulers And Units

This set of preferences affects the measurement system Paint Shop Pro uses to deal with image files. It lets you choose between the measurement methods of pixels, inches, and centimeters. It is also the place to set the Default Resolution value (Paint Shop Pro's default is 72 dpi because on-screen images cannot be displayed at a higher resolution).

Miscellaneous

A few other options not easily grouped into categories are seen here. You can set things like the Recent File Listing option, which determines the number of file names shown in the File menu directly below the Preferences submenu (the files listed are the ones you've most recently opened and edited). Another preference worth mentioning is the Show Splash Screen When Application Starts option, which allows you to disable the splash screen that is seen every time Paint Shop Pro starts.

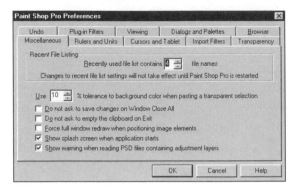

File Format Associations

Also accessible under the Preferences submenu is the File Format Associations dialog box. With this dialog box, you can tell Windows which type of file you want opened with Paint Shop Pro when you double-click on a file name (such as from Windows Explorer). This is a handy feature; you can decide which files you want Paint Shop Pro to handle and which ones you want to leave to other applications.

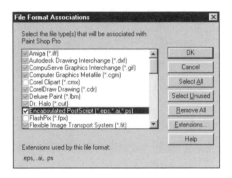

Chapter 2
Working With
Selections And Color

- Explore the various selection tools and options

- Discover the secrets to making good selections

- Learn the basics of working with color in the digital realm

By Joshua Pruitt

Two Important Concepts

So far, you've familiarized yourself with the basic painting and drawing tools—what they are and how to use them—as well as how to get around in the Paint Shop Pro interface.

The first part of this chapter is devoted to selections—that is, learning to select, or *isolate*, certain portions of an image. Zeroing in on a targeted area of an image, whether to move, remove, or manipulate it in some way, can be a challenge, but knowing how to use the tools at hand can make the task much easier.

In the second part of the chapter, I will briefly introduce another important aspect of creating great digital art—the manipulation of color.

Working With Selections

To put it simply, a selection is a portion of an image that you choose to work on, or edit, separately from the rest of the image. Selecting is one of the most basic image-editing operations. You can protect areas that you want to leave untouched and apply your effect or alteration only to the area you have defined as a selection.

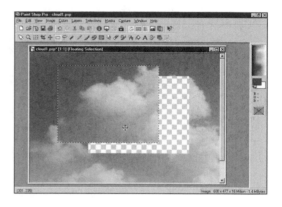

Selection Tools

Obviously, working with graphics often involves the need to manipulate a certain part, portion, range, or area of the image. In Paint Shop Pro, this job is handled by using the selection tools, which include the following:

1. *Mover*—Moves a selected area or object.

2. *Shape Selection tool*—Creates selections using any one of four simple shapes (Circle, Ellipse, Square, Rectangle).

3. *Freehand tool*—Gives you finer control over the selection process with more detail-oriented selection methods (Freehand, Point To Point, and Smart Edge).

4. *Magic Wand*—Selects areas by color properties (RGB Value, Hue, Brightness).

Making A Simple Shape Selection

In your day-to-day editing tasks, you'll find that you will want to select an area in a general basic shape—such as a rectangle or circle. With the Shape Selection tool, these basic shapes are also the easiest type of selection to make.

1.

Create a new image window in which to practice making selections. Begin by clicking on the Shape Selection tool. You'll notice that the Tool Options dialog box includes a drop-down menu of the available selection shapes. Choose Rectangle to start.

2.

Click once in the image and drag the cursor across and down. This will create a rectangular outline to illustrate your new selected area.

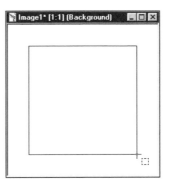

3.

Release the mouse when the rectangle is the size you want it to be. Your new selection will be designated by an animated marquee, or "marching ants," consisting of moving dashes that dance around your selection area. The animated marquee shows you the parameters of the selected area and indicates that your selection is active.

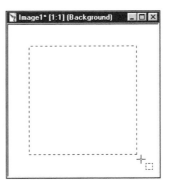

Common Selection Options

When you make selections, there are two main tool options you can use to your advantage—Antialias and Feather. In addition, the Numeric Edit Control can be used to adjust the intensity of the feather effect.

Antialias

Antialias, as described briefly in Chapter 1, smoothes the pixels along the edge of an object or selection, giving a cleaner, smoother effect that is often more realistic. Noticeable rough edges may appear on circular or elliptical selections. You can frequently see a jagged edge formed by the individual pixels in such a selected area after moving or pasting it elsewhere. If you select the Antialias option before making the selection, the area will look a lot better in most cases (although there are times when a crisp selection is more desirable).

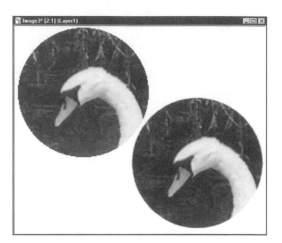

Feather

The effect of the Feather option is similar to that of Antialias—except that the effect is much more pronounced with the Feather option. The Feather option's purpose isn't necessarily to give a cleaner, smoother edge, but to take it a step further to give a fuzzy, blended border to the selection. (This can be an invaluable effect for photo manipulation.)

Numeric Edit Control

You can control the level and intensity of the blended feather effect with the Numeric Edit Control—this widget, which is also present in a number of other tools, gives you the option of altering a value in a number of different ways: by typing it in the text box, by using the slider (accessed from the button with an upside-down triangle), or by using the little black line underneath that also acts as a slider control. The value is, of course, measured in pixels.

Adding To A Selection

Along with the simple options given—Square, Rectangle, Circle, and Ellipse—more complex shapes are possible, and indeed pretty easy to make.

1.

You can use any of the shapes available in combination with each other to add to or subtract from an existing selection area. This can create more useful or interesting selections. First of all, select a rectangular portion of your image.

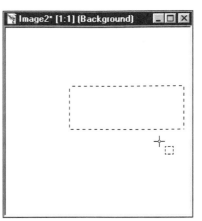

2.

Add a circular "end" to your rectangular area by using the Circle shape from the Tool Options dialog box. Holding down the Shift key while forming your circular selection not only adds to your existing selection, it also merges your selections into one singular selected area. When you use the Shift key to add to a selection, a plus sign will appear next to your cursor.

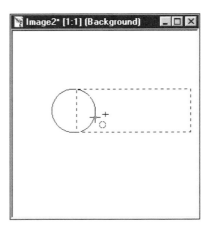

3.

You should now have a selection that has been augmented with your new shape.

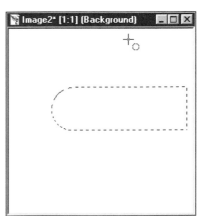

Multiple Selected Areas

The selected areas may connect to each other to form a single selection, but when you use the add to selection technique, they don't have to connect. You can have many separate selections within one image this way. Applied changes affect the multiple selected areas as if they are one selection.

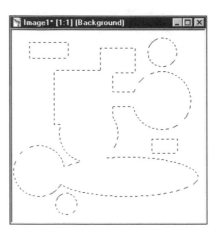

Subtracting From A Selection

You can subtract from selections in a similar fashion.

1.

First, make a selection as you normally would with the Shape Selection tool.

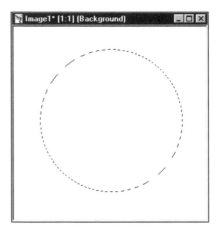

2.

Use the selection tool to make another selection, but this time hold down the Ctrl key (this will create a little minus sign next to you cursor) while dragging your selection area.

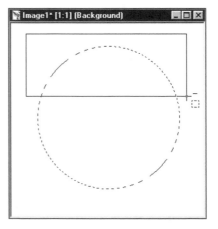

3.

Now your selection will consist of the original selection minus the overlapping area you selected by using the subtract from selection technique. Fairly simple, eh?

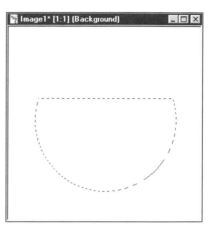

Freehand Selections

 The Freehand selection tool gives you finer control over your selection area. You can use it much as you would use the drawing tools—you simply draw your selection area with the mouse.

1.

Open an image and choose the Freehand selection tool. Your cursor will normally appear as a little lasso icon. Use the mouse and begin drawing around the object you wish to select.

When using the Freehand selection tool, drawing slowly around the object will usually give you a more precise selection area.

2.

Once you've drawn around the area of your selection, releasing the mouse button will cause the tool to connect the starting and ending points of your selection, closing off the area and finishing the selection process. Obviously, for a clean, smooth selection, you will want to try to end your selection as close to the starting point as you can. Drawing your selection freehanded like this can be a little clumsy with a mouse. (If you happen to have a pressure-sensitive art tablet, this is one great use for it.)

Fortunately, you can use the add and remove functions just as you would with any selection—by using the Shift and Ctrl keys. This can help you "clean up" that selection a bit if it's not as perfect as you would like the first time around.

Freehand Options

For those objects that are somewhat difficult or impractical to select in a freehand manner, the Freehand tool gives you a few more options to work with. If you'll look in the Tool Options dialog box, you'll see that, in addition to the Freehand option, you can choose Point To Point and Smart Edge.

Point To Point

Point To Point is a good selection method when the object in question is fairly simple and somewhat angular. It works by using a connect-the-dots type of method.

1.

Open a blank image and select the Point To Point option for the Freehand tool. Click once on your image where you want the selection to begin. Move the cursor over a bit and click again. This will draw a straight line from your starting point to your new point.

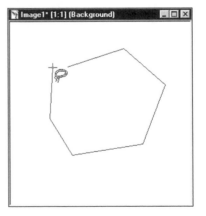

2.

Keep this process going until you're finished with your selection, at which point a click of the right mouse button will tidy up the ends and activate the selection area.

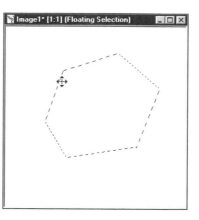

3.

The Point To Point function is a specialized tool that can make a difficult selection process easier. To make the point-to-point selection process much more accurate, use many small lines instead of fewer larger ones during the selection process. This way, you can handle an irregular shape with relative ease. In this example, even the curves were selected fairly easily using the point-to-point method.

Smart Edge

The Smart Edge is an example of a sophisticated selection tool that can make up for the difficulties you may experience using the freehand method of drawing with the mouse. It basically uses your input as an approximation and tries to come up with an educated guess as to which areas you actually want selected. It does this by comparing the adjacent pixels near your selection area and then readjusting the selection position (the marquee line) to line it up between pixels of differing color values (high contrast areas).

Using Smart Edge

In most situations, the Smart Edge tool works best for selecting subjects in high contrast to their surroundings (a light subject on a relatively dark background, for example). Muddy or low-contrast images are not the best choice for use with this particular tool.

1.

In this example, I want to select a complex object (the swan). Fortunately, the subject is definitely in high contrast to its surroundings. Making this selection should be fairly simple.

2.

First, find a starting point and draw like you would with the Freehand tool. You will notice that this time, your select tool draws a small box, indicating the pixels that will go under "comparative analysis." (Try to get your desired edge right in the middle of this box if you can.)

3.

When you've selected a satisfactory area, click the mouse button. This will lock the selected line area into place (much like the Point To Point tool), drawing the selection right along the edge of contrast. Keep this process going as you select the entire object. When the selection is complete, click the right mouse button to finish off the selection and activate it.

4.

I've noticed that the selection area may often be drawn in a little "too tight" around the object, cutting off some of the object around the edges where it blends in with the background. If this happens, you can easily fix it by expanding the selection a bit, by one or two pixels. You can do this with the Selection| Modify|Expand menu item. Simply select your pixel value (less is more here) and click on OK.

Magic Wand

Sometimes, selecting an area by drawing around it is exactly what is needed. However, other times you'll want to cover a large area—one with many similar, though not necessarily exact, pixels. Not to worry—the Magic Wand tool can cover this nicely.

Working The Magic

The Magic Wand works by selecting pixels of equal or similar hue and/or luminance values. If, for example, your image includes a reddish area, clicking the area with this tool would select all the pixels that match a red or ruddy hue.

Magic Wand Options

You can set the range of selection by modifying the Tolerance level. The higher the tolerance is set, the more different pixels will be included in the selection (the less *picky* the tool behaves, you could say). Match Mode determines how the pixels will be compared—by RGB value (color), by hue, or by brightness level. The All Pixels option, also in the Match Mode drop-down menu, simply selects everything (as does the Selections|Select All menu option).

1.

In the image shown here, I'm not satisfied with the hue and saturation of the background—and although I want to change the look and feel of the grass, I want to leave my subject (a certain wily dog I know) unmodified.

2.

The best way to do this is to select the area including everything *except* the dog. This really isn't as difficult as it sounds, thanks to the Magic Wand. In this particular image, clicking the area above the dog's head didn't select the entire area I wanted. Perhaps the Tolerance level wasn't set high enough. No matter—I'll simply select more pixels by using the add to selection technique (just as I can with any other selection tool). I do this by using the Shift key and clicking on more unselected pixels.

3.

If there are still a few errant pixels left, I can use the Freehand tool with the Shift key (add to selection) to select the remaining ones. Now that the entire background is selected, I'm free to use any color alteration or deformation I need on the grass portion of this image. If, after doing so, I want to make alterations to the dog, I can invert the selection by choosing Selections|Invert.

Modifying Selections

In addition to creating selections, you may find that you want to modify—or change—existing selections in any number of ways, such as moving, cutting, repositioning, and so forth.

Moving A Selection

Once a selection is made, it's a simple task to move it into a new position within your image. With a selection tool activated, simply move your mouse over the active selection (your cursor should turn into a quad-arrow icon), click and hold with the left mouse button, and drag your selection to any position you like.

Repositioning A Selection Marquee

This is where the Mover tool comes into play. Let's say you have a selection area you're satisfied with, but you want to move only the marquee into a slightly different position without disturbing your image. To do this, simply activate the Mover tool, right-click on the selection area with your mouse, and drag it to its new position. A left-click of the mouse will move the layer behind the selection (if you have an active layer). This tool has other applications, but it can be quite helpful in manipulating selection areas this way.

Cropping A Selection

Cropping involves "cutting away" excess areas of an image, leaving only the selection as the entire contents of your new image. To do this, you simply use the Image|Crop To Selection menu item. An irregularly shaped selection will be cropped to the outer edges, and the spaces will be filled in with your background color.

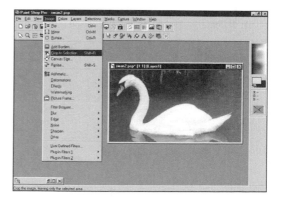

Deactivating A Selection

Once you've finished working with your selection, or if you're simply dissatisfied with it and want to try again, you will need to deactivate it. There are a few ways to do this. You can begin by simply making a new selection from scratch in an area not occupied by your current selection. You can also deactivate it by clicking with your right mouse button anywhere in the image or by using the Selections| Select None command.

Cut And Copy

You can cut or copy your selection and use it elsewhere in the image or within another image altogether by using the Edit|Cut and Edit|Copy menu items (or the Cut and Copy buttons in the toolbar). When you cut or copy a selection, the portion of your image marked by the selection is placed in your clipboard, ready to be pasted into any application that can handle image data.

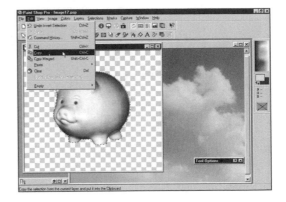

You can also use the shortcut keys: Ctrl+X for cut and Ctrl+C for copy.

Edit|Paste

To place your copied data elsewhere, simply activate your new image or area, and choose Edit|Paste (or click on the Paste icon). This will place an exact duplicate of your selection within the new area.

Edit|Paste|As New Image

Edit|Paste|As New Image creates a new image window within your workspace containing only the copied selection area. This is sometimes a wise thing to do when you want to experiment with the selected area without risking damage to your original file.

The Selections Menu

The Selections menu has a few more options that can be helpful at this point.

Hide Marquee

If for any reason you want to hide the "marching ants" marquee while you modify your selection, Selections|Hide Marquee will do that for you. Keep in mind that this option does not deactivate your selection—it merely hides the marquee from view.

Modify Options

In the Selections|Modify menu, there are options to adjust the size and smoothness of your selection. Contract shrinks your area by a given pixel value, Expand enlarges it, Feather adds a soft, feathered effect, and Select Similar selects pixels in your image with similar ranges of luminance and color values (much like the Magic Wand does).

Loading And Saving

If you don't want to lose your selected area after modifying your image, you can save the selection parameters to disk (using Selections| Save To Disk) to load at a different time or even into another image. All selection parameters are saved as SEL files (files with the .sel extension). Selections|Load From Disk will load your saved selection into your image. You can also save a selection to an alpha channel within an image (Selections|Save To Alpha) and load it back into the image via Selections|Load From Alpha. This is a good way to store selections in an open image or a PSP file. However, the alpha channel will be lost once you save the image to a file format that does not support them, such as GIF or JPEG.

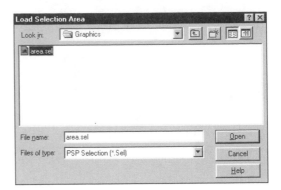

Floating Selections

If you move a normal selection, the area behind your selection's previous position will be filled in with your background color (or in a layered image, with a transparency). However, there are times when you'll want to reposition the contents of a selection without disrupting the contents behind the selection. If you choose Selections|Float, your selection will "float" above the image; when you move the selection, the image will remain intact.

Defloat

For what it's worth, selections brought in from the "outside" (such as pasted selections, text selections, and so on) are always created as floating selections. You can use the Defloat option (from Selections|Defloat) to make a selection behave like a standard selection.

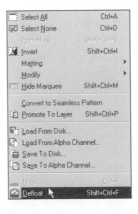

Working With Color

Colors are vastly important to graphic design work—they can say a lot about your composition, and the simplest alteration in color can have a tremendous effect on the tone of your work. For example, black-and-white images have an aesthetic that is still appreciated in forms of digital media—even though it may seem somewhat antiquated. Likewise, a color that is slightly "off" in your image can have a negative effect on your entire composition. Needless to say, humans are generally perceptive of color, and therefore it is something that demands close attention.

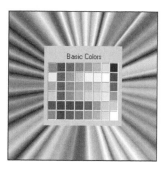

The Color Models

The two main color models Paint Shop Pro uses to describe and represent color are RGB (Red, Green, Blue) and HSL (Hue, Saturation, Lightness). Familiarization with these color models will help you better understand the digital design process.

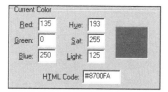

RGB

Computer monitors and televisions use light to produce color. As such, the colors are *additive* in nature—that is, adding two colors together creates a lighter color, and a combination of all colors produces white. Monitors and televisions utilize three colors (activated by electron beams inside a phosphor tube) to produce light—red, green, and blue. All colors represented on the screen are but a combination of these three colors. It makes sense, then, to store graphical data in this way.

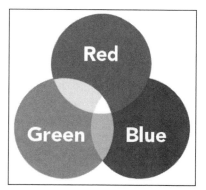

RGB images are optimized to display correctly and most accurately on monitors. This is the way most images are handled in Paint Shop Pro and how they are displayed on screen (such as on Web sites). You will likely do most, if not all, of your image creation in and for this format.

RGB Adjustments

It's easy to adjust your image's or active selection's RGB values directly.

1.

Choose Adjust|Red/Green/Blue from the Colors menu and the corresponding dialog box will appear.

2.

The Red/Green/Blue dialog box includes sliders to adjust the Red, Green, and Blue channels individually, as well as an image preview window, two zoom icons, and a Move Image icon that works inside the preview windows exactly like the Arrow tool. The Auto Proof option lets you preview the effect in the actual image before you commit to the changes.

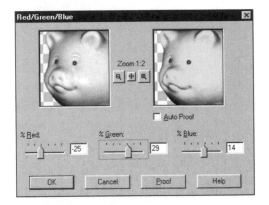

HSL

HSL—short for Hue, Saturation, Lightness—is another model that Paint Shop Pro uses to represent color. Everything is still displayed and stored in RGB. HSL merely describes color in a way that makes it easy for the designer to manipulate; you can change the color by manipulating the Hue, Saturation, and Lightness values (the image data itself is still stored and displayed in RGB format). The HSL dialog box can be accessed from Colors|Adjust|Hue/Saturation/Lightness. And, like the RGB dialog box, it includes sliders to control any one of these three values.

Hue

A hue is considered to be a pure color (red, blue, yellow) that has no mixture of white or black to create shades (pink, maroon, midnight blue, and so on). The Hue slider will adjust this value in either direction, starting with 0 (your original hue).

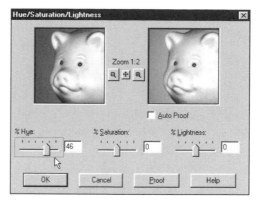

Saturation

Saturation represents the intensity of a color. The full lack of a color results in gray, whereas full intensity results in a full color. So manipulating this slider will give you either a richer or more washed-out color, depending on which way you move the slider.

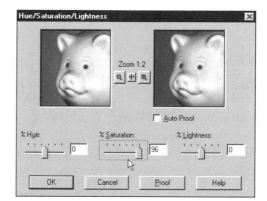

Lightness

Lightness is the quality of light within a color. A pure color exists at 50 percent lightness. Therefore, 100 percent lightness is equal to white, and 0 percent lightness is equal to black. Adjusting this slider can make your image appear to be obscured in darkness or awash in bright light.

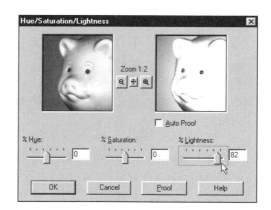

The Color Dialog Box Revisited

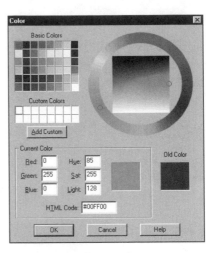

The Color dialog box (covered in Chapter 1) uses both RGB and HSL to represent color. This gives you a tremendous amount of control when choosing and matching colors. You can set colors manually by value in RGB and HSL (values range from 0 to 255) and even use hexadecimal (RGB representation) for use in HTML, which is great for color-matching in Web pages.

The Color Wheel

Paint Shop Pro's color wheel, in the upper-right section of the Color dialog box, uses HSL to represent color. The wheel itself consists of Hue values, and the box inside allows you to adjust Saturation (left to right) and Lightness (up and down). This gives the graphic artist one of the most accurate and definitive digital representations of color. It truly is a remarkable design.

Grey Scale

Another color model used by Paint Shop Pro is Grey Scale. It simply refers to the use of black-and-white images. The use of grayscale images can add flavor and character to a number of projects, such as Web sites. Likewise, it makes for a cleaner job when documents with graphics are printed on a black-and-white printer (which cannot interpret color data anyway). Creating grayscale images is quite simple. A process of desaturation is used to literally wipe out the colors; the filter removes all hints of color, but leaves luminance values intact. It works just like turning down the Saturation value in the HSL dialog box except the process is automated. To convert an image to grayscale, simply choose Colors|Grey Scale.

Color Depth

Bit depth refers to just how much color information an image stores. Paint Shop Pro handles a maximum of 24-bit depth, which is about 16 million individual colors per image. (These colors are used and stored in the image even if your video card can only display 16-bit or 8-bit color on screen, so technically, you can still paint in a higher color depth than your hardware may support. Working in 8-bit video just involves a lot of guesswork and is probably more hassle than it's worth.) When creating new images, you will be given color depth options from the Image Type drop-down menu.

Changing Color Depth

There are times when you may want to save an image with considerably fewer colors than those in which you created it. The GIF format, for example, requires that you save in 256 colors (8-bit) or less. Even if you don't *have* to save with fewer colors, reducing the color depth of an image—from 64,000 to 32,000 colors, for example—can not only make the file size smaller (which is important for downloads), it can also make the image easier to view on less capable video hardware (16-bit cards as opposed to 32-bit cards, for example). You can frequently reduce an image one notch without a significant noticeable loss in image quality. You can adjust color depth choosing the Colors|Increase Color Depth and Colors| Decrease Color Depth menu options.

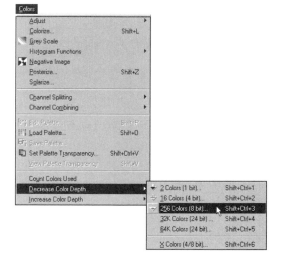

Counting Colors Used

If you're not sure how many colors your image initially has, Colors|Count Colors Used will do the trick.

Indexed Color

If you do have an image with 256 colors or less, Paint Shop Pro will let you take a peek at all the available colors within the image in the form of an indexed palette. Choose the Colors|Edit Palette menu option. This will bring up the Edit Palette dialog box. You can sort the colors by one of three methods: palette order, luminance, or hue. Each color is given a palette index, which is simply an identifying number. You can also save and load specific palettes or sets of colors to use in other similar images. You can do this from the Colors menu as well.

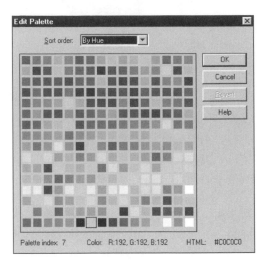

If black boxes appear grouped together at the end of the palette, they represent spots that have no assigned color value (when you have less than 256 colors, such as 216 colors, for example).

Transparency

Transparency is a mode used to define pixels that are invisible so that other elements can show through (such as a background on a Web page). Paint Shop Pro also uses transparency when working with layers, which will be covered in Chapter 3. Very few image formats can store transparencies when you save them, and of them, GIF is probably the only one that you will use outside the design process. PSPs and PSDs (Photoshop files) are mostly used for editing graphics, and they store all kinds of information, such as transparency, alpha channel, layers, masks, selections, and so on. Paint Shop Pro uses a light and dark checkerboard pattern to illustrate transparency. You may have seen it after cutting a selection. If you open a GIF with transparency, you will likely see the same kind of checkerboard area.

Various Color Effects

You can also modify the colors in your image in effective and often drastic ways with these quickly accessible color options.

Negative Image

To reverse all pixel color values to their exact opposites, simply choose Colors|Negative Image. This can produce a neat visual effect, or it can be useful for cleaning up those hard-to-see pixels on clean, white backgrounds, and so forth.

Solarize

Colors|Solarize turns a certain portion of your pixels to their negative value and leaves pixels of other values unaltered. You can adjust the amount of negativity by using the Threshold slider control. The amount of luminance inherent in each pixel determines whether or not it will be turned negative, based upon the Threshold value.

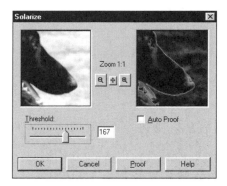

Colorize

Colorize simply allows you to create a monochrome image with a uniform hue. In addition to choosing a hue, you can adjust the saturation. This creates an effect almost like a black-and-white image, but with a color tint. (Old sepia-tone photographs come to mind.)

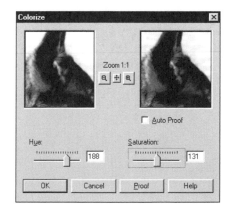

Chapter 3
Introducing Layers

- Learn the basic concepts of digital layering

- Perform layer functions to explore the ins and outs of the Layer palette

- Get acquainted with Blend Mode functions

- Discover adjustment layers—something new to Paint Shop Pro

By Ramona Pruitt

The Power Of Layering

Layering is perhaps the single most effectual and ingenious feature a graphics program can have, and Paint Shop Pro 6 literally shines in this area.

With this latest version of the program, you have at your disposal not only the basic layering capability, which was introduced along with layer blend modes in the last version, but also the new additions of adjustment layers and vector layers.

This chapter focuses on the fundamentals of layering by examining just what layers are and how they work, and by taking an in-depth look at the functions and options of the Layer menu and palette.

What Are Layers?

Imagine that you have a supply of transparent acetate sheets—like the kind used on overhead projectors. You could draw images or words on the separate sheets and then arrange them to appear as one image by overlaying one sheet on top of another. You could keep changing and adding to the image by adding more sheets to the stack.

Up To 64 Layers Available

Layers in the digital realm work in essentially the same way, but with even more versatility. By using a separate layer for each image element, you have control over the individual element's opacity and placement within the image, and also the ability to blend the element's pixels with underlying layers in various ways. In Paint Shop Pro, an image can contain up to 64 layers.

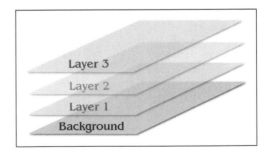

Creating A Layered Image

The best way to learn about layers is to dive right in and create a simple layered image.

1.

First, open a new image window in a medium size with the background color set to white. The image must be in either grayscale or full color in order to be able to add raster layers, which are the type I will focus on in this chapter, so choose full color. It is usually best to work in full color and then convert if needed upon completion.

2.

Your Layer palette is probably already open. If not, click once on the Layer Palette icon in the toolbar to open it.

Toggle Layer Palette

3.

All images have at least one layer—the background layer. If you take a look at the Layer palette, you'll see that your new blank image already has a layer; it's named Background by default. Hold the cursor over the layer name, and a thumbnail preview will pop up showing the contents of the layer.

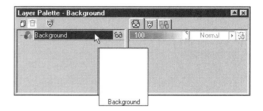

4.

There are several ways to add more layers. One way is to paste something from the clipboard into the image as a layer. Open another image or picture and choose Copy from the Edit menu, which will place the image in the clipboard. Then, activate the image containing the white background layer (by clicking on the title bar) and choose Edit|Paste|As New Layer.

5.

The image I chose to paste is a simple picture of a cloudy sky. Observe that there are now two layers in the Layer palette—the original background layer and another layer called (by default) Layer1. Notice how Layer1 has become the highlighted layer in the palette. This means that it is the active or current layer and any changes made to the image will apply only to this layer.

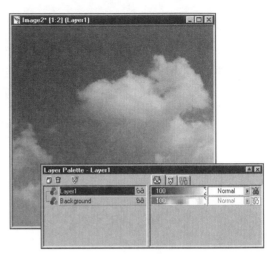

6.

In the Layer palette, just to the right of the layer name, you will see a button with a tiny pair of glasses on it. This is the Layer Visibility toggle. By clicking on it, you can hide a layer from view. When the layer is not visible, the button will have a red "X" over the tiny glasses as a reminder that the visibility is toggled off.

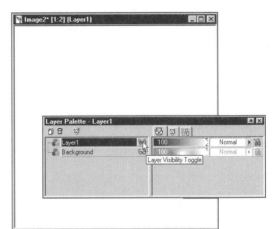

7.

Clicking on the button again will bring the layer back into view.

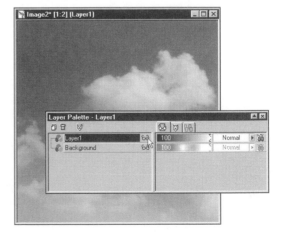

View Current Layer Only

To view just the active layer and hide all the rest from visibility, use the Layer palette to right-click on the name of the layer you wish to view and choose View|Current Only. Right-click the layer name again and choose View|All to bring them back into visibility.

Layer Opacity Control

To the right of the Layer Visibility toggle, you'll see a slider control set by default to 100. This is the Layer Opacity control. At 100 percent opacity, the layer is completely opaque and none of the underlying layers show through.

Reducing Layer Opacity

Reduce the opacity by pulling the slider to the left to allow the underlying layers to appear. The closer to zero you get, the more see-through the layer becomes, until at zero, it is totally transparent. Slowly reduce the opacity and notice how the white background shows through more and more as you go, giving a washed-out appearance to the upper layer.

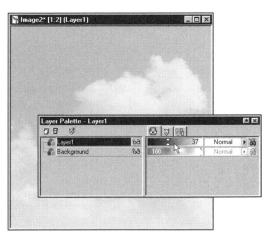

Creating New Layers

You saw how to add a layer by copying and pasting. Now, I'll show you some other ways to add new layers.

1.

In the upper-left corner of the Layer palette, click on the icon that looks like two little pieces of paper. This is the Create Layer button. Clicking on it will bring up the Layer Properties dialog box where you can set the options for the new layer.

2.

By default, your new layer will be created as a raster layer at 100 percent opacity with visibility enabled. Also by default, the layer will be given a name according to the order in which it was created. This layer is automatically called Layer2 because it is the second layer. You can change the layer name by typing a different name in the box.

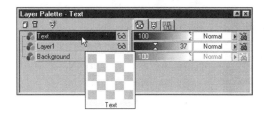

It is a good idea to get in the habit of naming layers descriptively. That way, when you have a multilayered image, you can see at a glance in the Layer palette just what each layer contains.

3.

You'll use this new layer to add some text to the image, so name the layer Text. Hold your cursor over this Text layer in the Layer palette and you will see (by the checkerboard indicator) that it has been created as a transparent layer—just like a new transparent acetate sheet on which you can draw.

4.

There are two other ways to create a new layer. One way is to use the Layers menu from the top menu bar (Layers|New Raster Layer).

5.

You can also create a new layer by right-clicking on a layer name. This will bring up many of the same options that are in the Layers menu. You can use whichever method you prefer; they will all lead to the same place, the Layer Properties dialog box.

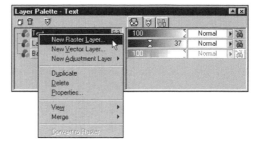

A new layer will always be added directly above the highlighted, or active, layer.

6.

To place some text in the new Text layer, activate the Text tool, then click once on the image to bring up the Text Entry dialog box, and type in a word or two. Choose a large font size and enable the Floating and Antialias options. Click OK to place the text.

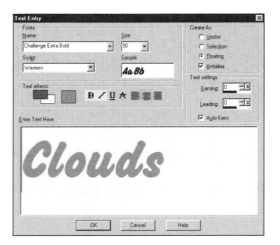

7.

Because you chose to place the text as floating, it will hover over the Text layer as a floating selection. While it is floating, you can use the cursor to grab the text and move it to the desired location.

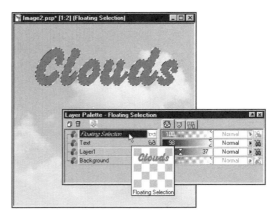

8.

This is also a good time to add effects to the text. In this illustration, I've used two of Paint Shop Pro's great built-in effects, Inner Bevel and Drop Shadow (both of which can be accessed via Image|Effects), to give the text a fancier look. You'll learn more about these effects in Chapter 5.

9.

The selection can be attached to the Text layer with the selection marquee still intact. Right-click on Floating Selection in the Layer palette and select the Defloat option. Defloating can also be accomplished by way of the Selection menu.

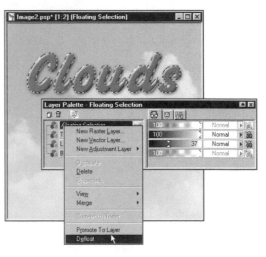

10.

A simple right-click will deselect the text (or choose Select|None) and allow it to become attached to the Text layer without the marquee.

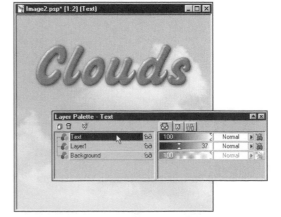

Ins And Outs Of Layers

The following sections offer more information about working with the functions and options available on the Layer menu and palette.

Duplicate A Layer

To duplicate a layer, you can either right-click on the layer name and click on Duplicate or use the Layers menu. This will create an exact duplicate, place it in the next spot up in the Layer palette, and name it Copy Of *Name Of Layer* (in this example, it will be named Copy Of Text).

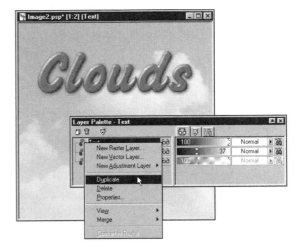

Flip The Active Layer

Duplicate your Text layer now so you can use the duplicate to create a mirrored text effect. After duplicating, go to the Image menu and choose Flip. Your image should now look something like the one here. Notice how the flip function affected only the active layer.

Moving A Layer

Reduce the opacity on the Copy Of Text layer and use the Mover tool to drag the layer so that the copied text is directly below the original text.

The Move tool cannot grab onto a transparent area of a layer. You must grab the portion of the layer directly on the image (the text in this case), or you will end up moving an underlying layer instead.

Moving Multiple Layers

The Layer Group option joins multiple layers into a group so that the chosen layers can move in unison. To see the Group options, click on the Group tab on the Layer palette.

Layer Group Toggles

Just to the right of the visibility toggle for each layer is the individual Layer Group toggle. As you click on a toggle, you will see it change from None to a number. A group consists of all of the layers that have the same number on their Group toggles. All of the layers in a group will move as one unit. If you keep clicking the toggle, the number will go all the way up to the number of layers contained in the image and then cycle back to None.

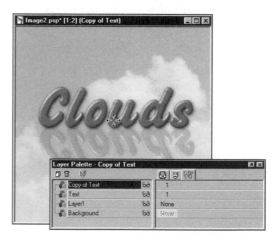

Promoting The Background Layer

The background layer is different from the others. It is stationary and cannot be grouped with others or even change position in the layer stack unless it is first converted to a regular layer. To do this, right-click on Background in the Layer palette and choose Promote To Layer. It will then be automatically renamed with a layer number and function just as the other layers.

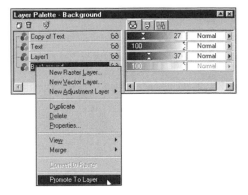

Repositioning Layers

There are two ways to reposition layers within the layer stack. You can simply grab an active layer by its name in the palette and drag it into the desired position, or you can click on Layers|Arrange, which will bring up four different options from which to choose.

Lock Transparency

When transparency is locked, you are restricted to editing data-containing pixels in the layer; you can't edit transparent areas. On the far right side of the Layer palette, each layer has an icon that looks like a tiny padlock and, by default, will have a red "X" over it. This is the Lock Transparency button.

1.

To see how this works, make your Text layer the active layer by clicking on the name. For now, leave the red "X" on the Lock Transparency button. The "X" means that the Lock Transparency function is off. Activate the Paintbrush tool, choose a large brush, and paint a few strokes on the Text layer. Notice how the paint is distributed anywhere you paint it in on that layer.

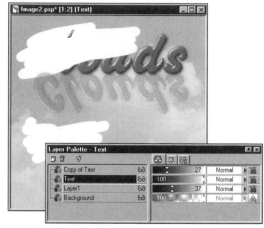

2.

Now click on Edit|Undo Paintbrush (or use the Undo icon) to restore the image. This time, click on the Lock Transparency button to enable it. The red "X" will disappear and you will see only the lock. Paint a few brush strokes on the same layer, but this time, you will notice that any portion of the layer that is transparent is now protected from your brush. Only the area that already contained information will accept the paint.

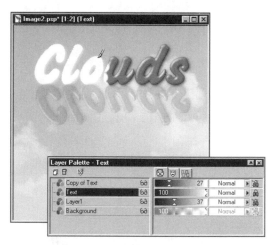

Deleting Layers

If you decide you no longer need a particular layer, it is easy to remove. Just right-click on the layer name and choose Delete. You will find the Delete option on the Layers menu as well. Another way you can delete a layer is to click on the trashcan icon in the Layer palette while the layer to be deleted is active.

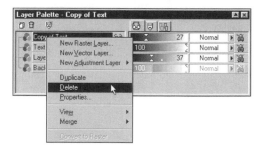

Promoting Selections To Layers

Sometimes you might make a selection on one layer and decide you would like to move it to its own layer. To do so, choose the Selections| Promote To Layer menu option. If it is a floating selection, you can promote it to a layer by right-clicking on the floating layer in the Layer palette and choosing Promote To Layer.

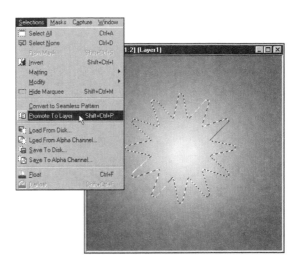

The Newly Formed Layer

When the selection is promoted, everything contained within the selected area is moved to a new layer named Promoted Selection, and the area surrounding the selection is transparent, by default, on the new layer.

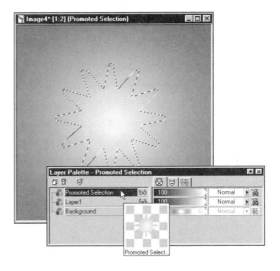

The Selection Marquee

If you wish to move the selection marquee to its own layer, but you don't want to move the contents of the selection, simply add a new transparent layer and make it the active layer. Once a selection is made, the selection marquee is functional on any layer that is active.

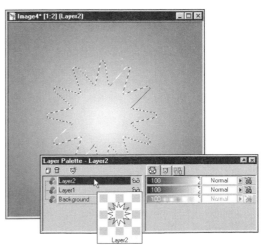

Copying Layers

To copy a single layer and move it to another image, choose Edit|Copy to copy any active layer just as you would copy an image. You can then paste it into another image as a layer or selection (with all nontransparent pixels becoming the selected area), or you can paste it as a new image. If you wish to copy the sum of all the layers as they appear together, use Edit|Copy Merged. This will make a copy as if the layers were merged, but it does not actually merge or affect the original layered image.

Merging Visible Layers

When you know you are finished editing certain layers, but would like to keep the other layers intact, you can merge the completed layers into just one layer by using the Merge Visible option in either the Layer palette or the Layers menu. Simply turn off the visibility (remember the tiny glasses icon) on all the layers you wish to keep separate, and then right-click on a layer name and choose Merge Visible.

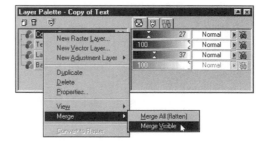

Merging All Layers

When you have edited all layers and you are ready to merge them into a single one-layered image, use Layers|Merge|Merge All (Flatten) or right-click and choose Merge All. *Flatten* is the term used for merging all layers, so when you see the term *flattened image*, it simply means a single-layered image.

Saving Layered Images

The PSP file format will save layer information to use later whenever the image is reopened, but most file formats don't support layers. If you forget to flatten and try to save in another format, you will be presented with a message reminding you that the chosen format will result in a flattened image; the image will be flattened automatically when you click on Yes.

Layer Blend Modes

Blend modes offer a means by which the pixels of a chosen layer can be blended with the pixels of all the layers beneath it. This blending can be done in a variety of different ways. By default, the mode of a layer is set to Normal.

Accessing Blend Modes

To access the list of blend modes on a layer, click on the small arrow to the right of the blend name box.

Blend Modes Defined

The layer whose blend mode you change is called the blend layer. Altogether, there are 17 blend modes from which to choose. Here I will introduce the specific functions of each of the different modes with a brief description of each:

- *Normal*—Uses all nontransparent pixels on the blend layer to cover the underlying layers completely. Normal can only be blended by reducing layer opacity.

- *Darken*—Compares color values in all layers and applies the darkest pixels found.

- *Lighten*—Uses the lightest color values of all layers.

- *Hue*—Applies the hue (color) of the blend layer to the underlying layers.

- *Saturation*—Applies the saturation (color intensity) of the blend layer to the underlying layers.

- *Color*—Applies the hue and saturation of the blend layer to underlying layers, but the luminance (lightness) is not affected.

- *Luminance*—Applies only the luminance of the blend layer to underlying layers, but the color is left alone.

- *Multiply*—Works by multiplying the color values in the blend layer with the values of all underlying layers, which results in darker colors.

- *Screen*—Think of this one as Multiply in reverse. Multiplies the inverse of color values to produce lighter colors.

- *Dissolve*—As opacity is reduced in the blend layer, the number of visible pixels is reduced resulting in a speckled appearance.

- *Overlay*—Combines the Multiply and Screen modes, depending on the color values of the underlying layers. Darker colors (values less than 50 percent) will use multiply, and lighter colors (with values of 50 percent or more) use Screen.

- *Hard Light*—Also uses both the Multiply and Screen modes, but here it depends on the color values of the blend layer itself rather than the underlying layers.

- *Soft Light*—Combines the Burn and Dodge blend modes, once again depending on the color values of the blend layer. Values less than 50 percent use Burn, and values over 50 percent use Dodge.

- *Difference*—Subtracts the blend layer's color from the combined color of the underlying layers.

- *Dodge*—Applies the lightness values in the blend layer to lighten the underlying layers.

- *Burn*—Uses lightness values of the blend layer to darken the values of underlying layers, just the opposite of the Dodge mode.

- *Exclusion*—Creates an effect similar to the Difference mode, yet softer. Also, when this mode is used, any blending with white on the underlying layers inverts the color values.

Example Blend Modes

To give you a quick idea of how a simple mode change can alter the look of an image, I'll use the original layered project from the beginning of this chapter and apply a couple of modes to one of the layers. Pull your original layer project up and follow along. The first thing I will do is raise the opacity back up to 100 percent on Layer1 so that you will be able to see the changes occur.

1.

Make the Text layer the active layer by clicking on the layer name. Bring up the blend mode list and click on Screen. Look at the difference the mode change made to the text in the layer.

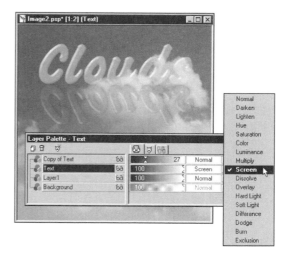

2.

Now change the mode to something a little different. Overlay is the example I've chosen here.

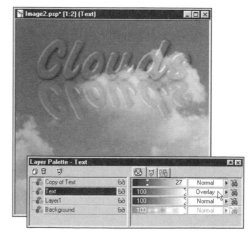

3.

Switch over to the Dissolve mode. Do not forget that this mode depends on opacity reduction to see any results. Because the modes are color dependent, some of them would not illustrate well in the grayscale constraints of this section of the book. Before moving on to the rest of the chapter, take some time to try out all of the blend modes on your image and see what you can create.

Be sure to take a look in the color section of this book to see full-color examples of all of the blend modes in action.

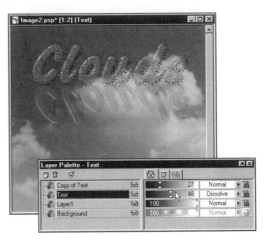

4.

Another place to set the layer blend modes, opacity, and so on is via the Layer Properties dialog box, which can be accessed at any time by right-clicking on a layer name and choosing Properties.

Blend Ranges

The second tab in the dialog box includes the options for changing the blend ranges. With the Blend Ranges controls, you can limit the pixels affected by the blend mode on both the active and the underlying layer with sliders similar to the opacity slider. Each slider has four arrow controllers. The two upper arrows control the values at which the opacity will be 100 percent, and the two lower arrows control the values at which the opacity will be 0 percent.

Layer Types

You have probably noticed by now that all of the layers you have been working with have had a little RGB symbol just to the left of the layer names in the Layer palette. This identifies them as raster layers (because raster layers can only be added in full color or grayscale), but there are other types of layers as well.

Adjustment Layers

An adjustment layer is a different type of raster layer. These layers are designed to make color corrections or "adjustments" to an image while keeping the individual layers completely unchanged. This gives you the freedom to experiment with various adjustments without worrying about losing your original image data. The adjustment layer types include Brightness/Contrast, Channel Mixer, Color Balance, Curves, Hue/Saturation, Invert, Levels, Posterize, and Threshold.

1.

Open a new image and I'll show you how to add and manipulate adjustment layers. Right-clicking on a layer and choosing New Adjustment Layer will bring up the list of adjustment layer types, which can also be accessed by choosing Layers|New Adjustment Layers. Here I've chosen to use the Brightness/Contrast option.

2.

When you click on an option, the Layer Properties dialog box will appear with an extra tab containing various settings according to the adjustment desired.

3.

By checking the Auto Proof option located at the lower-right corner of the dialog box, you can see the changes in the image as you drag the sliders to make the adjustment.

Once you're finished, click on OK to apply the changes to the adjustment layer.

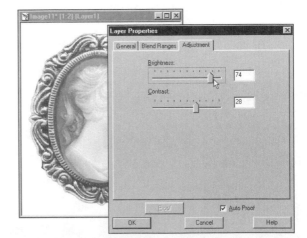

4.

Now take a look at the Layer palette. Because you are working with a single-layered image, the adjustment layer has been added directly above the background layer. Adjustment layers are always placed directly above the layer that is active at the time they are created, and they are by default named the same as their function. They can be moved within the stack just as other layers. The adjustments will affect only the layers located beneath the adjustment layer. Adjustment layers can be identified easily by the icon to the left of the name, which is a square cut diagonally in half with white on one half and black on the other.

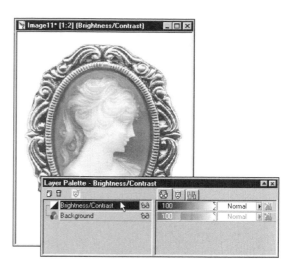

5.

You can bring up the Layer Properties dialog box at any time to reset the adjustment layer settings by right-clicking on the adjustment layer and clicking on Properties, or by using the Layers menu.

Editing Adjustment Layers

Delete the Brightness/Contrast layer so you can add one more type of adjustment layer for practice. This time you will learn not just how to add these layers, but also how you can further edit them. Keep your original image, but this time, right-click the layer name and choose New Adjustment Layer|Invert. You will notice that the resulting dialog box offers no settings for this particular adjustment.

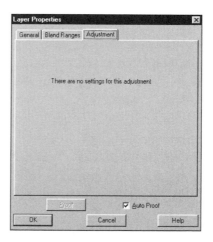

1.

As you can see, the Invert adjustment simply gives the image the appearance of a photographic negative. Notice that, by holding the cursor over the Background layer name in the Layer palette, the adjustment has not affected the original layer at all. The adjustment layer itself contains all of the Invert information.

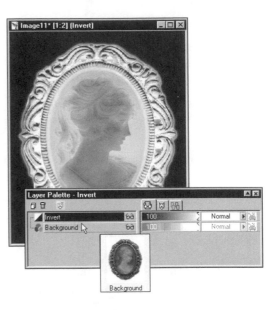

2.

Adjustment layers can be edited, but it works a little differently than editing a regular layer. Hold the cursor over the Invert layer name in the Layer palette and you will see that the adjustment layer appears there as solid white.

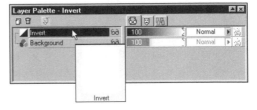

3.

When an adjustment layer is active, the colors in the Color palette will change over to grayscale only. Edit the adjustment layer by using the grayscale colors to add or subtract areas from the layer. An adjustment layer is similar to a layer mask in this regard. (Layer masks will be covered in detail in Chapter 4.) Basically, painting in black erases the adjustment layer information, painting in white replaces it, and the adjustment effect varies when you paint in shades of gray. Choose black as the foreground color in the Color palette and try painting in the center of the adjustment layer. Notice how the Invert effect disappears only in the painted area.

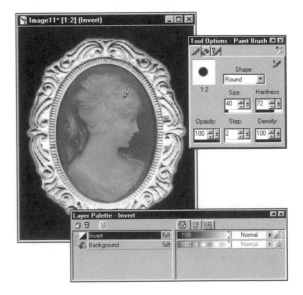

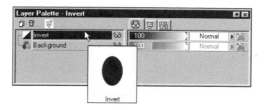

4.

Once again, hold the cursor over the adjustment layer in the Layer palette. This time, you can see just where the black was used to erase that portion of the adjustment layer.

5.

Shown here is a side-by-side comparison of the original image and the adjusted image. Adjustment layers made it simple to make a drastic change to outer portions of the image while leaving the central part intact.

In a nutshell, adjustment layers are quite handy. Take some time to experiment with the possibilities of this wonderful new addition to Paint Shop Pro.

You can also change the appearance of adjustment layers by use of the opacity slider and blend modes.

Vector Layers

Vector layers, identifiable by the icon of a square with nodes on each corner, work similarly to the other types of layers. They are also a new addition to Paint Shop Pro and will be covered in depth in Chapter 7, which also includes the necessary information about the difference between raster and vector graphics.

Chapter 4
Masks Unveiled

- Become familiar with the concept of masking

- Create a simple gradient mask

- Explore the tools used in the masking process

By Ramona Pruitt

Intro To Masking: A Primer

The first three chapters of this book focused on the most basic tools and functions of Paint Shop Pro—the ones you need to know to really get started using the program. For the next few chapters, you will learn about some of the more captivating program features—the ones that can help to turn a simple image into a fantastic one.

This chapter will zero in on the masking tools. Masking is a process in which parts of an image or layer can be virtually covered and protected from change, while other parts of the image or layer are left unprotected for editing purposes. Masks can be used for a variety of special applications.

The Basics Of Masking

Think of a mask as basically a grayscale channel that you can attach to a layer while you make changes, much like masking tape or a stencil is used in painting. You can attach it permanently or save it for later use in the same or a different image or layer. A mask is a lot like a selection, but it can be much more versatile because it can allow changes to be made based on varying degrees of opacity.

256 Shades Of Gray

Masks can be made from entire images, selections, and channels, or they can be made from scratch using the masking and painting tools. A mask can contain up to 256 shades of gray; white is totally transparent within the mask (meaning that the white areas of the mask will allow the image to show), and black is totally opaque (thus masking off those portions). All the shades of gray in between white and black have varying degrees of transparency (or masking capability) according to their lightness or darkness. When you're editing a mask, the Color palette will automatically default to the 256 shades of gray.

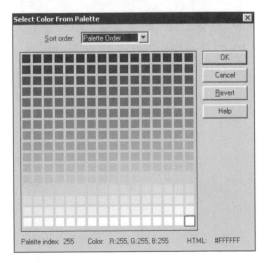

Masking: An Illustration

Masks can be confusing at first, but once you understand how they work, you'll realize just how useful they can be. Before you jump right into examining the masking tools and their options, take a look at what can be accomplished with a mask.

1.

Open or create a couple of images of the same size (similar to the ones shown here) and work along with the following steps to perform a quick and easy masking task. This will give you a basic idea of just how a mask operates. For this example, I will begin with a plain object image, which I will refer to as Statue.

2.

The second image used here is a simple cloudy sky pattern (which I will refer to as Pattern). The first step is to copy the Pattern image to the clipboard (Edit|Copy). Activate the Statue image (by clicking on the image's title bar) and paste the copied Pattern image into it as a layer (Edit|Paste As New Layer).

3.

With this new layer as the active layer, go to Masks|New and choose the Show All option. This step has added the mask, but you won't be able to tell the difference in the image at this point.

4.

Next, use the Masks menu again and activate the mask-editing mode (Masks|Edit).

5.

Use the Color palette to set the foreground color to white and the background color to black. Then use the Flood Fill tool with the Linear Gradient fill style to fill the mask with a gradient using the following gradient settings:

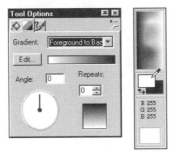

- *Gradient*—Foreground To Background
- *Angle*—0
- *Repeats*—0

6.

At the top of the image, notice how the areas of the edited mask that were filled with the black end of the gradient allow the lower (Statue) layer to show through. I have used the black to mask off, or hide, that portion of the upper (Pattern) layer. The gradient gradually masks off less and less as it progresses toward the white bottom portion, leaving the Pattern layer visible in those areas. The result is a nice blending of the two images.

Options For Creating And Editing Masks

Now that you've seen a mask in action, open a single, nonlayered image and make several copies to experiment with. We'll explore some different ways masks can be generated and manipulated. I'll use one of my original images to illustrate here. Choose Masks|New.

Experiment With Masks

The first two options, Hide All and Show All, allow you to create a solid mask over the entire image. The mask can then be edited to make the desired changes.

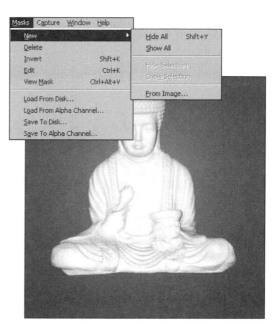

Hide All

When you choose the Hide All option, a solid opaque mask is formed over the entire layer. Your layer is then, in essence, *hidden* under the mask. In a nonlayered image, this leaves only the checkerboard transparency indicator visible because there is nothing else under the hidden layer. You can edit the mask by first activating the Masks|Edit function and then using the Paintbrush tools to remove the areas you wish to unmask. Set your foreground color to white, activate the Paintbrush, and watch what happens when you paint in the masked area. The image shows through the portion of the mask you are painting in white.

To see the mask, click on Masks|View Mask. It will appear as a semitransparent red overlay (simulating the look of rubylith film used by artists for retouching photos).

Show All

The Show All option works just the opposite of Hide All. You create a solid transparent mask, meaning you can view your entire layer through it. You can then edit the mask by painting in the areas you want masked (covered). This time, click on Masks|Edit and set your Paintbrush to black to paint in any area you want covered by the mask.

When editing any mask, just remember that painting with white removes the mask and painting with black adds to the mask. Light shades of gray equal less masking and darker grays equal more masking.

Hide Selection

The next two available options in the Masks| New menu, Hide Selection and Show Selection, allow you to use selected areas to create masks. You will need to create a selection in your image to see how these options work. In the example, I've made a simple circular selection. Then, I chose the Hide Selection option in the Masks menu to form a mask over the entire contents of the selection while leaving the unselected areas of the image unmasked.

Show Selection

Choosing the Show Selection option gives the opposite result, a mask that is created over the areas outside the selection, leaving only the selected area unmasked.

From Image

The last option in the new mask menu (Masks| New|From Image) allows you to create a mask from the currently active image or from an image open in another window. When you choose From Image, the Add Mask From Image dialog box opens.

The first thing you'll notice in the dialog box is a drop-down menu from which you can choose the mask image source. You can choose This Window, which is the default, or you can choose to create the mask from any other images that are open, which will be listed by name in the drop-down menu.

Next, you are given three specific choices for how you wish the mask to be created:

- *Source Luminance*—More than likely, this is the choice you will use most often. A mask is really a grayscale version of the image from which it was created. When a mask is formed using the source luminance, the luminance (or lightness) value of the grayscaled pixel color will determine the degree of masking.

- *Any Non-Zero Value*—This option creates the initial mask with no gradation in masking. All color-containing pixels are completely masked. Only pixels with a zero color value (as in totally black, or RGB 0,0,0) are left unmasked.

- *Source Opacity*—With this option, the degree of masking is defined by the opacity of the layer.

To create the mask using the inverse of the transparency values, check the Invert Mask Data option.

Invert Mask

You can also invert the mask at any time by simply clicking on Masks|Invert. This will change the black areas to white and vice versa.

Layer Palette Options

You can also create a new mask directly from the Layer palette. When you left-click once on the mask icon located directly above the layer list, a new Hide All mask is created. Right-click on the icon to pull up the Masks|New menu options if you wish to create a different kind of mask.

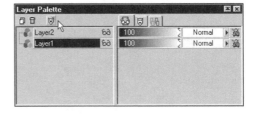

Thumbnails

Once you have a mask in place, you'll notice that another mask icon has appeared directly to the right of the masked layer's name in the Layer palette. Hold the cursor over this icon to view a thumbnail version of the mask.

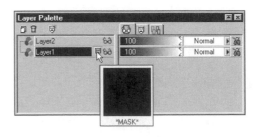

Mask Options Tab

On the right side of the Layer palette, there is a mask options tab (identified as such by the same trusty mask icon), located in the center of the three options tabs. Clicking on this icon gives you access to two toggles, the Enable Layer Mask toggle and Link Mask toggle.

Enable Layer Mask Toggle

The Enable Layer Mask toggle establishes whether a layer is viewed with or without its mask. When this option is on, the visible appearance of the layer is determined by the mask only. When the option is toggled to the off position (designated by a red "X" through the icon), the layer can be viewed through the mask.

Toggle on (view mask only)

Toggle off (view layer and mask)

Link Mask Toggle

The Link Mask toggle links the mask to the layer so that, if the mask is moved with the Move tool, the layer will move along with it. The Flip, Rotate, and Mirror functions also treat the mask and layer as a single unit when the Link Mask option is on. When the Link Mask option is toggled off (with the red "X" through the icon), the mask can be moved independently.

Toggle on (move layer with mask)

Toggle off (move mask only)

Saving And Loading Masks

Once you have a mask you like, you may want to reuse it later. There are two ways to save a mask. You can turn the mask into a file and save it to your computer's hard disk, or you can save it as an alpha channel within the image.

Saving Masks To The Hard Disk

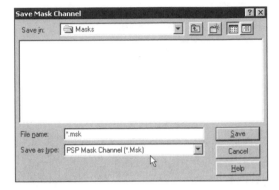

Paint Shop Pro has a special file format (.msk) to use when you're saving a mask to the hard disk. When you use this format, you will be saving the mask as a file that can later be loaded as an image. To save a mask this way, go to the Masks menu and choose Save To Disk. This will bring up the Save Mask Channel dialog box. You then just need to decide which folder on your hard drive you wish to store the mask in, give the mask a name, and click on Save.

Saving Masks As Alpha Channels

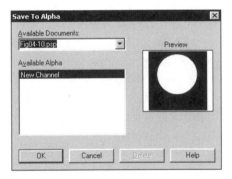

Your other option is to save the mask as an alpha channel, which means it is saved as a grayscale channel within the image. The mask will be available and intact as long as the image is open. If you want to save the image and yet still be able to access the alpha channel later, it must be saved in the native Paint Shop Pro format (.psp). Most other formats will not hold channels and will therefore lose the mask information. To save to a channel, go to Masks|Save To Channel to bring up the Save To Alpha dialog box. Here you will see your original image name listed under Available Documents and a preview window showing your mask shape. In the Available Alpha list, you'll notice a New Channel option.

New Channel Dialog Box

Double-click on New Channel (or click on OK) to bring up a New Channel dialog box, where you can name the mask channel.

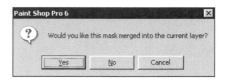

Merging Masks

Once you have saved the mask using either of these methods, it will still show in your image until it is manually deleted. If you choose Masks|Delete, you will be given the option to merge the mask into the current layer. Choose Yes to attach the mask permanently to the layer, and choose No to delete it. However, this only deletes it from the current image. If you have saved it to either your hard disk or an alpha channel, you can still access it until you delete from there also.

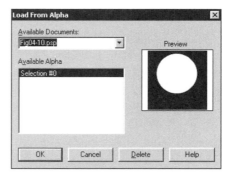

Loading Masks

The process for loading masks that you have saved is similar to the process for saving. First, select the layer in which you wish to place the mask, go to the Masks menu, and choose either Load From Disk or Load From Alpha to bring up the appropriate dialog boxes to make your choices.

Changing A Mask Into A Selection

One other available mask option allows you to change a mask into a selection. This option is accessed through the Selections menu and works by forming a selection that contains the unmasked image areas. If you want the selection to contain only the masked-off portions, just invert the selection (Selections|Invert).

Now that you're discovering the versatility of masks, you're no doubt coming up with all sorts of ways you can put them to use and wondering how you ever got along without them. You will visit masks again in the "Projects" section of this book, which includes hands-on tutorials to teach you more masking techniques.

Chapter 5
Filters, Effects, And Deformations

- Get acquainted with the basic Paint Shop Pro filters and the Filter Browser

- Explore the array of cool effects built into the program

- Enter the abstract world of image deformations

- Learn to manipulate images with the Deformation tool

By Joshua Pruitt

Enhancing Images With Ease

Filters, effects, and deformations give you added functionality to enhance and manipulate images in new, interesting, and appealing ways. Some of them attempt to reproduce and emulate real-life effects—such as pencil and charcoal drawings, chiseled sculptures, textured surfaces, and so on—and others simply create looks that are, well, weird and wonderful. Either way, they are a lot of fun to play with, and they can also provide you with smarter and easier ways to give your images extra touches of character.

Filters

Filters allow you to perform basic image-manipulation tasks with ease. The filters work by applying complex mathematical alterations based on color values; each pixel's color is compared to surrounding pixels and then adjusted according to the effect at hand.

Using Paint Shop Pro Filters

Paint Shop Pro filters can be accessed from the Image menu—between the line breaks beginning with Filter Browser and ending with Other.

If you find that filter options are grayed out, or simply do not work, keep in mind that many filters and effects only work on grayscale and full-color images.

Applying A Filter

To apply a filter, use the submenus as shown. Some filters will prompt you with a dialog box before proceeding, whereas others will apply the effect without any further input.

Filters that prompt you for more input are noted by ellipsis points (...) after the name in the menu.

Using Zoom Preview

Many of the filter, effect, and deformation dialog boxes in Paint Shop Pro 6 can be previewed with the new Zoom Preview features. You can use the Zoom Preview controls to alter the size and position of the image within the preview windows.

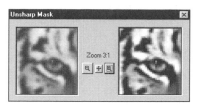

There are two buttons, marked by magnifying glasses with plus and minus signs, that are used for the zoom in and zoom out functions. Zooming in and out during preview can give you greater control over the adjustments of image quality. The original image is displayed in the left window, and the effect applied is displayed in the right preview window.

Navigation Frame

Clicking on the Zoom Preview crosshair button (the one in the middle) brings up a window to manipulate the *navigation frame*. The navigation frame is simply an area representative of what can be seen within a preview window. You can drag this selected area around with your mouse to reposition the viewing area within the preview windows.

Blur Filters

Blur filters all do pretty much the same thing—they compare pixels to their neighbors and average the values, thereby reducing the contrast between them. The Blur, Blur More, Gaussian Blur, and Motion Blur filters focus primarily on high-contrast areas (where areas of variant luminosity meet), whereas the Soften and Soften More filters apply the same effect more generally. All Blur filters are available from the Image|Blur submenu. The Blur and Blur More filters will apply a preset blur on your image. Blur More simply applies a slightly higher-intensity blur effect.

Gaussian Blur

The Gaussian Blur effect prompts you for more input—specifically, it asks how much of the effect you wish to apply. This filter gives you quite a bit more control over the amount and variance of the applied effect. To control the amount of blur effect, use the numeric edit control labeled Radius to increase or decrease the blur value. This controls the amount of blurring applied to any given pixel or edge.

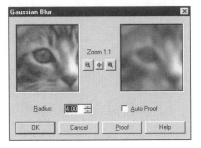

Motion Blur

The Motion Blur filter uses the blur effect in a directional manner to achieve the illusion of motion (such as when a photographic shutter can't quite keep up with the speed of an object in motion). In this dialog box, you can adjust not only the intensity of the blur, but the direction in which the blur effect is applied. Either use the dial control to select a direction or enter in an Angle value.

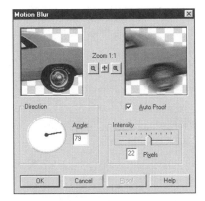

Soften And Soften More

The soften filters apply a blur more evenly across the entire selection or image. This effect is useful for creating that soft, warm glow you see frequently on retouched photographs—it removes harsh details without disrupting the composition too much. Soften More, of course, applies the effect with just a touch more intensity.

Edge Filters

Edge filters increase and augment the areas of very high contrast within an image. The result is that edges between objects tend be drawn in a highly visible and well-defined manner. The Edge Enhance and Enhance More filters increase the contrast along edges and lines of variant luminance.

Find All

Find All looks for areas of high contrast and displays the lighter portions while removing the rest of the image and replacing it with black.

Find Horizontal And Find Vertical

The Find Horizontal and Find Vertical filters do pretty much the same thing Find All does, except that they only focus on edges that exist in a given general direction—horizontal or vertical. That is, Find Horizontal displays high-contrast edges that flow along a horizontal plane, and Find Vertical does the same thing for edges that run vertically.

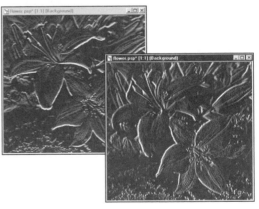

Trace Contour

Trace Contour is also similar to Find All, but its effect is more like a negative—it finds areas of high contrast, traces lines around those edges, and replaces the rest of the image with white. You can use it to create an interesting "sketched" effect.

Noise Filters

The Add Noise filter simply adds pixels of variant colors into the image to make it look grainy. To add noise, use the % Noise slider to increase or decrease the randomization factor—you will see the results in the right preview window. The Random option adds pixels of any color and position at random to your image. The Uniform option only uses colors from within the palette of colors already existing in your image and places them uniformly throughout.

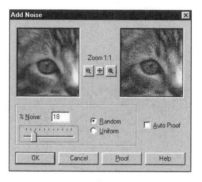

Although the Add Noise filter is used primarily to degrade images, it can be used to improve them as well. By using the Uniform setting and setting the % Noise value to a small number (1 through 3), you can actually remove color-banding from some images.

Despeckle

The Despeckle filter works just the opposite of the Add Noise filter—it removes excess noise and graininess from a given image—great for removing those pesky photographic anomalies. Except in extreme circumstances, this effect is usually very subtle.

Median Cut

The Median Cut filter has the same goal as Despeckle, but it uses a different, and more exacting, method to accomplish it. It essentially compares the color value of a given pixel with the values of the pixel's neighbors (of which there are eight, excluding edge pixels) and sets the color value of the pixel to the median, or average, value of all the bordering pixels. It does this to the entire image one pixel at a time. This makes for a more precise noise reduction method. It also means that there can be a significant reduction in *detail* on certain images.

Sharpen Filters

The effect of sharpen filters is opposite that of the Blur filters—they *increase* the contrast between edges of variant luminosity. Sharpen and Sharpen More both simply sharpen a blurred or unfocused image, with Sharpen More applying the effect more intensely.

Unsharp Mask

The Unsharp Mask filter is used to sharpen images with as little extra noise as possible (for a cleaner effect). The Radius value determines how many pixels are examined by the filter for the effect in each pass. Essentially, a higher value is better for larger, high-resolution images and vice versa. Strength determines the strength of the sharpening effect. Clipping adjusts the "sharpening eligibility" of adjacent pixels by how much contrast exists between them.

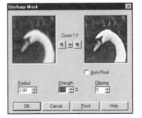

Other Filters

The Image|Other menu option refers to a grouping of filters that do not easily fit into any other category.

Dilate

The Dilate filter exaggerates the influence of lighter portions of an image, while toning down the darker areas. This creates a surreal, painted effect.

Emboss

The Emboss filter grays out the image and then highlights the most prominent edges with color to give it a textured appearance.

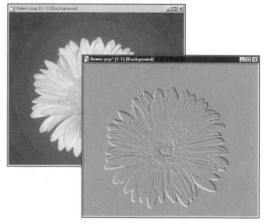

Erode

Erode works just like Dilate, except that it enhances the darker areas. This, too, creates a painted effect, which in some cases resembles watercolor.

Hot Wax Coating

The Hot Wax Coating filter uses your foreground color to create the illusion that your entire image is coated in a layer of melted wax.

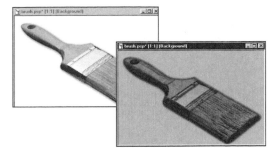

Mosaic

Mosaic creates a pixelated effect by creating large blocks of color. You can adjust the relative size of these blocks by using the Block Height and Block Width sliders. The Symmetric option links the Block Height and Block Width options together (to create perfect squares). If you uncheck this option, you can choose different values for height and width.

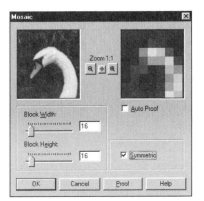

The Filter Browser

With many of these filters, you don't have access to a dialog box of any sort—the effect simply applies itself immediately. Fortunately, you can use the Filter Browser to preview any number of effects in a small preview window before using them. You can get to the Filter Browser by choosing Image|Filter Browser. Simply select the effect you wish to preview and click on the OK button when you're satisfied with your selection. This will either apply the effect or bring up the appropriate dialog box.

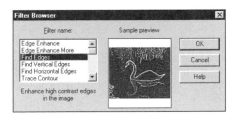

Importing Third-Party Filters

Paint Shop Pro supports a full variety of third-party plug-in filters, such as User Filters, Kai's Power Tools (shown here), Eye Candy, Blade Pro, and so on—most of the Photoshop-compatible plug-ins will work within Paint Shop Pro. Simply install the plug-ins (according to the instructions provided with the filters) where PSP can find them (see "Plug-in Preferences" in Chapter 1), and they should be listed under Image|Plug-in Filters. You may have more than one of these submenus, depending on just how many filters you have installed.

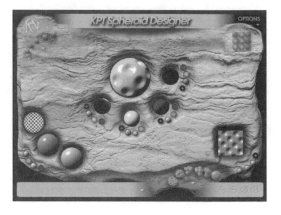

Effects

Paint Shop Pro comes with a wide selection of effects that you can apply to your images for various interesting and unique results that would likely be difficult to accomplish otherwise. Many of the effects work in much the same way, using the same style of dialog box, similar options, and so forth, so I won't cover every single one. They are available from the Image|Effects menu option.

Buttonize

Using the color set as the background color in the Color palette, Buttonize adds a border around the edge of an image or rectangular selection to create an effect that looks like a 3D button. Choose Buttonize from the Image|Effects menu. You can adjust the height and width of the shaded border by pixel value. The Opacity slider controls how visible the border is (contrast). The Solid Edge option creates a hard, crisp border, whereas the Transparent Edge option creates a softer, more blended border.

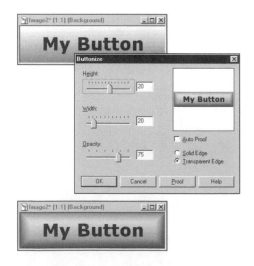

Blinds

The Blinds effect gives a "window blinds" look and feel to your image by creating a series of gradated lines over it. You can adjust the width and opacity of the blinds using the standard slider controls. Clicking on the color box will bring up the Color dialog box, from which you can choose a color for your blinds. Uncheck the Horizontal option to create blinds that run vertically. Uncheck the Light From Left/Top option to make the lighting effect appear as if it is coming from the bottom up.

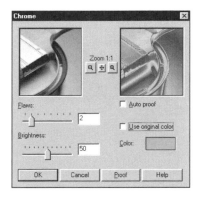

Set Opacity to 50 and Width to 1 or 2 to replicate a recently popular lined "camcorder" effect.

Chrome

The Chrome effect gives objects a metallic sheen. In this dialog box, the Flaws slider controls the number of dark to light variances (transitions) in the image (affecting the complexity of the effect). Use the Brightness slider to adjust the relative shininess of the effect. You can use the image's own colors for chroming (which is a bit more subtle) by checking Use Original Color, or you can use a solid color by selecting it from the color box—the default is white (for a silvery tone).

Mosaics

Both Mosaic effects—Glass and Antique—redraw your image to make it look as if it were made up of a composite of materials (glass or tiles, respectively). You can adjust the number of columns and rows of objects that make up your image (as well as their symmetry, or lack thereof). You can also adjust various settings in the Mosaic Settings section, such as Grout Width (the space between tiles or glass), Grout Opacity, and various texture options.

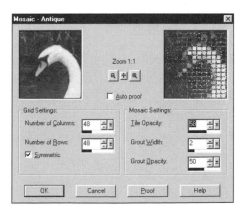

Kaleidoscope

This is an effect that is extremely fun and entrancing. It can keep you from getting any work done! Essentially, it replicates the effect of a kaleidoscope by taking a slice of your image and duplicating it into a circular shape. There are many options to adjust here, and changing an option's value even slightly can render an entirely new image. The Image Sector settings on the left side of the dialog box determine how the slice of the image is chosen (from which portion of the image). The options in the Kaleidoscope Settings section, on the other hand, adjust how the image slice is drawn into its new symmetrical shape.

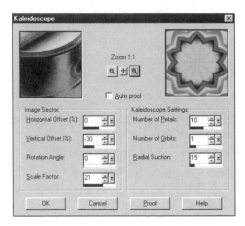

Drawing Effects

Paint Shop Pro has four effects that emulate the look and feel of real textured, hand-drawn images. These effects include Black Pencil, Charcoal, Colored Chalk, and Colored Pencil. To use a drawing effect, you need only adjust two slider controls. Detail controls how many strokes are drawn (too many can make an image unrecognizable) and how minute they are; Opacity controls how much of the original image is allowed to show through. By allowing just a bit of the original colors to show through, you can emulate the effect of using colored pencils and chalks for shading.

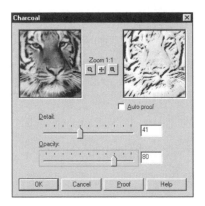

Drop Shadow

The Drop Shadow effect is perhaps one of the easiest to use and yet one of the most useful. It generates the illusion of depth by emulating a shadow, which of course is produced by light sources.

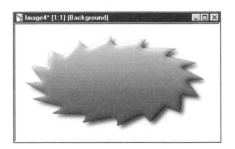

Using Drop Shadow

To use Drop Shadow, you must first have an active selection because this is an effect that you'll want to apply to a particular object or selection, not an entire image (creating selections is covered in Chapter 2). Once you've activated a selection, bring up the Drop Shadow dialog box (Image|Effects|Drop Shadow) to create a custom drop shadow. You can choose the color (black in most instances), the opacity, and the blur, as well as the vertical and horizontal offsets, which control the alignment of the shadow offset in pixels from the edges of the selection.

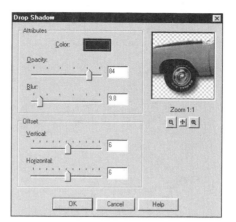

Inner Bevel

Like the Drop Shadow effect, Inner Bevel is applied to an active selection rather than to a whole image. Essentially, it emulates a 3D shape by adding curvature, lighting, and shadow to a selected object.

Using Inner Bevel

After selecting your object and bringing up the Inner Bevel dialog box, you will see a Bevel drop-down menu in the Bevel area to the left. From this drop-down menu you will choose the 3D shape you want your selection to emulate. The Width slider affects the strength of the curvature. The Image area in the middle of the dialog box controls options for the look and feel of the 3D effect, such as Smoothness, which refers to how rounded the beveled edges are, and Shininess, which controls the reflective quality of the surface. The Light area affects the lighting itself, such as its direction, color, and intensity. Use the Angle control to select the light-source direction, which is measured in circular degrees. From the top of the dialog box, you can also choose from a collection of presets.

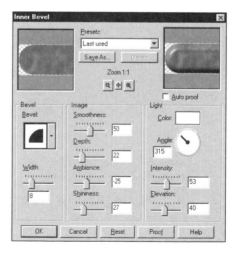

Outer Bevel works much the same as Inner Bevel, except that it applies the beveling effect to the outside of the selection.

Tiles

Tiles, much like Mosaics, create a composite image from textured geometric shapes. You can choose the style of the shape, such as Hexagon, Square, or Triangle, from the Tile Shape drop-down menu. All options in the Tile area of the dialog box to the left deal with the tiles themselves—their size, shape, and angularity. The Image area controls the tiles' texture—the quality of the curvature, the reflective quality of light, and so on. The Light area controls aspects of the lighting source itself.

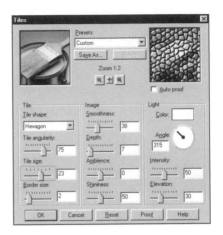

Deformation Effects

Deformations provide a way for you to alter your image easily by simply manipulating the data already present within the image into new positions. This can create the illusion of perspective or depth or other interesting effects. Deformations are available from the Image|Deformations menu.

Circle

Circle, as its name accurately implies, skews the image into the area of a circle, thereby creating an effect that resembles a convex glass lens (such as those installed in front door peepholes).

Cylinder

The Cylinder-Horizontal and Cylinder-Vertical deformations simply stretch the image from the center toward the edges in a cylindrical direction. These deformations use a dialog box with one option, % Effect, which edits the amount of deformation you wish to apply.

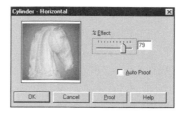

CurlyQs

The CurlyQs filter applies curls to a number of rows and columns within the image. In the Grid Settings portion of the dialog box (on the left), you can alter the frequency of the rows and column themselves—and whether or not you want them equidistantly spaced, which is determined by the Symmetric checkbox. The other portion of the dialog box adjusts the properties of the curls themselves—their size, curve strength (tightness), and relative direction.

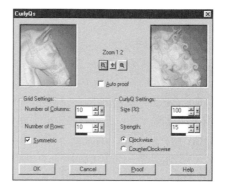

Perspective

Perspective-Horizontal and Perspective-Vertical both give the illusion of perspective by stretching the edges of the image to unequal sizes (either along the top and bottom or along the left and right, depending on if Horizontal or Vertical is used). You can use the dialog box to adjust the Difference value, which is the ratio between the short side and the long side of the altered image.

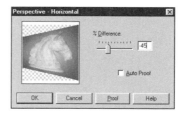

Pinch And Punch

Pinch and Punch work similarly, but with opposite results. Pinch pulls color toward the center of the image, whereas Punch pushes color toward the edges of the image. The % Effect slider control adjusts the intensity of the effect.

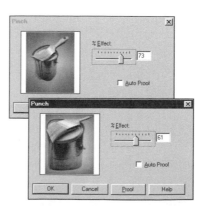

Ripple

Ripple manipulates color to create the illusion of liquid waves. The Amplitude and Wavelength options affect the intensity of the waves, and the Center options on the right side of the dialog box affect the actual position of the center of the wave effect.

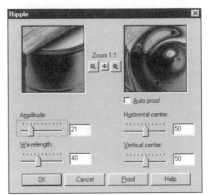

Rotating Mirror

Rotating Mirror splits the image in half and displays a mirror image of one side of the image on the other side. By adjusting the Rotation Angle value (measured in degrees), you can rotate the line along which the image is split. You can use the Offset values to adjust the position where the split occurs (depending on whether you're using the Vertical or Horizontal Offset option, a positive value moves it to the right or up, and a negative value moves it to the left or down, respectively).

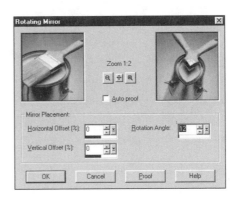

Deformation Browser

The Deformation Browser simply allows you to preview each and every deformation effect before applying it. In this regard, it works exactly the same way the Filter Browser works. To get to the Deformation Browser, use the Image|Deformations|Deformation Browser menu option.

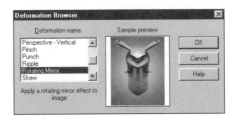

Manual Deformations

In addition to using predefined deformation filters, you can also manipulate and form the image by hand. The main tool you'll use to do so is the Deformation tool, which is available from the Tool palette.

1.

The Deformation tool enables you to perform many different types of skewing, resizing, and rotating operations on any object. To enable it, however, you must have an object *on its own raster layer*, or as a floating selection, otherwise, the option for this tool will be grayed out. Once you do have an object or selection on its own layer, however, clicking on this tool will create a deformation guide around the object (make sure the layer on which the object resides is the active layer). You can also see that the Tool Options dialog box has the options to either apply or cancel the deformation operation.

Deformation tool

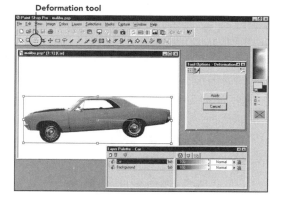

2.

You can now click and drag any one of the control points (the little squares) on the edge to resize the image horizontally, diagonally, or vertically. After deforming the shape, you can either click on the Apply button to commit the changes or click on Cancel to start again.

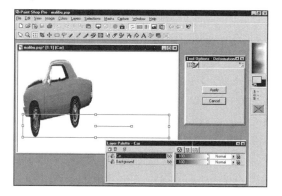

3.

You can also use the Ctrl and Shift keys to add deformation functions to the resize handles. For example, to skew the image, hold down the Shift key while clicking and dragging one of the control handles—the rectangular shape next to your cursor should change to reflect this shape change as you hold down the key. Holding down the Ctrl key, on the other hand, will give you a perspective effect, and Ctrl+Shift will give you a cumulative effect.

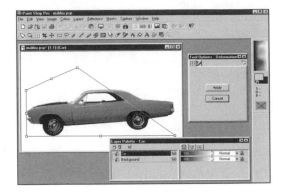

4.

You can use the control handle in the center to move the selection, and the control handle at the end of the center bar will allow you to rotate the object.

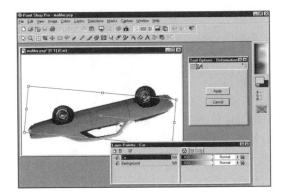

The Deformation Settings Dialog Box

By double-clicking on the Deformation Tool button in the Tool palette, you can bring up the Deformation Settings dialog box. From here, you are able to enter absolute values, in pixels or percentages, concerning the placement and position of the active object, such as X and Y position (actual pixel positions within the image), scale (size relative to the original), shear (skew), perspective, and rotation angle (measured in circular degrees).

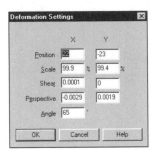

Flip, Mirror, Rotate

Flip, Mirror, and Rotate, available at the top of the Image menu, do what their names imply—they deform an image by flipping it upside down, mirroring it, or rotating it at any angle. The Rotate item will prompt you for a rotation angle and a direction (right or left).

Add Border

Add Border simply prompts you with a dialog box, increases the size of the image by the pixel values specified for each side (Top, Bottom, Left, Right), and then fills in the extra space with your current background color.

Resize

Resize, available from Image|Resize, gives you many options for safely (without losing too much image quality) altering the physical dimensions of your image. You can resize either by absolute pixel size or by relative size as a percentage of the original image. Actual/Print Size lets you deal with size in inches, centimeters, print resolution, and so forth.

Resize Types

At the bottom of the dialog box is the Resize Type drop-down menu, which gives you four separate resize methods—Pixel Resize, which destroys unneeded pixels as necessary (this option is not good for most situations); Bilinear, which retains as much image quality as possible when resizing down (by using interpolation to approximate proper color placement for fewer pixels); Bicubic, which reduces distortion when resizing larger; and Smart Size, which tries to guess which algorithm is best suited for your resizing situation (which, in practice, will usually be Bilinear). The Maintain Aspect Ratio option ensures that the resized image will have the same length-to-width proportions as the original.

Chapter 6
Introduction To Web Graphics And Animation

- Learn the concepts surrounding the creation and use of Web graphics

- Learn about common Web graphics formats, including graphics compression and transparency

- Become acquainted with JASC's Animation Shop and simple animation concepts

By Joshua Pruitt

Paint Shop Pro As A Design Tool

Paint Shop Pro has become extremely popular in recent years and one of the biggest contributing factors to its continued success has been the birth and rise of the Hypertext Transfer Protocol (HTTP), or more generally, the World Wide Web, and the proliferation of Web sites as a whole.

It seems that everyone these days wants to create a Web site of some sort—whether it be an *e-commerce* site, a showcase of artwork or craft, an *e-zine*, a dispenser of journalism, a community-based fan site, or simply a personal home page dedicated to the family cat.

People are now empowered to present their knowledge, expertise, products, and services to a worldwide audience. But given the amount of competition nowadays, the presentation of knowledge can be almost as important as the content itself (minimalist aesthetics aside...). Indeed, even a small-time shop can appear as large and professional as any of the Big Boys out there, provided that the information online is presented in a clean, consistent, and pleasing manner. The best way to accomplish the task of building a professional-looking Web site is through the use of powerful Webmasters' tools—and Paint Shop Pro 6 is one of the best items a site designer can have in his or her creative PC toolbox.

Web Site Essentials

In this chapter, instead of dealing with actual Web design, I'll concentrate on working with the various Web file formats and their options (without which no graphical Web sites can be built), as well as give you an introduction to animations.

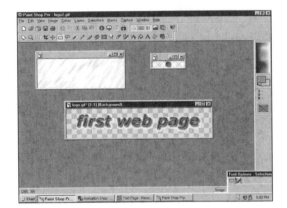

Although it's not within the scope of this book to explain all the details of creating Web sites, I will briefly cover some of the basics.

Hypertext Markup Language (HTML), the language that describes all Web sites internally, is a *markup language*—that is, it describes a set of parameters and properties by which elements on a Web page are displayed (such as fonts, italics, bold, alignment, image location, and so on). Sometimes people who are new to the Web design process have the notion that a Web page is constructed as one big page or image, kind of like an Adobe Acrobat, Illustrator, or Word file. But in actuality, the individual graphical elements—that is, the graphics files themselves—are not embedded in one file; they are instead separate files that are assembled for viewing within a Web browser (sometimes those coming from print design workshops have this conceptual problem; my advice is to forget everything you've learned because Web graphics function quite differently). It is indeed the Web browser that assembles these elements and displays them in a coherent manner (as defined by the Webmaster with HTML).

Sample Site

For example, the simple site shown here consists of a few small elements—a header logo, a background image, and some buttons. The source for the Web page HTML (usually saved as an *.html or *.htm file) appears as follows:

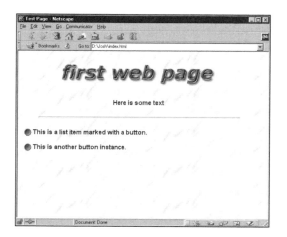

```
<html>
 <head>
  <title>Test Page</title>
 </head>
 <body bgcolor="#ffffff"
background="back.gif">
  <div align="center">
   <img src="logo.gif" alt="first web
page" height=110 width=475>
   <p>
   <b>Here is some text</b>
   <p>
   <hr width="85%">
  </div>
  <br>
  <div align="left">
   <img src="button.gif" height=20
width=20 align=texttop>
   <b>This is a list item marked with a
button.</b>
   <p>
   <img src="button.gif" height=20
width=20 align=texttop>
   <b>This is another button
   instance.</b>
  </div>
 </body>
</html>
```

Web Site Design Tasks

It's your job as a burgeoning Web site designer to do a few things:

1. Come up with some content (obviously).

2. Think of a way to present this content appropriately yet pleasingly.

3. Create the graphics to present the content.

4. Put it all together.

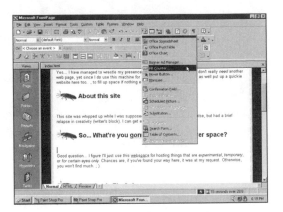

Eye-Catching Graphics

Although it can't really help you with content or "style," Paint Shop Pro is just the tool needed to create the eye-catching graphics for your Web site. As far as putting it all together goes, you can either jump right in and do the HTML markup by hand (using notepad.exe or an equivalent simple text editor), or you can acquire one of the many good WYSIWYG graphical HTML editors, such as Netscape Composer, Microsoft FrontPage, Adobe PageMill, HotDog Pro, and so on. All of these applications are capable and fairly easy to use.

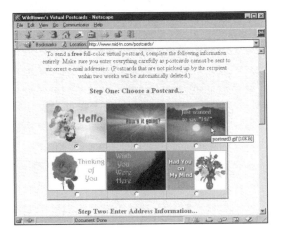

By the way, WYSIWYG—pronounced wizzy-wig— stands for "What you see is what you get." It's a fairly common term used to describe a graphical user interface.

Web File Formats

Web sites don't use just any graphics format for the images you see online (bitmaps, files with the .bmp extension, are a no-no). In fact, there are but a few main formats used with HTML on Web sites today—popular for the most part for their high compression (which translates to smaller file size).

Creating images for Web sites is a balancing act—obviously, you want the highest-quality images possible. At the same time, a high-color, high-quality image can have a large file size—which is how much hard drive space it consumes. The reason this is a concern is simple—the larger the image, the longer it will take to download. And because the majority of people use 56Kbps modems or less for their connection to the Internet, you'll want to make sure that your images do not take too terribly long to download (lest your audience become frustrated and move elsewhere). For someone using a 14.4Kbps modem (the slowest acceptable modem speed today), it simply becomes impractical to view a lot of large images.

GIF Images

GIF stands for Graphics Interchange Format. Here are the pros and cons of using GIF images:

- *Pros*—GIF is perhaps the most popular format in use on the Web today. It sports an extremely small file size and a lossless compression algorithm (which means no quality is lost during the compression process). In addition, it has transparency and animation support and has been around and established for quite a while.

- *Cons*—The drawback is that GIF only supports 256 colors. This is really not a lot when you are talking about high-quality, colorful, photo-realistic images. That's why the GIF format is best used for headers, logos, buttons, and things that do not require a lot of color variation to be effective (as well as objects that are suitable for transparency and simple animation). High-color photographs are best not saved in GIF format.

JPEG Images

JPEG stands for Joint Photographic Experts Group. There are also both pros and cons with using JPEG images:

- *Pros*—JPEG is popular because, in addition to supporting a fairly high level of compression, it supports a full palette of more than 16 million colors. This alone makes it a great choice for working with photographs and other high-definition images that require a lot of color.

- *Cons*—The drawback is that JPEGs use a *lossy* compression algorithm. Some image quality is always lost when a JPEG is compressed to reduce file size. So in setting the level of compression, you have to make a compromise between quality and bandwidth. (You have probably seen highly compressed JPEGs that have a "blocky" appearance.) Also, the JPEG format does not support transparency as GIF does—which makes it a poor choice for logos, buttons, and other navigational elements.

PNG Images

A relative newcomer to the Web design scene, Portable Network Graphics (PNG) embodies the best of both file formats, but there also are some issues to be aware of:

- *Pros*—It uses an advanced lossless compression algorithm, it supports full-color images, it supports transparencies (but only at 256 colors), it has a higher compression ratio at 256 colors than GIF has, and it has about the same file size, but much, much better image quality at high color, than JPEG. All in all, it is the better format.

- *Cons*—The problem with PNG at this point is simple—it is still too new. Only the most recent browsers—such as Internet Explorer 4, Netscape 4, and above—support PNG at all for viewing in Web pages (and not everyone upgrades their browsers on a regular basis). Older browsers require the assistance of a plug-in.

  In situations where you have little control over what kinds of browsers your viewers use (which is most situations), you may want to wait a bit on the PNG format until more people adopt it (chicken and egg syndrome, perhaps). If, however, you are working in a controlled environment, such as the company local area network (LAN), then there is little reason not to use the latest and snazziest in Web design, including newer file formats such as PNG.

Saving And Exporting Web File Formats

All this talk about compression and file size may seem a bit confusing, but Paint Shop Pro actually makes working with Web file formats fairly simple.

Adjusting And Saving JPEGs

The most straightforward method to save an image as a JPEG file is to use the File|Save As menu. Select JPEG-JFIF Compliant from the Save As Type drop-down menu in the Save As dialog box, name your image, and then click Save.

Options

Clicking on the Options button before clicking Save will allow you to manipulate various options for your JPEG file, such as encoding, compression level, and so forth. And although this dialog box does fulfill its intended purpose, it is admittedly a rather unintuitive tool for *optimizing* your images for use on the Web. Previewing the image and potential file size as you manipulate compression would be a nice feature (otherwise, it is anybody's guess as to just how well that compressed image looks before you save it). Fortunately, the Paint Shop Pro JPEG Saver is a useful new tool that allows you to do just that.

Using The JPEG Saver

Because the JPEG format lets you adjust the level of compression to use for saved images, balancing file size and image quality can be tricky. However, the JPEG Saver dialog box makes this process a breeze.

You can find the JPEG Saver dialog box by choosing File|Export|JPEG File. From here, you can not only save your image in JPEG format, but you can also adjust the amount of compression needed *dynamically* in order to balance between file size and image quality—to make the task of creating and optimizing images for the Web that much easier.

Once the dialog box is opened, you have two choices: You can either tweak the graphic by hand, or you can use the JPEG Compression Wizard.

Adjusting JPEG Quality

As stated earlier, the JPEG format uses a *lossy* compression algorithm, which means that to save space, some image degradation is to be expected. Because this ratio can be adjusted, you can avoid creating a poor-quality JPEG image simply by not overdoing the compression. Your image should be as small as it can be (in file size) and still look good (if the image cannot be reduced to an appropriate file size for the Web, reducing the physical dimensions via Image|Resize may be a better option than continuing with the compression).

JPEG Saver Dialog Box

Tweaking the compression ratio by hand is a matter of manipulating the Set Compression Value numeric edit control box on the Quality tab. Increase the value (1 to 99) to increase compression (thereby decreasing file size—and image quality).

The dialog box gives you a preview of your image, both compressed and uncompressed, with the corresponding estimated file sizes below the preview windows (measured in bytes). You can see in the example that my image has been reduced to about 55K, which is much more suitable for a Web image than the original 756K, and my image *didn't lose any visible quality*. In this particular example, when the compression ratio is set just one step higher, you begin to see a noticeable amount of image quality loss. Of course, your mileage will vary. As you can see, this is a great tool for tweak freaks who want to squeeze as much as they can out of an image.

Decompression Format

The second tab in the JPEG Saver dialog box—Format—lets you choose which *decompression* format you want your JPEG image to be encoded with when saved. This affects how your image will appear as it downloads over the wire into your visitor's Web browser. (This effect is especially apparent on slower Internet connections.)

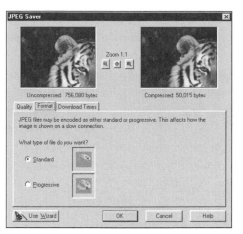

Standard Format

Standard format simply decodes and displays the image line-by-line as it is downloaded into your Web browser. In this example, the image in question is approximately 50 percent downloaded from the remote server.

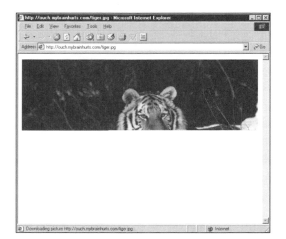

Progressive Format

Progressive format, on the other hand, utilizes a completely different method during decompression. Instead of showing the image line-by-line as it downloads, progressive format displays the entire image at once, albeit very blurry and pixelated at first, and progressively rescans the image, filling in all the missing color and detail information, until the image is complete.

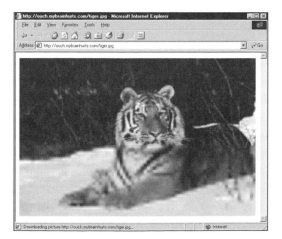

Some Webmasters choose to use this method because it allows the client to see pretty much what a large image is going to look like before it finishes downloading, therefore, he or she may choose to peruse the rest of the page as the image finishes filling itself in.

As a bonus, JPEG progressive format frequently acts indirectly as a type of mild compression, resulting in a slightly smaller file size as well.

Estimating Download Times

The third tab, Download Times, gives you a list of download time approximations according to current compressed file size and type of download speed (28.8Kbps modem, 56Kbps modem, 128K ISDN, and so on). This can be a useful utility when you're trying to determine proper file size for your particular audience. Keep in mind, however, that the values represented here are approximations only and cannot account for other variables that affect bandwidth, such as network traffic, time of day, and so on. Nevertheless, this area can give you a good gauge to adjust your pages and images to fit within a reasonable bandwidth frame.

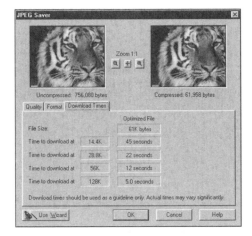

JPEG Wizard

If you don't really want to fool with all this hand tweaking, you can use the JPEG Wizard to walk you through the steps. To use the wizard, click on the Use Wizard button in the JPEG Saver dialog box.

When the JPEG Wizard dialog box appears, the first step is to select relative image quality and compression. Once you select a suitable setting, click on the Next button.

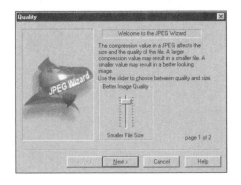

Preview In JPEG Wizard

Step two of the wizard gives you a preview window of your image (on which you can use the Zoom Preview controls) as well as the file size. If you are not satisfied with the quality or the file size of the image, you can always click on the Back button to choose a new compression setting and try again.

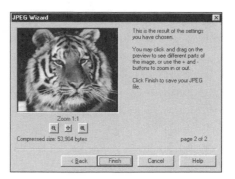

Once you're satisfied with your image thus far, you can click on Finish and save your JPEG file.

Saving Your JPEG

Click OK from the JPEG Saver dialog box or Finish from the JPEG Wizard to bring up the standard Save As dialog box. From here, you can name and save your image as you normally would.

Working With GIFs

GIFs are useful because they are so widespread and relatively small. Working with GIFs can at times be challenging, however, because you are limited to an 8-bit, 256-color palette. Not all images translate well to this color depth. (Sometimes reduction to 256 colors is almost unnoticeable, and other times it is disastrous. It all depends on the composition of the image and how many colors of variant hue the image had to begin with.)

Reducing Color Depth

To save any image as a GIF, the first thing you have to do is reduce the color depth to 256 colors or less (you can also use this as a gauge to determine whether or not the image is in fact *suitable* for saving in this format or if it would be better as a JPEG). You can do this by choosing Decrease Color Depth from the Colors menu.

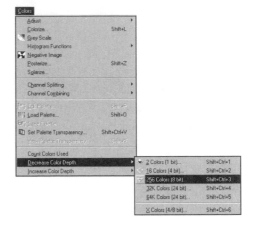

Remember that it is always best to do a color reduction as the last step of composition before saving. This allows you to work in full color (which is easier) and lets you test the reduction process on the final image.

Decrease Color Depth Dialog Box

The Decrease Color Depth-256 Colors dialog box gives you many options for the color reduction process. The best way to determine the proper reduction algorithm for your particular image is to experiment with them and see which one *looks* best (common sense, eh?). Optimized Octree and Optimized Median Cut are similar color reduction methods that attempt to closely match your colors within a 256-color palette. In practice, there is little real visible difference between them, and determining which one is most suitable for your graphic is usually a trial-and-error process (using Edit| Undo). Either one will suffice in most instances because they both match your colors within the reduced gamut pretty accurately.

Web-Safe Palette

Standard/Web-Safe refers to a specialized re-duction method that stems from the days when most users had 256-color VGA monitors. When you use this method to decrease the color depth, the colors in your image are approxi-mated to fit within 216 specific predefined colors used on 256-color displays, for a per-fect, albeit very limited, color match (the other 40 colors are reserved for the operating system).

Using The Web-Safe Palette

Using the Standard/Web-safe option has the effect of making images look slightly better on these 256-color displays (a full-color image on an 8-bit display may end up a bit dithered). However, because the majority of users nowa-days view Web sites and such with 16-bit or better displays, the slight quality gain achieved for 8-bit displays by doing this may hardly be worth *degrading* the image drastically for high-color viewers. This issue can still be a cause for a bit of contention with some graphic art-ists. Again, the "know your audience" maxim applies here as well (at least until 8-bit moni-tors disappear completely). Personally, I see its usage less and less often as time goes by.

After reducing your image color depth, you can view the colors within your indexed palette by choosing Colors|Edit Palette.

Reduction Method

The options in the Reduction Method section refer to how Paint Shop Pro matches colors in reference to the other colors in your image.

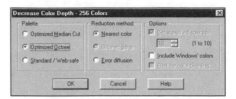

For example, Nearest Color simply reduces a pixel to its nearest value within a 256-color gamut, regardless of what that color may be or how it looks against its neighboring colors. On the other hand, Error Diffusion uses a process called *dithering* that tries to resolve areas of gradation by matching the *overall* image more closely to the original, thereby *simulating colors* using closely located pixels in a certain fashion (much like many newspaper comic strips still use white and red dots together to achieve the illusion of pink). This leads to a more accurate depiction of gradated (changing) color against the original, but it also results in a more speckled, distorted image, that is, an image with lots of pixel "noise." This can actually reduce image quality in some instances. My general rule of thumb is, if the amount of colors within a GIF requires the use of the Error Diffusion option, JPEG may be a better option.

Ordered Dither

Ordered Dither is an option only to be found within very limited palette schemes, such as the web-safe palette. It dithers pixel colors in a predefined, highly patterned fashion (this emulates the newspaper look and feel very well). You may want to intentionally enable this option simply for the effect. Again, use whatever looks best. Experimentation is key with color. Once you've chosen your color reduction method, click OK to try it out. Fortunately, any changes made in regards to color can be reversed with Edit|Undo, which makes experimentation relatively painless.

Transparency

One of the most utilitarian things about using the GIF format for Web design is the fact that it supports transparency. This means that, within a 256-color palette, you can define *any one color* to appear *invisible*, thereby allowing any background image or color within your Web page to "show through" (they appear just like layer transparencies in Paint Shop Pro itself, but there are some fundamental differences). This allows you to create images that have the appearance of blending in with the rest of the composition or that appear to be any number of shapes other than the standard rectangle, while allowing the background image to appear directly around your object's borders for a seamless look.

Transparency Example

In this simple example, the GIF transparency has allowed the textured background to show through the spaces within my funky navigational aid.

Defining A Transparent Color

To select a color as transparent, first of all, make sure that you have merged all your active layers (Layers|Merge|Merge All—otherwise, you'll have channel information that the GIF format cannot save or use) and then reduce the image color depth to 256 colors or less.

Set Palette Transparency Dialog Box

Once you've done this, select Colors|View Pal-
ette Transparency (in order to see your changes),
and then select Colors|Set Palette Transparency.
This brings up the Set Palette Transparency
dialog box.

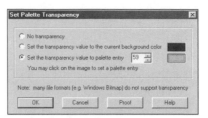

Select Color From Palette

You can select which color you want defined
as transparent by either setting it to the current background color or by using a specific
palette entry. To use a specific palette entry,
click on the color box next to the Set The Transparency Value To Palette Entry option. This will
bring up a palette window in which you can
select the exact color you want transparent.
Then click on OK in both dialog boxes. Your
transparency should now appear as the Paint
Shop Pro checkered field. When this image is
viewed in a Web browser, the selected color is
simply ignored and treated as if it were transparent.

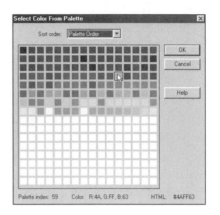

Avoiding Jaggies

It is wise to keep in mind the general color of
the background over which your transparent
GIF will be placed during the creation process—
especially concerning light and dark areas. You
want to achieve a good blend into the transparent area, which does not generally happen
when you place an image made upon a white
background (now transparent) in Paint Shop
Pro over a dark Web background and vice
versa. GIF does not support semitranslucent
pixels and blending over layers like PSP files,
so avoiding the jaggies is a concern here.

Transparent GIF Saver

The Transparent GIF Saver, like the JPEG Saver, gives you an easy way to manipulate, optimize, and save GIF files from one convenient central location. This dialog box works almost exactly like the JPEG Saver—except that instead of dealing with compression ratio, you're dealing with the number of colors used (the fewer colors, the smaller the image) and transparency. Select File|Export|Transparent GIF to bring up the Transparent GIF Saver dialog box.

Transparency

The first tab, Transparency, works much like the Set Palette Transparency dialog box. The color box next to the Areas That Match This Color option allows you to select the transparent color in much the same way you selected it in the Set Palette Transparency dialog box (the Tolerance option sets the level of color matching—a higher level selects a wider range of similar colors for transparency). Your changes will be reflected in the Compressed Preview Window.

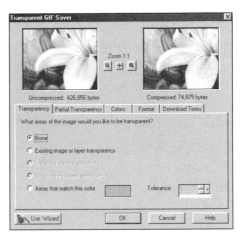

GIF Saver Color Adjustment

The Colors tab lets you adjust the amount and distribution of color, which, incidentally, affects file size (color reduction acts as a sort of compression in this case). Lowering the number of colors within your image can improve the file size but degrade the content as well.

The dithering numeric edit control lets you adjust with variant degrees between the Nearest Color and Error Diffusion reduction methods, the former represented with a lower value. The lower value results in possible color banding, whereas the effect of a higher value is possible graininess. The ability to adjust this dynamically with preview capabilities is a wonderful feature.

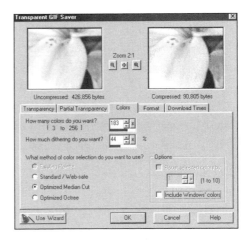

From this dialog box, you can choose between the standard palette reduction methods, previewing the effects of their implementation, as well.

Format

Like JPEGs, GIFs too can be encoded in one of two different decompression methods. There is but one major difference—instead of "Progressive" and "Non-progressive," proper GIF parlance is to refer to them as "Interlaced" and "Non-interlaced."

From the Format tab, you can also choose which format revision you want to use to save your file, GIF87a or GIF89a. GIF89a is the format that supports transparencies and animations. The other version offers no real advantages that I am aware of, other than perhaps backward compatibility with some older software.

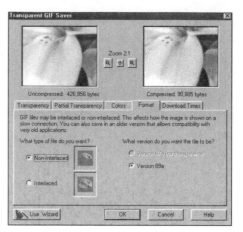

GIF Wizard

The GIF Wizard can help you complete the appropriate tasks by asking you questions within five easy steps. Simply click on Use Wizard to begin.

1.

In the first step, you're asked whether or not transparency is to be represented within this image. If so, select the Convert Matching Colors To Transparent option, click on the color box to bring up the Paint Shop Pro color picker dialog box, and click on Next when you're finished selecting the color you want to be shown as transparent within your image.

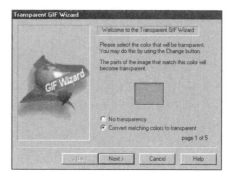

2.

In the second step, you're asked what you think the general background color of your Web page will be. This does not have to be an exact match because many patterns are textured and variant, but it should be pretty close. This helps the wizard automatically try to reduce the possibility of jaggies that are caused by creating a transparent image geared for laying atop one shade of color and displaying it atop another completely different shade, as described earlier in this chapter.

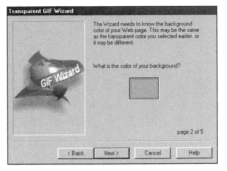

3.

The next step asks you whether you want to reduce to an optimized 8-bit palette ("No, choose the best colors") or to the web-safe palette (Yes, use Web-safe colors only") geared for 8-bit monitor displays.

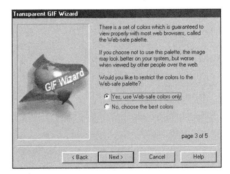

4.

Step 4 is where the adjustment of compression and color takes place. As before, the smaller the image, the fewer the colors, and hence, the poorer the image quality.

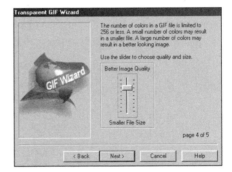

5.

And the final step lets you preview, save, or go back and readjust your settings. Click on Finish to bring up the standard Windows Save dialog box, from which you can name and save your completed image.

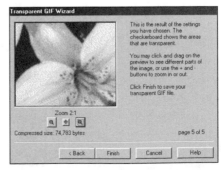

Animation Shop

Paint Shop Pro comes with a fantastic helper application called Animation Shop. It works in concert with Paint Shop Pro to enable you to create animations with ease. You can get to it from within Paint Shop Pro by using File|Run Animation Shop.

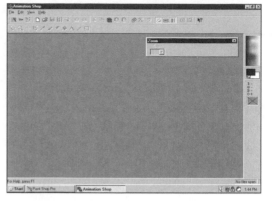

The interfaces and concepts behind Animation Shop are similar to those behind Paint Shop Pro, so if you can use Paint Shop Pro, you can learn to use Animation Shop with relative ease.

What Is An Animation?

Simply put, an animation in digital format works much like animations in the real world—it is nothing more than a series of sequential images displayed one after another, quickly enough to create the illusion of motion. This is exactly how animations such as cartoons that use animation cels work (at least until digital animation more or less took over the industry). An animated flip book, such as you may have made in elementary school, also works in this manner.

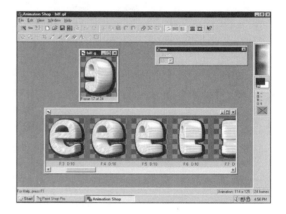

The Animation Shop Interface

Animation Shop uses a lot of the same types of tools that Paint Shop Pro uses. The icons on the toolbar, which give you access to the general image editing, saving, and viewing functions, are as follows (if the Toolbar is not present on your screen, you can get it back with View|Toolbar):

1. Animation Wizard

2. Banner Wizard

3. Export Frames To Paint Shop Pro

4. New Animation

5. Open Animation

6. Save

7. Save Frame As

8. Print

9. Undo

10. Redo

11. Cut

12. Copy

13. Paste As New Animation

14. Paste As New Frames

15. Paste Into Selected Frame

16. Propagate Paste

17. Delete Frames

18. Duplicate

19. Toggle Tool Palette

20. Toggle Style Bar

21. Toggle Color Palette

22. View Animation

23. View Frames

24. Help

The Tool Palette

The Tool palette, which gives you access to various color, pixel, and shape editing tools, appears as follows (you can view the Tool Palette via View|Tool Palette):

1. Arrow

2. Zoom

3. Registration Mark

4. Crop

5. Dropper

6. Brush

7. Eraser

8. Flood Fill

9. Text

10. Line

11. Shape

Creating Animations

To create a custom animation, you need to create your various frames in Paint Shop Pro and then assemble them in Animation Shop (Animation Shop also has many options for creating various animated effects from scratch, especially for text banners and transitions). This can be done by hand, but by far the easiest way to assemble an animation is by using the Animation Wizard.

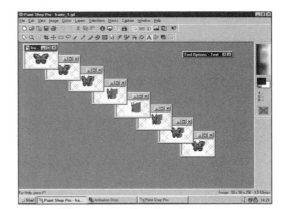

The Animation Wizard

The Animation Wizard leads you through the image-assembly process step-by-step. To open the Animation Wizard, simply click on the Animation Wizard button or use the File|Animation Wizard menu item.

1.

The first dialog box asks you the dimensions of the cumulative animation. You can simply allow it to be the size of the first frame (which is easiest), or you can define the size explicitly. It's not uncommon to build an animation with frames of the same size as the original images, but you may also wish to work with a canvas that is slightly larger than the animation content itself (to give yourself some elbow room, so to speak). Once you have set your values, click on Next to continue.

Remember that View|Image Information in Paint Shop Pro will give you the exact size of your image in pixels.

2.

Next, the wizard will ask you whether you want the background of the animation to be transparent (as in a transparent GIF) or simply a solid color. You can choose a background color by clicking on the color picker box. Clicking Next will set your value and take you to Step 3.

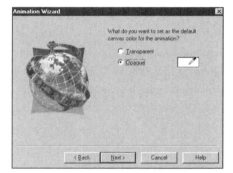

3.

This step determines where your content is displayed within the frames. This really applies *only* if you've set the dimensions of your animation larger than the original images in Step 1. If, for example, your frames were 30 by 30 pixels, but your animation is set at 100 by 100, this step will place the original 30 by 30 images either at the upper-left corner or directly in the middle of each frame, depending on which radio button you choose. It also determines what is displayed in the free space surrounding the image within the frame,

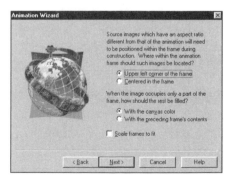

either the canvas color from Step 2 or a transparent space through which the contents of the previous frame(s) show through.

Scale Frames To Fit applies if you have image frames that are *larger* than the size of your total animation. Once you have set your values, click Next to move on to Step 4.

4.

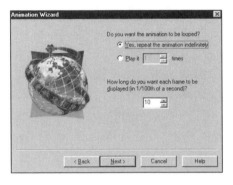

Step 4 enables you to set animation timing and looping information. Looping refers to how many times an animation sequence is repeated. You can loop the animation indefinitely or set the repeat value to a specific number of times (a value of 1 plays the animation only one time).

The other value set within this step is the play rate, measured in 1/100ths of a second. The lower the value, the faster the animation will play. In general, 10/100ths, or 1/10th of a second, is a pretty standard play speed for many animations. Click on Next when you've set your values.

The more frames you have, coupled with smaller movement per frame and a faster play rate, will result in a smoother animation. Unfortunately, it also results in a larger file size.

5.

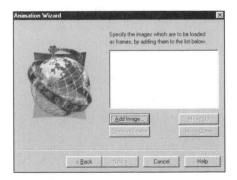

Step 5 is where you enter in the frames that you have created separately in Paint Shop Pro. First, click on the Add Image button. This brings up the Open dialog box, from which you will select the images that will comprise your animation frames.

6.

In the Open dialog box, browse to the directory in which you have saved your frames, select them, and click on Open. This will place the image(s) within the list box in the Wizard dialog box.

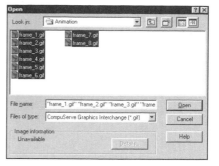

Instead of selecting the images one at a time by clicking on Add Image again and again, you can select all your images at once very easily by using the following method. Select the first image with your cursor, hold down the Shift key, and then click on the last image in the list.

7.

Now your image(s) should be listed within the list box in Step 5. If you need to, you can use Add Images again to select more frame images until they are all within the list.

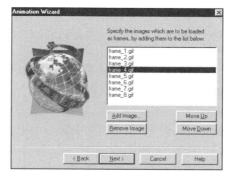

You can use the Move Up and Move Down buttons to place the images in the correct order for the animation (descending order displays the files in the animation first to last). Click Next when you're ready.

8.

The last step simply shows you that all the variables are in place and that the wizard is ready to build the animation for you. If you need to change any of the values for any reason, now is the time to do it. You can go back to any of the previous wizard screens by clicking on Back. Click on Finish when you're ready to build the animation.

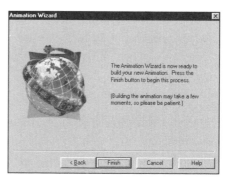

9.

Once the wizard finishes, the animation will be displayed within the film-style frame display, which makes animations easy to deal with by showing all of the frames next to each other in the order they'll be displayed. From here, you can edit the animation frame-by-frame using the tools in the Tool palette just as you would in Paint Shop Pro.

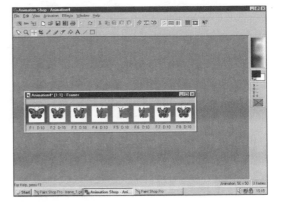

10.

You can now use the View Animation button (also available from the View| Animation menu) to see the animation in action. Viewing the animation will help you determine if variables such as animation frame rate, looping, and background color are really suitable for your animation.

11.

If you're not satisfied with any of the values for some reason (if your animation is choppy, too slow, or whatever), they're easy to change.

For one thing, each individual frame does not have to have the same play rate as the others. You can manipulate effects in your animation, such as speeding up, slowing down, or pausing certain frames, for example.

To alter the play rate value for each frame, first use the Arrow tool to select the frame you wish to alter, then use the Animation|Frame Properties menu item.

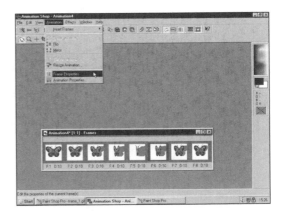

12.

This will bring up the Frame Properties dialog box. Here you can set the frame rate for the selected frame. In this example, I've slowed the display speed down to 20/100, or 1/5th of a second. You can also use the second tab to insert simple comments about your frame; the comments will be viewable only from within an animation graphics program. You could use this space to insert copyright information, for example.

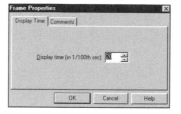

13.

Likewise, you can use the Animation|Animation Properties menu item to set the canvas background color and looping properties, as you did in the wizard. You can insert internal comments here as well.

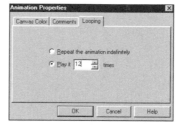

Animation Effects

In addition to simply creating images by importing frames from Paint Shop Pro, you can apply numerous effects and transitions to single images that you may have lying around to create dazzling effects in a snap. You can find these many features and effects from the Effects menu.

Image Transitions

An image transition is an effect that gradually alters an image from one state to another, using such methods as *wipes*, *splits*, and so forth. You've probably seen image transitions before if you've ever watched a PowerPoint presentation or something similar.

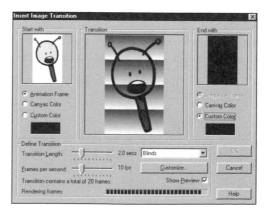

Open an image and select Effects|Insert Image Transition. This will enable you to create image transitions with ease, using either one or two separate images. You can use the drop-down menu in this dialog box to select the type of effect you want to use and the Customize button to set any effect variables. The two slider controls on the left will adjust animation length and frame rate, respectively.

Insert Image Transition

There are two small frame previews in the dialog box, one on the left, and one on the right, representing the starting and finishing states. The preview box in the center shows the effect in action. If your starting image consists of one frame only (nonanimated), it will appear as the first frame on the left, and you can choose the ending color or image on the right. If you want to transition between two images instead of an image and an ending color, place both images in the same animation as separate frames, select them both using Shift+Arrow, and then select the menu item; the images will appear in sequence on the right and on the left (you can easily create a two-frame animation sequence with the Animation|Insert Frames|From File menu item).

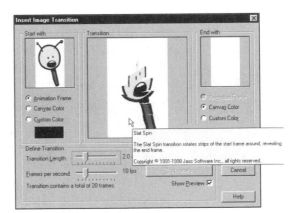

Hold the cursor over the effect preview window or the drop-down menu for a second or two to see a tool tip that describes what the effect does in detail.

Image Effect

Available from Effects|Insert Image Effects, the Insert Image Effect tool works very much like the transition effects tool, except that it simply applies more general animation effects to your image. These effects are very useful if you want a quick and easy way to put an object into motion, such as motion blurring, compression, rotating, underwater waves, and so on.

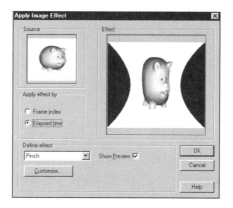

Apply Image Effect

If you want to apply an image effect to a single frame within an animation or to a set of selected frames within an animation, instead of creating an entire animation from one image or frame, you can use the Apply Image Effect dialog box (choose Effects|Apply Image Effect). This way, you can add some motion to your object within an animation for a specific number of frames as you wish.

Text Effects

The text effects tools work exactly like the image effects tools, except that they enable you to create animated effects using text rather than images. (Such effects include a scrolling marquee, bouncing text, moving shadows, and backlighting.) The addition of a little animation to text can really attract attention to your message.

Optimization Wizard

At this point, you are ready to save that animation—but before you do, you may want to
run it through the Optimization Wizard first.
This wizard optimizes your graphic for file size,
much like the JPEG and Transparent GIF Sav-
ers in Paint Shop Pro. It does this by reducing
colors, eliminating unnecessary pixels (pixels
that have the exact same value as they did in
the previous frames), and so forth. When you
create GIFs for the Web, you can make your
clients much happier by optimizing your GIFs
so they are smaller.

1.

To use the Optimization Wizard, find the
File|Optimization Wizard menu item. This will
bring up the Optimization Wizard.

In Step 1 of the wizard, you are asked in which
animation format you want your animation
saved (when you are creating animation for
the Web, GIF is your only choice here). The
When Finished options allow you to specify
whether you want the animation you're working on replaced with the optimized version or
created as a new animation.

*It is my opinion that you should always use the
Create A New Animation From The Optimized Animation option. You wouldn't want that animation
you've been working so hard on to be replaced if for
some reason the Optimization Wizard did something
to your animation that you didn't like. It's always better to be safe than sorry.*

2.

In the second step of the wizard, you can adjust the balance between image size and quality. The label box to the right contains all the image's information, including color information, distribution, and so on.

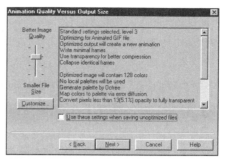

The option Use These Settings When Saving Unoptimized Files simply tells Animation Shop to automatically use these compression options when saving a file instead of running it through the Optimization Wizard first.

3.

Clicking on the Customize button enables you to exact very fine control over the optimization options as displayed in the wizard, such as color depth, reduction method, and other, more complex options. It's usually a safe bet to let Animation Shop handle the optimizations for you because it will never intentionally create any incompatibilities with browsers and such, but the option is there should you ever feel like you want more control.

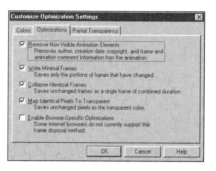

4.

After setting your options, click Next to start the optimization process. After the wizard has completed optimizing your animation, you will the see the message "Press Next to continue."

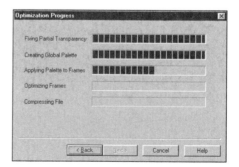

5.

The last step of the wizard shows you the results of the optimization and reduction process, in terms of file size in kilobytes and estimated download time for various connection speeds.

Click on Finish to set your optimizations. You may want to preview the animation again to make sure the changes have not altered your image in a negative way. If not, you are then ready to save your new animation.

6.

The Save button in the toolbar, as well as File|Save, will bring up the standard Save As dialog box.

Paint Shop Pro
Studio

*The following pages contain
color examples of the topics and
techniques presented in this book.*

Although it may be true that a picture is worth a thousand words, sometimes an image just doesn't say it all until it has been properly framed. The Picture Frame Wizard is a simple way to add beautiful and elegant frames to any image, and it's one of the many features new to Paint Shop Pro 6. Frames are covered in Chapter 8.

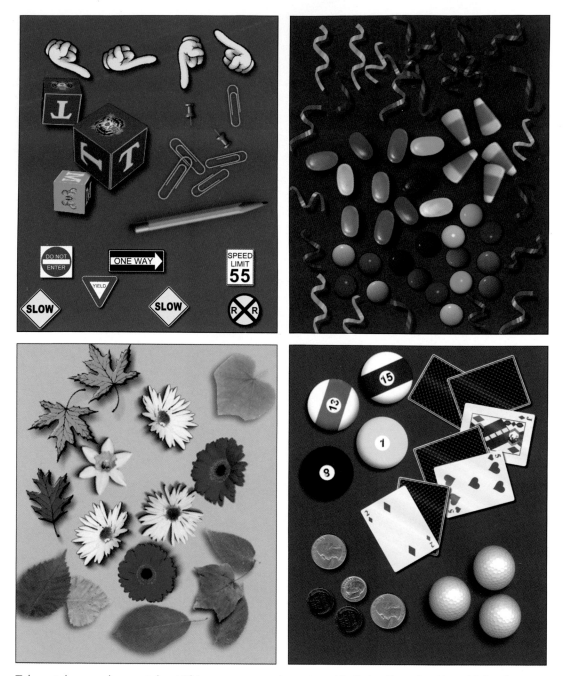

Tubes, tubes, and more tubes! This concept was introduced in Paint Shop Pro 5, and it has been growing in popularity. Chapter 8 shows you how to create original picture tubes to add to the tubes collection that is included with the program.

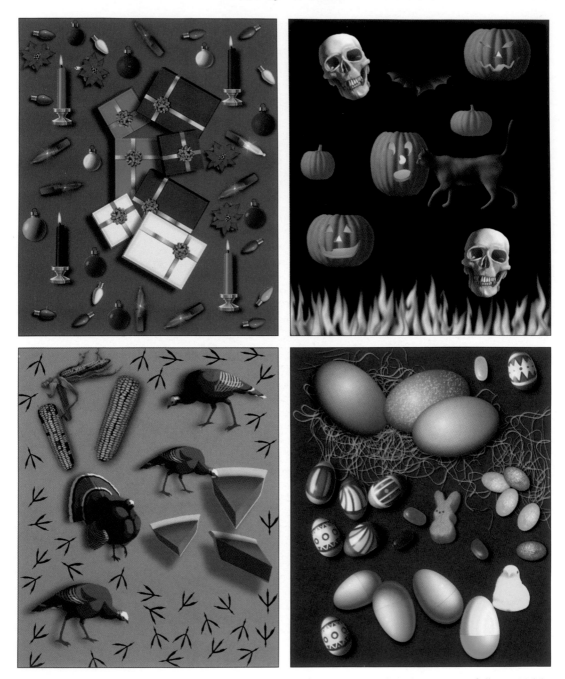

Decorating has never been easier. Since the advent of the picture tube, the creative folks at JASC have been providing tubes to enhance holiday and seasonal projects. These types of tubes are available for all Paint Shop Pro users to download from the JASC Web site, **www.jasc.com**.

Original Image

Unsharp Mask

Gaussian Blur

Edge Enhance

Add Noise

Emboss

Mosaic

Hot Wax

Find All Edges

Graphics programs use filters, effects, deformations, and color manipulations to transform images in one way or another. Paint Shop Pro 6 includes not only the essential filters—such as sharpen and blur—but it also contains a mind-boggling assortment of built-in artistic and enhancement effects. On this page and the following three pages, samples of these effects give you an idea of the magic that can occur with a click of a button. Also see Chapter 5.

Trace Contour

Colorize

Negative

Posterize

Black Pencil

Blinds

Buttonize

Chrome

Colored Chalk

Feedback

Glowing Edges

Kaleidoscope

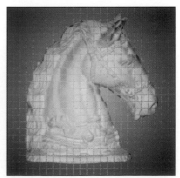

Mosaic-Antique

Mosaic-Glass

Neon Glow

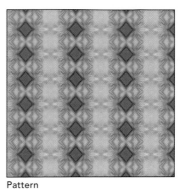

Pattern

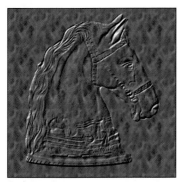

Sculpture

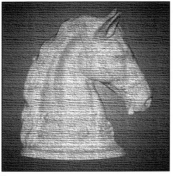

Texture

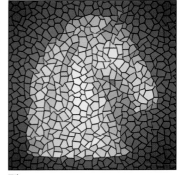

Tiles

Weave

Circle

Cylinder-Horizontal

Cylinder-Vertical

CurlyQ's

Pentagon

Perspective-Horizontal

Perspective-Vertical

Pinch

Punch

Ripple

Rotating Mirror

Skew

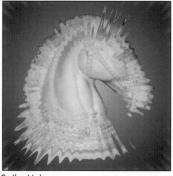

Spiky Halo

Twirl

Warp

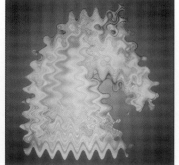

Wave

Wind

Original Layers

Darken

Lighten

Hue

Saturation

Paint Shop Pro's blend modes allow you to mingle colors when working with layers. The mixed colors often look very different from either of the two layers used to form the blend. The images on this page, and continuing on the next two pages, illustrate the results of applying different blend modes to a two-layered image. Learn about blend modes in Chapter 3, and use them in Chapter 9.

Color

Luminance

Multiply

Screen

Dissolve

Overlay

Hard Light

Soft Light

Difference

Dodge

Burn

Exclusion

Miraculous masks! You can use a gradient mask to achieve a simple, yet interesting, merging of images. The statue and cloud images were layered, and then a linear gradient mask was applied. See this project in Chapter 4.

A Chapter 11 project steps you through creating and using edge masks. JASC includes a variety of premade masks on the Paint Shop Pro 6 CD-ROM. Look for the Edges folder. A sampling of the premade masks is shown here. To apply an edge mask to a photo:

1. Add a new layer.

2. Fill the new layer with a color or pattern.

3. Go to Masks|New|From Image to choose the opened mask image.

4. If necessary, use Masks|Invert.

Is this one ready for the home for old photos?
Not with Paint Shop Pro 6 around!

The process begins with a Clone tool session to
remove flaws and scratches.

Gamma Correction greatly improves the color
balance.

Desaturating and recoloring can bring about the
trendy "black and white world" look.

Chapter 10 looks at photo restoration techniques. Here, a severely damaged photo
makes its way through the restoration process.

Chapter 12 reveals the processes involved in creating interesting text effects using the array of available tools and functions. This example illustrates the combination of vectors, gradients, layers, blend modes, and filters to create an eye-catching effect.

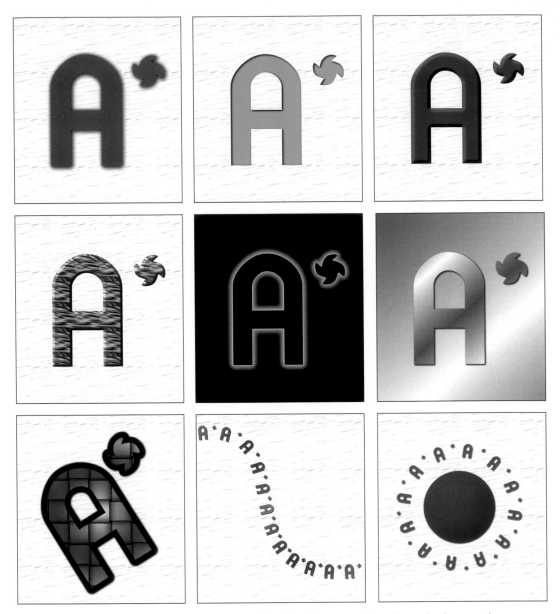

Other text effects covered in Chapter 12 include the classics, such as drop shadows and cutouts. But, the chapter doesn't stop there. You will discover how Paint Shop Pro 6 makes easy work of creating specialty effects, including glowing, beveled, metallic, and skewed text and text that follows paths.

Chapter 7
Introduction To Vector Graphics

- Compare the differences between raster and vector graphics

- Delve into the specifics of vector tools and layers

- Learn the ins and outs of node editing

By Joshua Pruitt

Vector Concepts

Vector graphics are a new feature in Paint Shop Pro 6. They allow you to create geometric shapes easily and then alter their shape, size, and position without losing any image integrity whatsoever.

Raster Defined

So far, you have been working solely with *raster* graphics. Raster graphics are graphics that consist of many individual elements, or *pixels*, of variant color. Because both monitors and printers display images by drawing dots (pixels), raster graphics are good for storing and editing image information in digital format. But they do have their limitations.

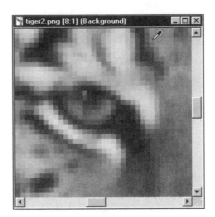

Vector Defined

Vector graphics, on the other hand, do not store graphical information in the form of individual colored pixels or dots. Instead, vector graphics are *object-based*; using various mathematical descriptors and formulas, each drawn shape is described in terms of size, shape, distance (from the edge of the image and between points), curvature, and so forth. Vector objects can easily be drawn, resized, rotated, deformed, reshaped, sketched, or skewed—larger or smaller and to any resolution or size—without *any* loss in image quality. Each time a vector shape is altered, the program redraws the shape and displays it on the monitor (or printer) in pixel form.

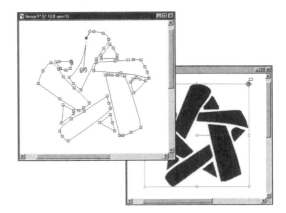

Working With Vectors Layers

On a vector layer, as opposed to the standard raster layer, you deal directly with objects, not with pixels. Vector layers enable you to draw and edit vector objects. As such, you can only place a vector object on a vector layer, and raster elements on raster layers (any attempt to place a vector object on a raster layer will automatically create a new vector layer).

Vector layers are identified by a special icon in the Layer palette. The icon resembles a vector square with editing nodes on each corner.

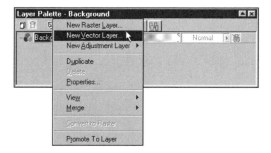

Vector Layer Icon

Creating A Vector Layer

To create a new vector layer, right-click on the layer title area in the Layer palette and select New Vector Layer, or simply use the Preset Shapes, Draw, or Text tool to create a new vector object, which will be automatically placed on its own vector layer.

Vector Objects

A vector layer is different than a normal layer in that you can place more than one vector object on any given vector layer at a time. On any vector layer with active objects, you should see a small plus sign to the left of the vector layer icon indicating that multiple objects may be contained within that one layer. Click on the plus sign to change it to a minus sign and reveal the objects.

Working With Vector Objects

A number of the standard Paint Shop Pro creation and editing tools allow the option of working in vector mode.

1.

Perhaps one of the easiest shapes to create is the circle. First of all, select the Preset Shapes tool, and then select Circle from the Shape Type drop-down menu in the Tool Options dialog box. Make sure you set your style to Stroked and that the Create As Vector option is checked. Then, start from the middle of your image, click and drag, and begin drawing.

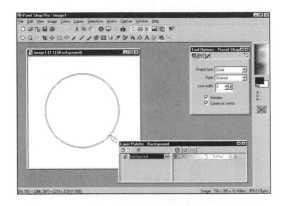

2.

Now, you'll notice a couple of things:

- A new vector layer has been created for you.

- Your new vector object has an outline with various control points. You can use these control points to adjust the size and shape of your object.

To use the control points, activate the Vector Object selection tool from the toolbar.

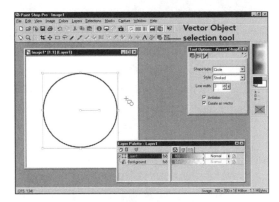

3.

Place your cursor over the control point at the top and center of the new vector object outline (until you see the double-arrows cursor), and click and drag the control point to resize the object vertically.

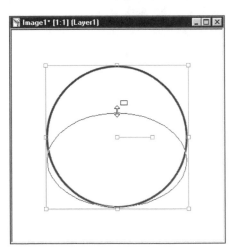

4.

Likewise, place your cursor over the center point on either side and drag to resize horizontally. Dragging the corner control points will resize the shape diagonally. This will stretch and resize the image. To maintain aspect ratio (proportions) while you size diagonally, click and drag the corner control points using the right mouse button.

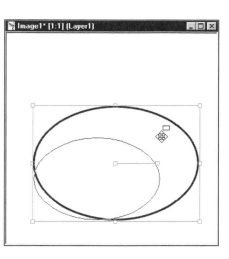

5.

Now place your cursor directly over the control point in the center of your shape outline. You should see a four-pointed Move icon. Click and drag to move your shape into any position.

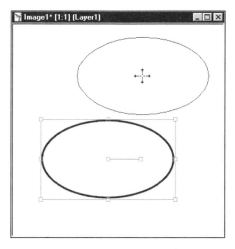

6.

To rotate your object, place the cursor over the point extending from the bar in the center. You'll see a Rotate icon in the cursor area. Clicking and dragging will move the object in a circular motion.

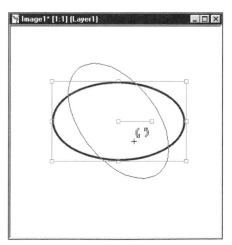

Additional Deformation Options

There are a few more simple shape deformation options at your disposal. Again, use the Preset Shapes tool to draw a shape. This time, use the Stroked And Filled option to create a shape that is filled with your background color.

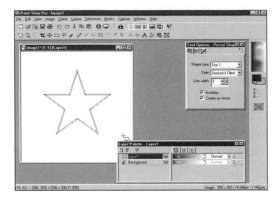

Hold down the Shift key while you form your shape area to keep the aspect ratio intact (in other words, the geometric shapes, such as the star, octagon, and so on, will be geometrically correct as they are formed).

1.

Activate the Vector Object selection tool, and place your cursor over the upper-right corner control point as if you're going to resize it diagonally as before. But before you do, hold down the Shift key. You'll see the cursor icon change from a rectangle to a rhombus. Using the Shift key allows you to alter the perspective of your shape to the right or left.

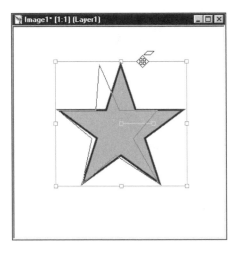

2.

Try the same thing, but this time hold down the Ctrl key before you drag. The cursor changes into a trapezoid, and the shape is skewed from both ends of the range of motion, resulting in a sort of pinching effect. If you go past the center of the image, a twisting effect will occur.

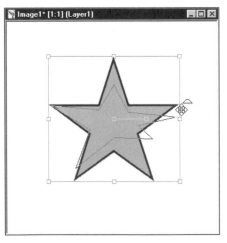

3.

You can hold down both the Shift and Ctrl keys at the same time while resizing the corners to achieve an additional distortion effect.

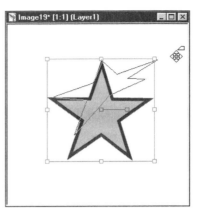

Editing Vector Object Properties

With vectors objects, you can change many properties that determine the look and feel of the shape dynamically by simply clicking a button.

1.

Once you have an object drawn, activate the Vector Object selection tool and right-click on the object. This will bring up the Vector Object context menu where you will click on Properties (clicking on the plus sign in the Layer palette and then right-clicking on the object there will bring up a menu with the Properties option as well).

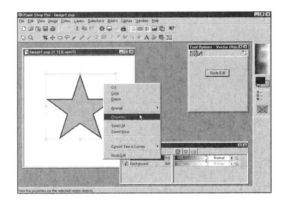

2.

This action brings up the Vector Properties dialog box. From here, you can change any of your original shape settings on the fly. You can change colors, line width, fill styles, and so forth without altering the integrity of the object. You can also change the name of your vector object as it's displayed in the Layer palette.

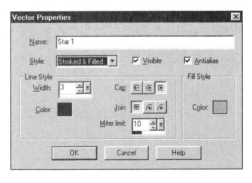

3.

Click on the color box in the Fill Style area. From here, use the standard Color dialog box to change the internal color of your filled object. Any changes made to your object from this dialog box are applied right then and there. The Cancel button will, however, revert the object to its original state if you change your mind.

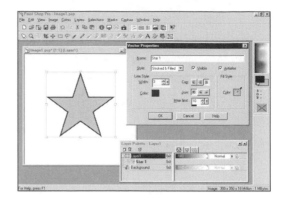

4.

Now change the line width to make it thicker. To do this, simply use the numeric edit control for the Width option under Line Style.

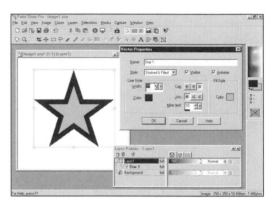

5.

You can also alter the look and feel of your object by changing the Join options. These three options, Miter Join, Round Join, and Bevel Join, affect the way in which corners are rendered and beveled.

By default, you've been using the Miter Join option, which produces sharp, clean corners. Choosing the Round Join button changes all of the outside bevels of your stroked line to round, smooth corners.

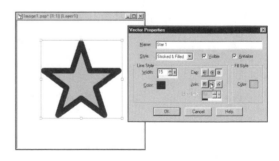

6.

You can choose the Bevel Join button to create corners that are cut off and flattened. The Miter Limit field, which only works with Miter Join, draws a pointed corner unless the value is exceeded, at which point a Bevel Join is drawn. The Miter Limit value is a ratio between the length of the miter (from the inner corner to the outer corner) to the width of connected lines themselves.

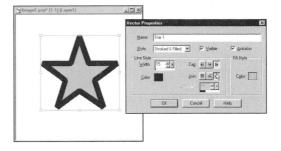

7.

Once you get your shape manipulated to the form you like, you can edit it further and then save it by converting the vector layer to a raster layer (so you can perform raster-based painting and color operations on your shapes) and then by merging the layers. To convert a vector layer to a raster layer, right-click on the vector layer in the Layer palette and select Convert To Raster.

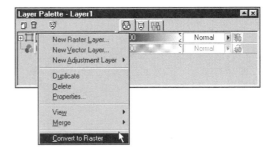

The only file format that supports saving vector information from within Paint Shop Pro is PSP. With any other format, an attempt to save vector information automatically converts the vector objects to raster format.

Vector Node Editing And Paths

With Paint Shop Pro's vector capabilities, you can not only draw simple lines and shapes, but you can also edit them and create new shapes in a more sophisticated manner by using the Node Edit function.

Every vector object, whether it's filled, stroked, or both, contains a *path*—the outline defining the shape and position of the object in 2D space. Each path comprises one or more *contours,* which in turn define the curvature of the outline (a circle has one contour). You can control the curvature, and therefore the overall shape of the object by editing *nodes* (also known as control points), which enable you to alter and tweak the contours of your objects.

1.

To begin using the vector node editing functions, select your object with the Vector Object selection tool, right-click on the object, and select Node Edit from the menu.

A Node Edit option is also available from the Tool Options dialog box when the Vector Object tool is used.

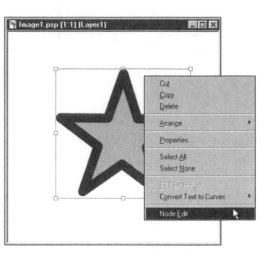

2.

When you're in Node Edit mode, your shape will be outlined, and nodes for editing and adjusting your shape will appear at the end of every contour.

All the nodes in this illustration control lines. Each node has a line "before" and "after" that are, in turn, affected by changes in the node's position. The node influence ends where the adjacent node begins.

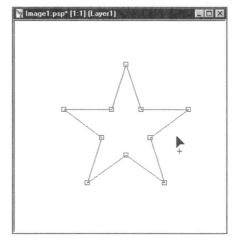

3.

The easiest place to start with node editing is to move a node in a drawing. To do this, place your cursor over one of the nodes—the cursor will now have a four-pointed arrow icon—and then click and drag the node to the position of your choice. You will see that the two lines connected to the node are affected by its movement and adjust accordingly.

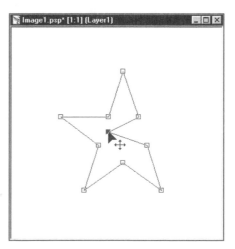

4.

You can also select and move any number of nodes as a group. First, use the cursor to select a node. This node will turn black, indicating that it is selected. Hold down the Shift key and select another node, then another, and so on. When all the nodes you want to work with are selected, release the Shift key. Now, if you drag a selected node in any direction, the others will move as well.

To select multiple nodes, you can also click on any area outside the nodes and drag to make an inclusive selection marquee around the nodes you want to select.

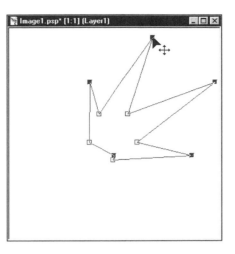

5.

If you want to remove a node from between any two nodes to create a straight path between them, you can use the Merge function. First, select the node you want to eliminate, then hold down the Ctrl key and place the cursor over the node. You'll see the word "MERGE" pop up next to the cursor.

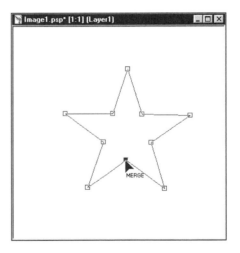

6.

Click with the mouse button while holding down Ctrl. The node disappears, and the line connects between the surrounding nodes.

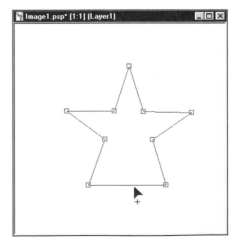

7.

The Ctrl key can be used to add nodes as well as to delete them. To do this, hold the cursor over the outline of the image. A wavy line should appear, indicating that you're in the right place.

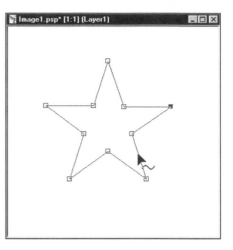

8.

Then, hold down the Ctrl key and position the cursor over the outline. When you see the word "ADD" pop up next to the cursor, click on the outline. The new node appears and takes over the editing functions of the neighboring lines.

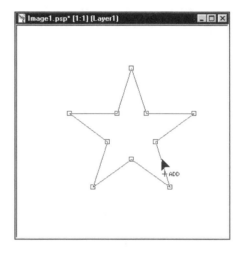

9.

Once you're done making your changes in Node Edit mode, you can exit it and return to normal view by either right-clicking and selecting Quit Node Editing, using the Ctrl+Q shortcut, or simply clicking outside the image window.

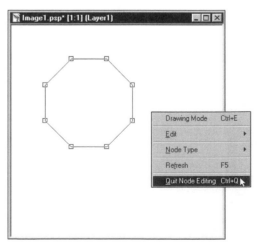

Editing Node Types

Generally, nodes allow you to edit your path in two ways—by using simple lines and with curves. The Node Type function—available while in Node Edit, from a right-click, then the Node Type submenu—allows you to alter your paths and contours fairly easily.

1.

Open or create another vector object composed of many angular points and straight lines.

Select one of the nodes that controls two straight lines. Right-click and choose Node Type|Curve Before. This converts one of your lines (the one left of the node) into a Bezier curve.

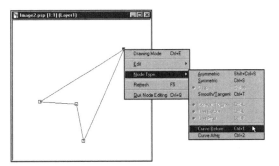

2.

You should now have a handle extending from the node. With this handle you can edit the shape of the curvature along your path. To do so, click and drag the point on the end of the handle to move it around to affect the contour. (Actually, all nodes have handles, and a handle can have a length of zero. When two handles from facing nodes have zero length, you have a straight line.)

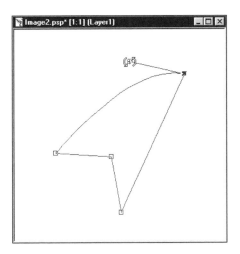

3.

Using the Curve After option from the Node Type menu will give you access to a control handle on the other side of the node.

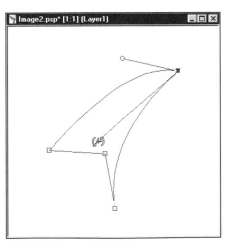

4.

You'll notice that the two node handles that affect the curvature along your path work independently of each other. This is because the nodes are of the Cusp type. You can alter this behavior by changing the node type:

- *Cusp*—Allows node handles to be adjusted independently of each other.

- *Tangent*—Puts handles tangent to a segment of the path. This is frequently useful when connecting a line cleanly to a curve.

- *Curve*—Operates such that both handles are dependent upon each other (that is, you can't move one without affecting the other). The result is a clean, smooth curve segment along the path. There are two categories of curve nodes, both of which are available from the Node Type menu, along with Cusp and Tangent:

  - *Symmetrical*—Both handles are always the same size; the position in which they're pulled doesn't matter.

  - *Asymmetrical*—The handles are along the same tangent, but the curves operate independently. The length of the handles may differ, giving you more control over the shape of the curvature.

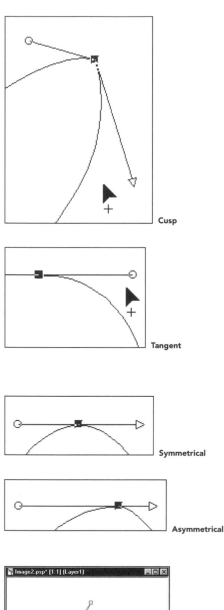

Cusp

Tangent

Symmetrical

Asymmetrical

5.

To revert the curves back into lines (returning the handle lengths to zero), right-click and choose Node Type|Convert To Line.

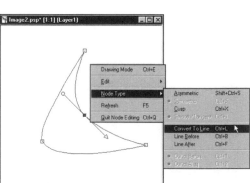

Further Node Editing

You can also access further editing functions by using the Edit menu from within Node Edit mode.

1.

In Node Edit, select and then right-click on any node to bring up the context menu. From there, select Edit|Break.

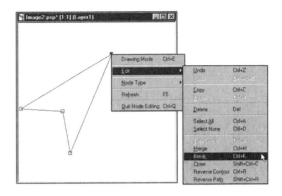

Standard functions, such as Undo, Copy, Select, Delete (the selected nodes), Paste, and so forth are accessible from this menu. Remember, clicking outside the image window closes Node Edit mode, so you can only access these kinds of functions here.

2.

This splits your node into two separate nodes as shown.

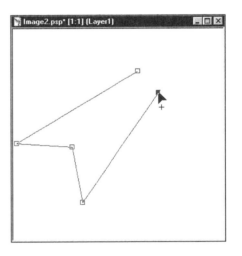

3.

If you want to connect any two disjointed points within your path, select one of the nodes and choose Edit|Close. This draws a line in between the two nodes.

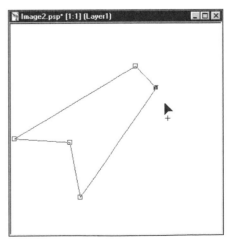

Creating New Nodes

In addition to manipulating and editing your nodes, you can add new nodes to give more dimension and detail to your shape.

To add new nodes in places other than strictly on your path, you have to enter Drawing mode. By default, Node Edit works in what is termed Edit mode. Simply put, Drawing mode gives you the ability to add new nodes and contours anywhere in your image window.

1.

To enter Drawing mode, right-click anywhere in the image window while in Node Edit, and select Drawing Mode from the top of the menu. Now you can add nodes. If you were to right-click again, the menu would highlight Edit Mode. Clicking there will, of course, bring you back into Edit mode, which prevents you from adding nodes. Essentially, you're always in whichever mode is the one *not* listed in the menu.

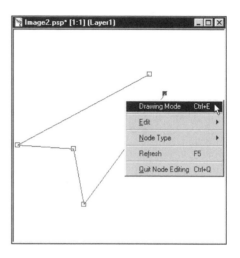

2.

To add a new node, click anywhere on the image window. This will create a new contour. You can continue adding nodes by clicking repeatedly; the paths are automatically connected. To change the contour of the nodes, hold down the mouse button and drag while you click.

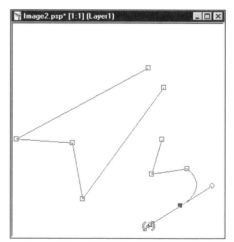

3.

If you want to join your contours in Drawing mode, just drag a node on top of another node, hold down the Ctrl key, and when the word "JOIN" pops up, click.

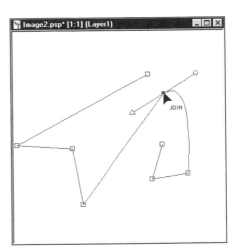

4.

If you want to work entirely within the existing contour, select the end point of a node that has been broken (disconnected from another node), and then click. A new node will be drawn with the path connected to the preceding point.

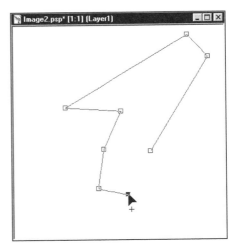

Using The Draw Tool As A Vector

With the Draw tool, you can also take advantage of vector capabilities, which makes editing and altering lines within your image much easier and more productive.

1.

To use this functionality, activate the Draw tool to draw a line, but select the Create As Vector checkbox in the Tool Options dialog box.

2.

Draw your line (Single Line type in this case) by clicking, dragging, and releasing. Now you will have a line, but you will notice the vector shape outline surrounding it. To access vector functionality, activate the Vector Object selection tool.

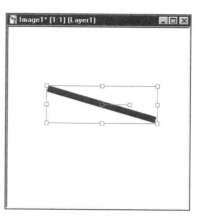

3.

The deformation options work with lines in the same way they work with shapes, and direct functionality over any type of line can be achieved by right-clicking and selecting Node Edit. This is useful when matching a line over an exact shape, giving you the ability to "trace" accurately.

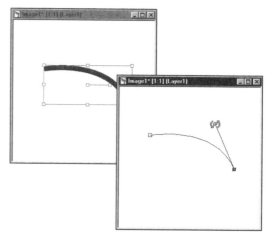

4.

When using the freehand line option of the Draw Tool, the Close Path option (in the Draw Tool Options dialog box) will automatically connect the beginning and end of your line area. This is useful for a filled—or stroked and filled—object because it is sometimes difficult to draw a complete path ending exactly where it started using the mouse.

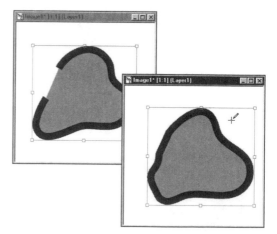

Other Line Options

There are three Line Cap styles to choose from under the second tab of the Tool Options dialog box (and the Vector Properties dialog box as well)—Flat, Round, and Square. Of course, they only apply if your line is thicker than one pixel.

- *Flat*—Starts drawing at the pixel where the cursor begins—and of course, it's flat.

- *Round*—Rounds off the ends of the line and extends the path out past where the cursor is positioned on both sides (start and finish).

- *Square*—Appears flat like the first option, but it extends past the start and end points of the path.

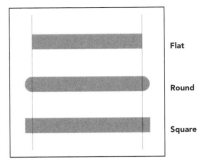

Flat

Round

Square

Working With And Selecting Multiple Vector Objects

When working with vector objects, you may choose to keep multiple objects within one vector layer. You can also select multiple vector objects and work on them as a group (so long as they are all within the same vector layer). Likewise, you can separate objects into different layers for different groupings.

Except when you're in Edit Mode, you can deform, move, copy, and otherwise manipulate many vector objects at once. But first, you need to select them. There are two ways to go about this.

1.

Activate the Vector Object selection tool and then drag a selection area around the objects you wish to group together. You will see the vector selection area encompass all the objects you've selected. You'll also notice that the names of the selected objects appear in bold in the Layer palette.

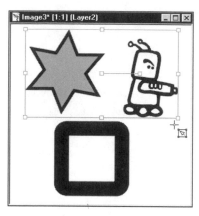

2.

You can also use the Ctrl key with a click to select each object in the Layer palette (selected objects will be listed in bold type). Another click will deselect the objects.

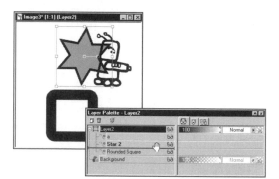

3.

You can position vector objects above and below each other in the same way you would manipulate layers, by clicking and dragging the selected objects to their new positions within the Layer palette.

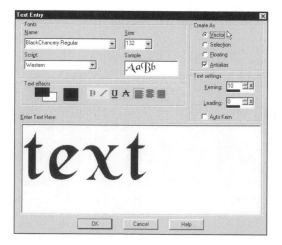

Vector Text

In addition to lines and shapes, text can also be created as vector objects by choosing the Vector option from the Text Entry dialog box.

Cool Text Effects

There are a lot of great vector text effects to explore. You will learn more about manipulating vector text and text paths in Chapter 12.

Chapter 8
Picture Frames And
Picture Tubes

- Learn to use the Picture Frame Wizard and create custom frames

- Discover picture tubes—learn how they function and how to create more of your own

- Explore the possibilities of making other objects using transparency

By Ramona Pruitt

Paint Shop Pro's Little Extras

In this chapter, you'll learn about two of Paint Shop Pro's specialty toys, the built-in picture frames and picture tubes. You'll look at how they work, discover ways to use them, and even learn how to create frames and tubes of your own from scratch. In addition, I'll show you how to create other transparency-based objects (similar to tubes and frames), which you can use to execute some easy and entertaining effects.

Using The Picture Frame Wizard

The Picture Frame Wizard, new to the version 6 release of Paint Shop Pro, is an easy-to-use application that will add a decorative frame around an image.

Making great frames requires little effort. Thanks to a simple user interface, all that is required is the push of a button. However, there are a few little tips and tricks you can use to make your frames even better.

1.

To use the Picture Frame Wizard, you will first need to open or create an image to frame. For illustration purposes, I will use a photo with an image size of 600 by 500 pixels.

The picture Frame Wizard was enhanced in a Paint Shop Pro update and in version 6.01 of the program. You can now choose to add a new frame either inside or outside the borders of an image.

2.

You can access the Picture Frame Wizard from the Image menu (Image|Picture Frame).

Because the Picture Frame Wizard works by adding a new layer, the image must be in either 24-bit color or grayscale for it to work. If the wizard appears grayed out in the Image menu, you will need to increase the color depth of your image to make the wizard available.

3.

To select a frame, use the drop-down frame selection menu to view the assorted styles. If you click on a style name, a preview of that particular frame will show up in the area to the right of the menu.

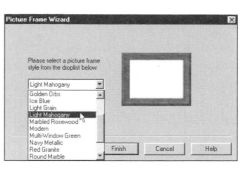

You can view all the frames quickly by using the up and down arrow keys on your keyboard to scroll through them.

4.

Choose a rectangular frame for this first framing project. Once you have a frame picked out, click the Finish button to apply it to your image.

If you had free space around the perimeter of your image, your frame probably looks all right. As you can see in the example shown here, though, the image I'm using has been partially covered by the frame, so the situation will need to be addressed.

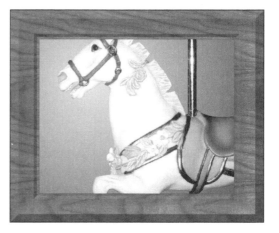

5.

The frame is automatically sized to fit within the borders of the image, so you'll almost always need to increase the canvas size of the image to create extra space surrounding the actual image area in order to accommodate the frame. Deciding how much to increase depends on the image size and frame chosen, because the width of the different frames will vary both by style and original image size. An easy way to estimate how much size to add is to go ahead and create the chosen frame and then use the image rulers (View|Rulers) to determine the approximate width of the finished frame.

6.

Use the Zoom tool to zoom in on the upper-left corner of the image. By holding the cursor at the inside corner of the frame, you can look at the dotted placement lines on the rulers to approximate the extra canvas size needed. In the image shown here, each side of the frame is taking up about 70 pixels. Therefore, a canvas size increase of 70 pixels for every side will add enough extra space so that, when the frame is remade, it will not cover the edges of the image.

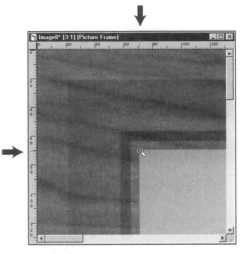

If the width and height of your image differ greatly, you'll notice the frames will be thinner along the longer sides.

7.

Once you know how much to increase the canvas size, delete the frame that was used for measuring. You can delete it by choosing Undo Picture Frame from the Edit menu, or you can delete the picture frame layer itself (Layers|Delete). With your image back to the way it was originally, enlarge the canvas by clicking on Image|Canvas Size and then entering new width and height amounts, calculated by adding the frame measurements acquired in Step 6 to the original image measurements. For example, with my original image height of 500, I added 70 pixels for the top side of the frame and another 70 for the bottom side (for a total of 140) for a total new height measurement of 640. With my original image width of 600, I added 70 each for both the left and right sides for a total a new width measurement of 740.

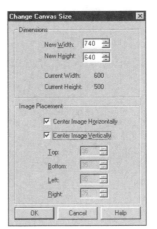

8.

Use the Picture Frame Wizard again and choose the same frame. This time, thanks to the canvas size increase, you'll notice that the frame doesn't cover important image areas. This is not an exact method because the size increase will also generate a bigger overall image (meaning that a frame that is slightly wider than the measurement frame will be formed). If you still have too much overlap, undo the frame again and add a little more to the canvas size.

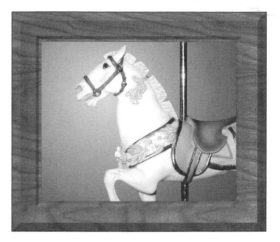

9.

Now try a different type of frame. Open a new image to work with or use a copy of your first image. This time, choose one of the round-shaped frames. You will notice that, upon choosing one of these types of frames, the Finish command is not available in the Picture Frame Wizard. Instead, you will see a Next button. Press it to bring up the next option.

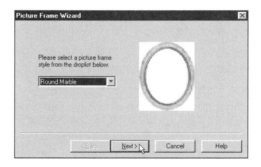

10.

When using any of the round- or odd-shaped frames, you will need to specify the color you wish to use to fill in the area where the frame does not extend to the edge of the image, such as the corners on a round or oval shape. Use the drop-down menu to choose either a color or transparent, and click on Finish to apply the frame.

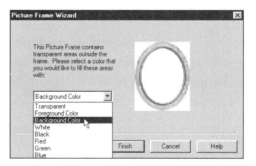

11.

Just as with the rectangular frame, some important image areas are going to be covered, as shown here, unless you increase the canvas size to create additional space around the image area.

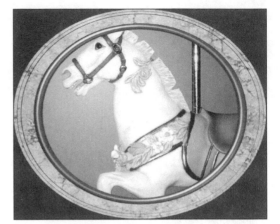

12.

To approximate the necessary canvas size increase for one of these frames, zoom in and place the cursor at the center of the inside edge on the narrowest portion of the frame; then use the adjacent ruler to determine the edge width of the frame.

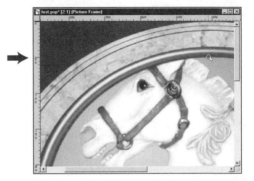

13.

Just as you did with the rectangular frame, either undo or delete the "measuring" frame, increase the canvas size by the measured amount, and then add the final frame.

Because the Picture Frame Wizard has added a layer for the frame, your image will have to be merged (Layers|Merge|Merge All) to save in a format that does not support layers.

Creating Simple Custom Frames

Even though Paint Shop Pro has provided some very cool frames, you may want to design some of your own.

1.

Frames contain transparent portions to allow your image to show through, so they are always created on a transparent background. And because they are resized on the fly, so to speak, you'll want to create them rather large so the frame quality will look good even if applied to a large image (sizing down always produces better quality than sizing up). Open a new, large-size image, 1,000 by 1,000 pixels, with Transparent as the background color.

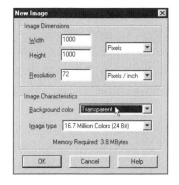

2.

In this lesson, you'll create a simple square frame. To select the frame portion, first use the Selections menu to choose Select All. Decide how wide you wish your frame to be and contract the selection by that many pixels (Selections|Modify|Contract). In the illustration, I'll contract by 125 pixels for a fairly wide frame. Now the center portion is selected 125 pixels away from each edge.

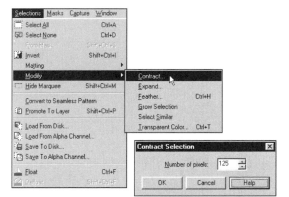

3.

Choose Selections|Invert so that the selected area is reversed to encompass the 125-pixel outer edge (which will become the frame), rather than the center portion.

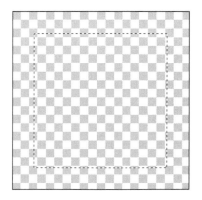

4.

This is the point at which you can really experiment and get creative if you like. You could fill the frame with a solid color or pattern and apply filters such as Sculpture, Texture, or Inner Bevel. For this practice frame, a gradient fill will do the job. Activate the Flood Fill tool now and choose Rectangular Gradient from the Fill Style drop-down menu.

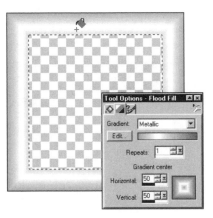

5.

Under the Flood Fill Options (accessed by clicking on the middle tab of the Tool options dialog box), choose the following settings:

- *Gradient*—Metallic
- *Repeats*—1
- *Horizontal*—50
- *Vertical*—50

Fill the selected area.

6.

This would make a pretty nice frame the way it is, but it could use a little extra decorative touch. Go to Image|Effects|Inner Bevel. Use the drop-down Presets menu and choose Frame (click on OK to apply). This preset will add a small groove to both the inner and outer edges of the frame, giving it a more realistic appearance.

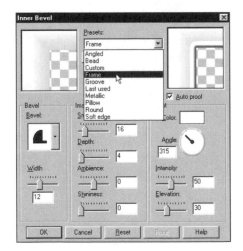

7.

Deactivate the selection (Selections|Select None). The frame is now ready to be saved so that it can be used in conjunction with the Picture Frame Wizard.

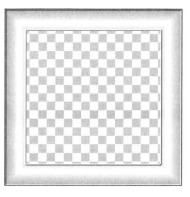

8.

The Picture Frame Wizard uses a file format exclusive to Paint Shop Pro; it's known as PFR (which stands for picture frame) and is an extension to the native PSP file format. To save custom-made frames in this format, you'll first need to associate the .pfr extension to the PSP file format. This is relatively easy to do. Go to the File menu to bring up the File Format Associations dialog box (File|Preferences|File Format Associations).

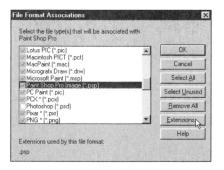

9.

In the dialog box, you'll see a list of all the file formats. Scroll through them until you find the one called Paint Shop Pro Image (*.psp). Click on it once to highlight it, and then click on the Extensions button on the right side of the dialog box.

10.

You will now see an Extensions dialog box in which you can choose to add or delete extensions to the PSP format. Choose Add and a box will pop up, prompting you to define the new extension. Type in "pfr" and click on OK.

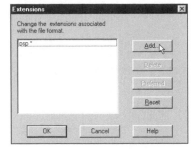

11.

You'll notice in the dialog box's inner window that "pfr" has been added to the list directly under "psp." Click on OK. Now you will be able to save your custom frames and view and select them through the Picture Frame Wizard, right along with the built-in frames.

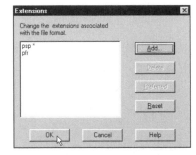

12.

To save, go to File|Save As. In the Save As dialog box, navigate to the Frames folder located within the Paint Shop Pro 6 program folder. Type in a name for your file in the File Name area and give it a .pfr extension. As illustrated here, I've chosen to name the new frame Light Metallic.pfr. Click on Save when you're finished.

13.

Now when you use the Picture Frame Wizard, you'll find the name and a preview of your frame in the wizard screen.

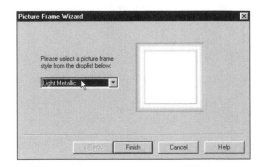

14.

Open an image and follow the measuring and framing steps you learned earlier in this chapter to see how your custom frame looks when put to use.

Because the custom frame you just made in this project is a light neutral color, it can be easily color-matched to complement your image through Colors|Colorize.

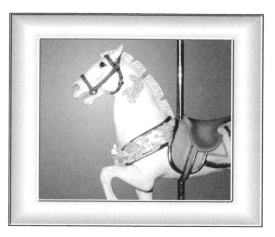

Creating More Complex Frames

It's a bit trickier to create round and oval frames than it is to create plain square frames, but it's not difficult once you learn how.

1.

Open a new image with a transparent background. Once again, make it large. The one shown here will be 1,000 by 800 pixels and will be used to make an oval frame. Activate the Shape Selection tool and choose Ellipse in the Tool Options window. Set Feather to 0 and keep Antialias checked.

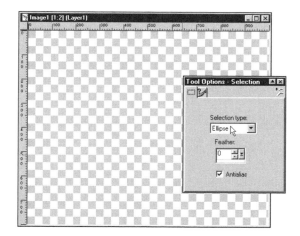

2.

Ellipses are formed from the center out, so place your cursor in the exact center of your image to begin the selection. Look at the status bar in the lower-left portion of your screen to see the X,Y position of the cursor for perfect centering. For this image, place it at 500, 400 and then click and drag it all the way to one of the corners so that the edges of the ellipse go all the way to the edges of the image.

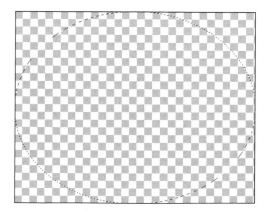

3.

Go to the Color palette and choose a frame color. Use the Flood Fill tool set to the Solid Color fill style to fill the selection. If you prefer, you can open a pattern and use the Pattern fill style.

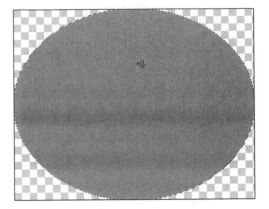

4.

The outer corner portions of the image will need to be masked off in order for the Picture Frame Wizard to present the option of which background color to use in those areas. Otherwise it will be transparent. To mask off the areas, begin by inverting the selection (Selections|Invert) so that the outer portions, rather than the ellipse, become the selected area. Then choose Masks|New|Hide Selection.

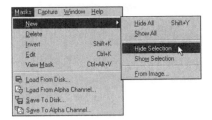

5.

The mask will need to be saved as an alpha channel within the image so that the Picture Frame Wizard will mask off that outer area each time the frame is used. Go to Masks|Save To Alpha and click on OK in each of the two ensuing dialog boxes, accepting the default name for the channel.

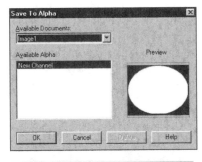

6.

To finish the frame, once again choose Selections|Invert. The inner portion of the ellipse will be selected as it was in the beginning. Decide how wide you wish the frame to be and contract the selection by that many pixels (Selections|Modify|Contract). The selection shown here has been contracted by 75 pixels.

7.

To eliminate this inner selected part and leave only the oval frame, you can either use the Delete key on your keyboard or go to the Edit menu and choose Cut. You will no longer need the selection, so use the Selections|Select None menu option.

8.

Now is the time to apply any special effects you might want to use before saving the frame. For this frame, I used the Texture filter with a Stucco preset followed by the Inner Bevel filter with the Round preset.

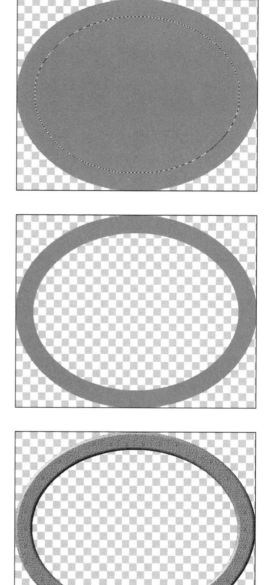

9.

Save the frame just as you saved the square frame. Use the File|Save As menu option. In the Save As dialog box, navigate to the Frames folder located within the Paint Shop Pro 6 program folder. Type in a name for your file in the File Name area and give it a .pfr extension. I've chosen to name this new frame Oval Stucco.pfr. Click on Save when finished.

10.

Test your new oval frame on an image. Use the measuring tips you learned at the beginning of the chapter to make sure the frame doesn't cover vital image areas.

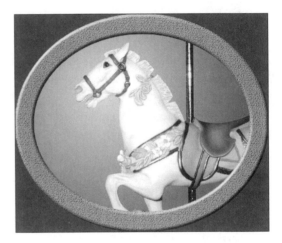

What Are Picture Tubes?

Let's suppose you're holding a tube of paint in your hand. When you remove the lid and squeeze the tube, you would certainly expect nothing to come out but a blob of paint, right?

But now, imagine that what you have is a *magic* tube of paint, and when you squeeze it, entire images pop right out, and you can use these images to *paint* with! In essence, that's what happens when you use Paint Shop Pro's picture tubes.

Tube Basics

If you were to rank all the Paint Shop Pro tools according to how much fun they are to play with, the Picture Tube tool would no doubt be right up at the top of the list.

1.

Paint Shop Pro 6 contains an array of built-in tubes. Each tube contains an assortment of similar "pictures" that can be placed into a new or existing image. For instance, the fish tube contains 12 different images of fish. Because tubes are initially created on a transparent background, they can blend right in to any background color or image.

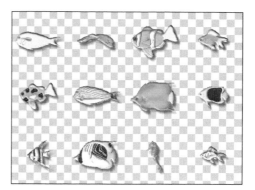

2.

You can use tubes any number of ways—to decorate photos and other images, to make Web graphics, or even to create entire tube paintings from scratch.

3.

When the Tube tool is activated (by clicking on the tube icon in the toolbar), you'll notice a drop-down menu of available tubes in the Tool Options dialog box. The dialog box also shows a thumbnail image of the first picture in the chosen tube.

4.

If you wish to view all of the images in a particular tube, you can do so in a couple of different ways. You can use the File menu (File|Open) and navigate to your Paint Shop Pro directory where you will find the tubes folder. Once there, just click on the desired tube and you'll be able to view the contents in the Preview window. Click on Open to bring up the full view if you need a closer look.

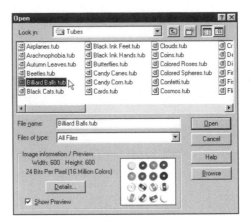

5.

To view the contents of all the tubes at once, you can use the Browse function (File|Browse) to navigate to the Tubes folder. Double-click on any of the thumbnails for the full-size view.

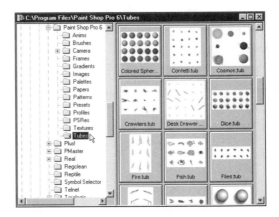

6.

Once you've seen the tubes that are available, open a new blank image and activate the Tube tool. Select a tube from the drop-down menu. Notice that with each click of the mouse in your image, a different picture from the tube will appear.

7.

Now that you see how the tubes operate, let's take another look at the Tool Options dialog box. Located directly beneath the Tube drop-down menu is an option called Scale. By default, this option will size the tubes at 100 percent (their original size), but you can change the scale to range anywhere from 10 percent to 250 percent.

150%

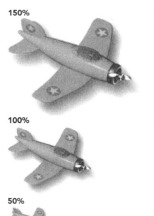

100%

50%

8.

Next are the Placement Mode and Selection Mode options. These options give you control over various means of picture placement. Using the Placement Mode, you can choose from Random or Continuous to control whether the tube images appear at either random or equal intervals when you place more than one. The Selection Mode lets you also control the image placement by Random (picking images from the tube at random), Incremental (placing the images from the tube in order from the first to last), and by such things as the direction (Angular) or speed (Velocity) that you drag the cursor. The Pressure option works only with pressure-sensitive pads.

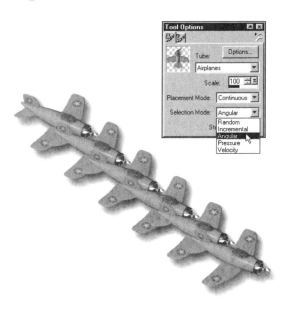

9.

Step refers to the pixel distance allocated between the images when you're painting with a continuous brush motion.

Creating New Tubes

Making your own tubes can be a handy way to save small, simple, oft-used images, such as decorations and Web page buttons.

1.

The first step in the creation process is to set up the grid size with which to make the picture cells. Begin by going to File|Preferences| General Program Preferences to bring up the Preferences dialog box.

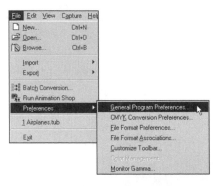

2.

On the Rulers And Units tab, you'll find the necessary options for setting up a grid. The Horizontal Spacing and Vertical Spacing values will be used to define how much room you will have for each picture in the tube. I've set both the spacing sizes to 200 and chosen pixels as the form of measurement. This will result in a 200-by-200-pixel square for each of my picture cells.

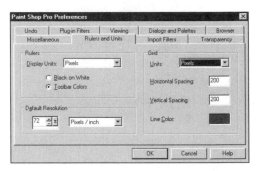

3.

To calculate the image size needed, first decide how many pictures will be created in the tube and the placement system, such as how many across and how many down. Multiply these numbers by the grid size (200 in this case) to get the correct height and width dimensions. For example, I'll make 12 pictures in my example tube, so I'll use 4 cells across and 3 cells down. My image width will need to be 800 (4 cells multiplied by the 200-pixel grid size) with a height of 600 (3 cells multiplied by the 200-pixel grid size). Tubes must be created on transparent backgrounds, so remember to specify Transparent in the New Image dialog box.

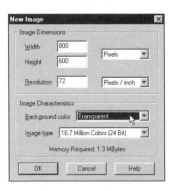

4.

Once the new image window is created, you will have to activate the grid to be able to see it. To do this, simply choose View|Grid.

5.

The blank image will now have visible grid lines to use as boundary lines while you're creating the pictures. The grid lines will appear in the color that was selected as the line color in the Rulers And Units tab in the Preferences dialog box.

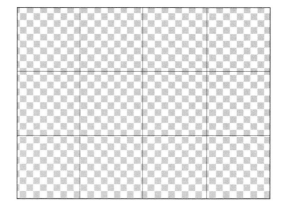

6.

To create the picture tube, place one image in each grid square. Each square represents one picture tube cell. In this illustration, I've used a dingbat font consisting of different chess pieces and applied some coloring and inner bevel effects to create the 12 different pictures, each contained in a cell.

7.

Once you've created the images for the tube, go to the File menu and choose Export|Picture Tube.

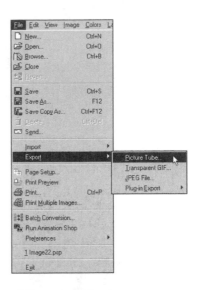

8.

The Export Picture Tube dialog box opens, giving you the necessary options to set for your tube, such as the number of cells across and down. Just type in the values that were used in Step 3. In the Step Size box, type the pixel width of the cells. Give the tube a descriptive name, click on OK, and you're finished.

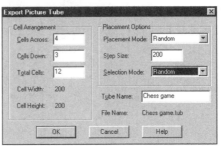

9.

The new tube will be automatically saved with the .tub extension and added to the list of tubes in the Tool Options dialog box.

10.

More tubes are available! By visiting the Paint Shop Pro Web site at **www.jasc.com/tubes**, you gain access to an ever-increasing store of royalty-free tubes made available by JASC. They include special holiday and seasonal tubes.

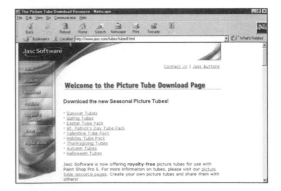

11.

While you're there, be sure to check out the design resources section for links to user-created tubes. Most user-created tubes can be easily added to the Tube folder in Paint Shop Pro 6 by either downloading and dropping them right into the folder or exporting them into the folder. And if you find you're rapidly becoming a tube-aholic (or *collector*, if you prefer), don't worry—you're not alone! You may want to join in on the Paint Shop Pro newsgroup talk at **comp.graphics.apps.paint-shop-pro**.

Stock Art, Custom Brushes and Picture Tubes

- Nikki's Brush Boutique – Custom brush tips for Paint Shop Pro 5.
- PhotoDisc, Inc. – High-quality yet affordable royalty-free digital stock photography.
- ArtToday – Image and font archive.
- DigArts Software – Professionally created Picture Tubes.
- Thomas Bosselmann's Picture Tubes – Includes a tube for the Euro – *Updated!*
- Free Tubes – Tubes, brushes, masks and more.
- The Page of Blues – Tubes, brushes and Blade Pro sets.
- The Tube Page – Pages of Tubes.

An Object Lesson

Working with frames and tubes has illustrated the advantages of the use of transparency in an image. A similar way to use transparency to your advantage is with the creation and application of reusable objects.

1.

A reusable object is one that is saved in a file format that supports transparency—such as Paint Shop Pro's native PSP format—and can be copied and moved to another image as a selection rather than a tube, with the added control that selections offer.

On the Paint Shop Pro CD-ROM, you'll noticed that, in addition to the executable program itself, there are a few extra folders. One of the folders is called Objects.

2.

Use the Paint Shop Pro Browse function
(File|Browse) to open the Objects folder and
take a look at what's in there.

As you'll see, the objects located in the folder
are purely for fun—things you can use to decorate photos with, such as hats, sunglasses,
neckties, and comical hairdos.

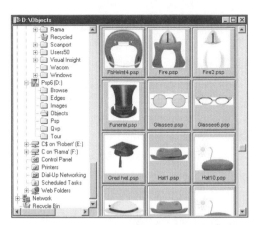

3.

The first step is to open an image or photo that
you'd like to embellish. To illustrate, I'll use a
photo of a very tolerant lion I know.

4.

Choose an object and open it by double-clicking on the thumbnail version in the Browser.
This will bring up a much larger version of
the same object. Use the Edit menu on the
toolbar to copy the object.

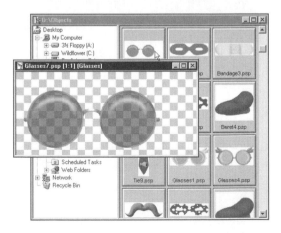

5.

Activate the photo image (by clicking once on the image's title bar) and choose Paste As New Selection from the Edit menu. Notice how the object is now located in your image as a floating selection, complete with flashing marquee. The program automatically selects any portion that is not totally transparent. If an object contains any partially transparent colors, like the lenses in this illustration, you'll notice your image shows through the partially transparent portions of the selection, similar to showing through a layer with the opacity reduced.

6.

Because the object is now a selection, you have the freedom to easily apply any desired changes—such as positioning, resizing, rotating, and applying desired effects—to allow it to fit in with your image.

If you wish to resize the selection (Image|Resize), make sure the Resize All Layers option in the Resize dialog box is unchecked or you will end up resizing your image along with it.

7.

Take a few minutes to try out some of the other objects in the folder, and then I'll show you how to create one of your own.

Creating An Object From Scratch

To get some practice, you'll utilize a few of the features new to version 6 to create a new object that can be saved and reused on any image.

1.

To begin, open a new image with Transparent selected as the background color. When creating an object, you may want to make it a little on the large size—notice my new image window is 500 pixels by 400 pixels, big enough to accommodate a large object. That way, just as with the frames, when you decrease the size of the object to fit in with another image, it doesn't lose as much quality as it would lose if you had to increase its size.

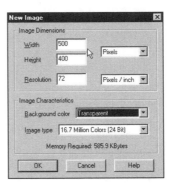

2.

Use the View menu to activate the image ruler (View|Rulers). Once the ruler is activated, notice how rulers appear across the top and left side of the image window. You'll use these as measurement guides when forming your object.

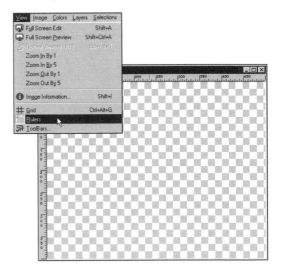

3.

Activate the Shape Selection tool and choose Rectangle as the selection type. Set the Feather option to 0 and leave Antialias unchecked.

4.

Hover the mouse cursor over the image and watch the rulers as you do so. You'll see that a line appears in each ruler designating the location of the cursor. Hover toward the upper-left portion of the image until the lines are at 50 on the left ruler and 100 on the top. Click and drag across the blank image until the ruler lines show 300 on the left and 400 on top to form a rectangular selection like the one shown here.

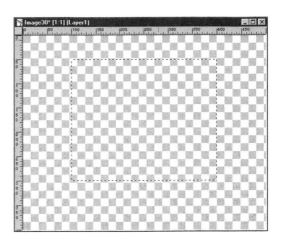

5.

Choose Modify|Expand from the Selections menu. This brings up a window where you can enter the number of pixels by which you'd like to expand the selection. Enter 10 pixels for this particular selection. When a rectangular selection is expanded, the corners will gain a rounded appearance.

6.

Next, choose a light gray color as the foreground color in the Color palette and use the Flood Fill tool with the Solid Color setting to fill the selected area.

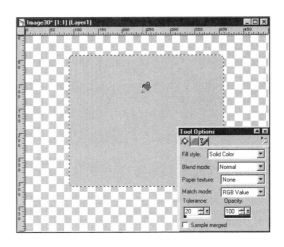

7.

Go to the Image|Effects menu and use the Inner Bevel effect to form a slightly rounded beveled edge along the inside of the selection marquee.

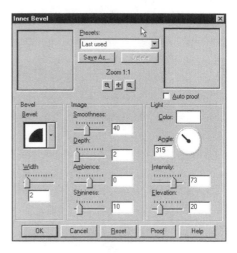

8.

Once you have the bevel, go to Selections| Modify again, but this time use the Contract option. Set the number of pixels in the ensuing options window to 30. The selected area will now be reduced in size by 30 pixels all the way around.

9.

Head back to the Image|Effects menu and use the Outer Bevel effect, this time to place a softly rounded bevel on the outside edge of the selection marquee.

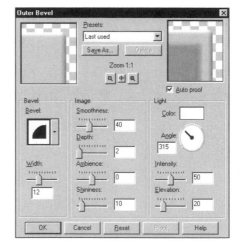

10.

Your selection should now look something like the one shown here.

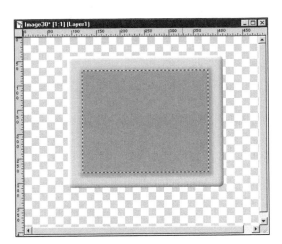

11.

Press the Delete key on your keyboard, and the remaining selected solid-gray center portion will be cut to transparency.

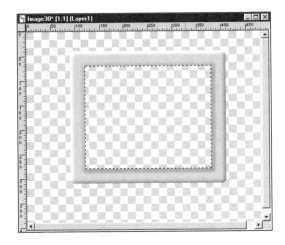

12.

Set the background color in the Color palette to a medium gray. Activate the Flood Fill tool and choose the Sunburst Gradient fill style. Click on the center tab in the Tool Options dialog box and choose Fading Background as the gradient. Set Repeats to 0, Horizontal to 30, and Vertical to 75.

13.

The effect you are shooting for now is for the background color (the medium gray) to fade into transparency toward the center point of the sunburst, rather than from the center out (as would happen with a left-click). To achieve this, right-click in the selected area to place the gradient. (You can apply any gradient in reverse by using the right-click method.) The object is now beginning to resemble a computer monitor with a light source shining on it from the upper left.

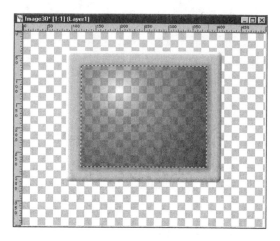

14.

Use the Rectangular selection tool to add on a control panel at the bottom of the newly formed monitor screen. After making the selection, fill with the light gray foreground color and use the Inner Bevel effect (Image|Effects| Inner Bevel) to add depth.

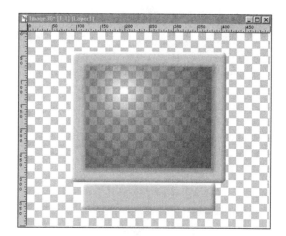

15.

Use the same technique to form a few control buttons of various sizes on the panel.

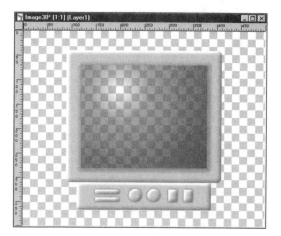

16.

Now your object is ready to be copied and used in a chosen image.

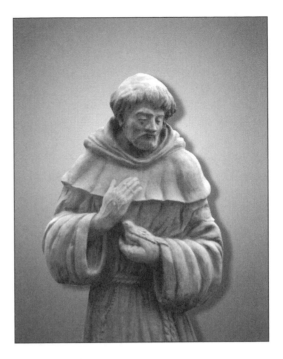

17.

With the object as the active image, choose Edit|Copy. Then activate the targeted image and choose Edit|Paste As New Selection. You can now position the object so that the "monitor" screen encloses the desired portion of the image. Resize the monitor object if necessary.

18.

You can use the still-selected object to your advantage to eliminate the unnecessary areas of the picture. Choose Selections|Invert to reverse the selected area from the object to the area surrounding the object. Choose a nice color or background pattern and use the Flood Fill tool to fill the now-selected outer area, thus capturing the subject inside the monitor.

Save the original monitor with the .psp extension. You can use it as a selected object and apply it to other images whenever you wish, or you can export it as a tube and use it that way.

Part II
Projects

Chapter 9
Layering In Action

Project 1: Turn an image into a puzzle using layers and basic Paint Shop Pro tools

Project 2: Create a layered stained glass image complete with a light shining through

Project 3: Produce a textured mat to complement a frame from the Paint Shop Pro Picture Frame Wizard

By Ramona Pruitt

Put Your Layer Knowledge To Work

You learned about the fundamentals of layering in Chapter 3, including the basic layering tools, functions, and concepts. Now it is time to get into some heavy-duty layering and really make use of the great tools you have at hand.

In this chapter, you'll take a step-by-step approach to this layering business and learn to use techniques and tools to create simple effects that can serve you time and time again in various graphic endeavors.

Project 1: A Puzzle

The first project in this chapter is a fun and easy lesson that you can use to create a jigsaw puzzle from just about any photo or image with outstanding results.

1.

This technique involves a bit of drawing, so unless you're used to drawing lines with a mouse, it may be easier if you begin with a fairly good sized image rather than a small one. The image I will use to illustrate the steps is a photo of a carousel horse with a pixel size of 600 by 480.

2.

As you recall from Chapter 3, your image begins as a single layer called Background by default. The first thing you will want to do is to promote it to a workable layer by right-clicking on the layer title in the Layer palette and choosing Promote To Layer.

3.

Your base image, now named Layer1 by default, has been turned into a layer that can be moved and manipulated just as any other layer can. Right-click again on the layer title, choose Properties to bring up the Layer Properties dialog box, and give the layer a descriptive name to make it easier to recognize later. I've named my base layer Horse. Click on OK once you've filled in the desired name.

4.

Right-click on the layer title again and choose New Raster Layer. Accept the defaults in the Properties dialog box and name this new layer Bottom Layer. By default, it will be placed directly above the first layer. Choose Arrange|Send To Bottom from the Layers menu to place the new layer at the lowest position in the layer stack, or you can position it by simply dragging the layer title.

5.

With the foreground color set to black (or a similar dark color of your choice), use the Flood Fill tool to fill the layer named Bottom Layer with solid color. Later on in this project, you will be cutting out portions of another layer, and you will want a background color to show in the areas where those portions are cut.

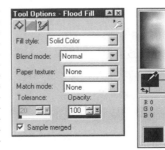

6.

Add one more new raster layer—name it Puzzle Lines. This layer will be used to create the puzzle pieces. Position the new layer on the top of the layer stack. You should now have three layers, and your Layer palette will look something like the one shown here.

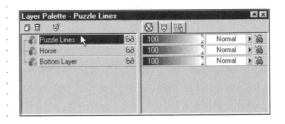

7.

Activate the grid by clicking on the View|Grid menu option. You will use this grid as a guide when drawing in the puzzle lines. Try to imagine each of the grid squares as a puzzle piece.

8.

If the grid squares are too small, remember that you can change the size by going to File|Preferences|General Program Preferences| Rulers And Units. There you can set the horizontal and vertical spacing to reflect the grid size you prefer. The larger you want your puzzle pieces, the larger the grid will need to be. Calculate the size vertically and horizontally so that the grid lines will fall right at the edges of the image.

9.

For example, my image is 600 pixels wide, so a horizontal grid spacing of 100 will give me exactly six squares across. With my image height of 480, a vertical grid spacing of 96 will give me exactly five squares from top to bottom. Shown here is my image with the visible grid lines in place.

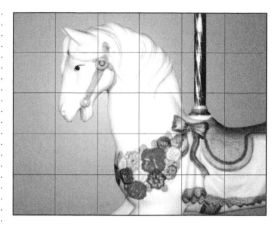

10.

With black or a dark color still set as your foreground color in the Color palette, choose the Draw tool from the toolbar. Use the Tool Options dialog box to choose the following options:

- *Type*—Freehand Line
- *Style*—Stroked
- *Width*—1
- *Antialias*—Checked

11.

Click on the top Puzzle Lines layer title to make it the active layer. With the Draw tool, slowly draw a line using the top grid line as a guide. Instead of just drawing a straight line all the way across, form a loop (as shown here in the zoomed-in shot) in the middle part of each grid square, first a loop going up in one square and then a loop going down in the next square. Continue drawing in this fashion until you are all the way across the image.

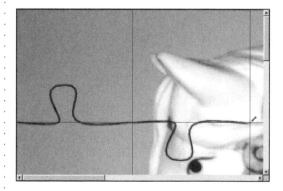

12.

Once you have the line all the way across the image, you can select it by clicking directly on the line with the Magic Wand tool (for the Magic Wand tool, set Match Mode to RGB, Tolerance to 0, and Feather to 0). Once selected, this line can be copied to the clipboard (Edit|Copy) and subsequently used to form the remaining horizontal puzzle lines.

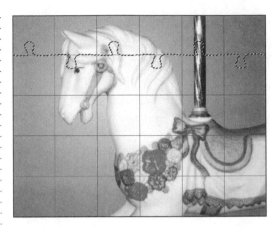

13.

To accomplish this, just choose Edit|Paste As New Selection. To make the puzzle more interesting, use the Image|Flip menu option to flip every other line after you paste it in. Use the Mover tool to position the lines along the horizontal grid lines. Your image will look something like the illustration here. See how the puzzle pieces are beginning to take shape?

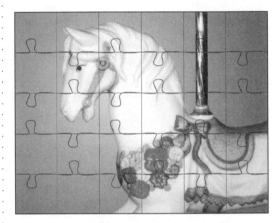

14.

You can use the same line to form the vertical lines for the puzzle. First, choose Edit|Paste As New Selection just as you have been doing, but to make the lines vertical, you can use the Image|Rotate function. In the Rotate options box, choose to rotate the selection by 90 degrees to the right. Because you only want to rotate the selection and not the entire image, leave the All Layers option unchecked.

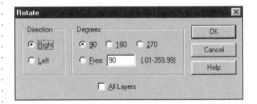

15.

After you paste and rotate each line, position it right along a vertical grid line just as you did with the horizontal lines. To make the vertical lines more interesting, use the Image|Mirror function to mirror every other line. Once you have pasted the lines along every grid line, turn off the grid (by clicking once more on View|Grid). Your image now has the basic puzzle shapes in place.

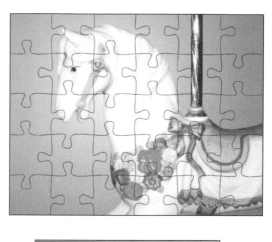

16.

At this point, you'll use a great little selection trick to select the entire collection of puzzle lines all at once. First, choose Select All from the Selections menu. This places the selection marquee around the entire layer. Now, with any selection tool activated, just a left-click in the image will bring the selection marquee into action and surround only the nontransparent pixels, which in this case are your puzzle lines. In the Layer palette, you will see that a new layer entitled Floating Selection is directly above the Puzzle Lines layer.

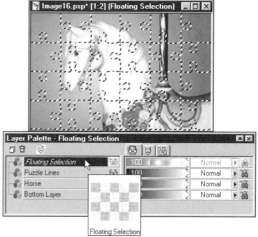

17.

Defloat the selection (Selections|Defloat) so that it is no longer hovering over the Puzzle Lines layer but yet is still selected. You will use this selection to give the puzzle pieces some depth with shading techniques so that they will appear more realistic. First, create another new layer (Layers|New Raster Layer)—name it Shading. With the Shading layer active, any changes you make to the selection will now apply only to this new layer.

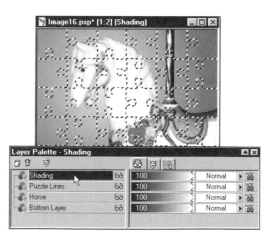

18.

Go to Image|Effects|Drop Shadow. In the dialog box, choose the following settings:

- *Color*—White
- *Opacity*—100
- *Blur*—Around 5 or so
- *Vertical Offset*—2
- *Horizontal Offset*—2

Click on OK to apply the settings. If you look at your image, you will see that a little depth has been added already by the addition of this white shadow on one side of the puzzle lines.

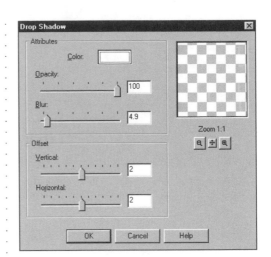

19.

Once again, Go to Image|Effects|Drop Shadow. In the dialog box, choose the following settings:

- *Color*—Black
- *Opacity*—100
- *Blur*—Around 5 or so
- *Vertical Offset*—Minus (-) 2
- *Horizontal Offset*—Minus (-) 2

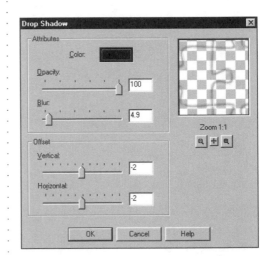

20.

Notice that by changing the Drop Shadow offset, the block shading has appeared on the opposite side of the lines, adding even more depth to the image. Deselect the lines with Selections|Select None (or right-click in the image).

21.

Now that the shading is in place, get rid of the Puzzle Lines layer (by right-clicking on that layer title and choosing Delete). This will remove the harsh black lines and give your puzzle pieces a realistic softly beveled look around the edges. You will have three layers left in the image—the layer named Bottom Layer, the Horse layer (or whatever you named your basic image layer), and the Shading layer.

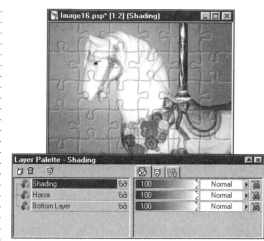

22.

At this point, you may want to make a copy of the Shading layer (Edit|Copy and Edit|Paste As New Image). Save it in the PSP file format to preserve the transparent portion. You'll be able to use it later in other images you wish to turn into puzzles by simply pasting it in as a new layer and resizing it if necessary.

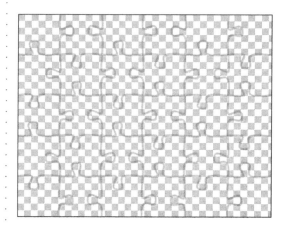

23.

Go ahead and merge the Shading layer and the basic image layer (Horse in my case). To do so, first use the Layer Visibility toggle to put the Bottom Layer into invisible mode. Then right-click on the Shading layer title and choose Merge|Merge Visible.

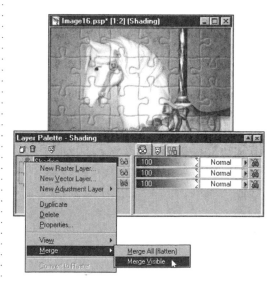

24.

Now your Layer palette will contain only two layers—the layer named Bottom Layer and a layer named Merged. Use the visibility toggle to restore visibility to the Bottom Layer.

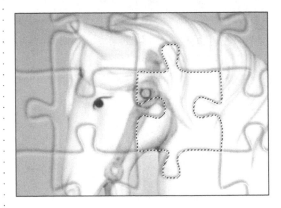

25.

Now your puzzle is looking good as a whole, but suppose you want to have a puzzle that is not all put together—maybe with a few pieces missing. On the Merged layer, use the Free-hand selection tool to select an area containing one of the puzzle pieces. You'll probably want to keep the Antialias option checked in the Tool Options dialog box for the selection tool to get a smooth edge. I prefer to zoom in closely and use the Freehand tool set on Point To Point for selections of this type, but you should use whichever selection style you feel most com-fortable with.

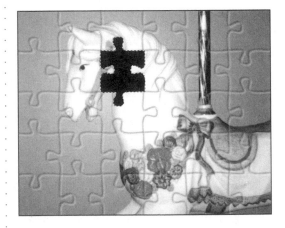

26.

Cut the selection (Edit|Cut). Because the Merged layer is the active layer, it's the only layer out of which the selected area is cut, leaving the Bottom Layer's dark solid color showing through.

27.

Choose Edit|Paste As New Selection. This will paste the puzzle piece you just cut; you can then manipulate it and place it somewhere on the puzzle to give the appearance of a work in progress. In the illustration here, I pasted the cut piece, used Image|Rotate to rotate the piece 45 degrees to the right, and applied a slight black drop shadow with the same shadow settings used in Step 19 to give the piece some depth. Finally, just merge all the layers into a single-layer image by choosing Layers|Merge|Merge All.

Project 2: Stained Glass

Everyone loves the look of stained glass, and it is amazingly easy to create beautiful *digital* stained glass images from scratch using Paint Shop Pro 6.

1.

Open a new blank image window in a size large enough to work in comfortably. Choose white as the background color.

2.

Each element of the stained glass will be created on its own layer to allow for greater control. The first thing you need to do is to make a new, transparent layer (Layers|New Raster Layer using the default settings) to begin your work on. (The plain white background layer will used later in this project, so leave it be for now.)

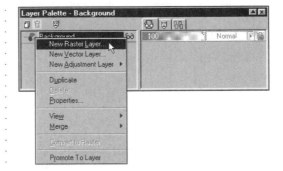

3.

The first element you will form is the lead that separates the panes of glass, so name the layer Lead. Set the foreground color in the Color palette to a medium-to-dark gray color (whichever you prefer) for the lead color.

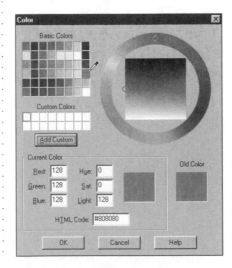

4.

You can use the Preset Shapes tool to make a beginning line shape that you will use for the formation of the basic image. Here I've chosen to use an octagonal shape and set the line width to 5. Because I chose the Stroked style, the shape will form as a 5-pixel outline. I like to use the Antialias option to avoid jagged edges.

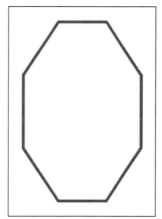

5.

Click and drag within the image area to form the shape. Once it is formed, you can use the Mover tool to place it in a central position. Remember, the Mover tool must grab onto a color area (the line shape, in this instance), rather than a transparent area.

If you have a touch of perfectionist in you, you can center the shape exactly within the image by copying it and pasting it as a new layer. Anytime something from the clipboard is pasted as a new layer, it lands perfectly in the center. Then, just delete the layer you copied.

6.

Next, activate the Draw tool. You'll use it to form more of the lead lines that will surround the beginning shape. Choose the Single Line type in the Tool Options dialog box and set the line width to 5 (or the same width as the line in the shape you just created) and the style to Stroked.

7.

One by one, draw in random lines beginning at the outer edges of your shape and going in different directions. Draw and connect the lines until you have a pleasing geometric-type array. Let your creative license take charge.

8.

Use the Draw tool now to draw a straight line from corner to corner along each of the outer edges.

9.

Now you will create a centerpiece. You can continue to use the Single Line type with the Draw tool to fill in a simple straight-line image, such as a cross or a geometric shape as shown here, or if you happen to be feeling especially creative, switch over to the Freehand Line type and create your own line-art masterpiece for the center. If you use the Preset Shapes tool to make your centerpiece, you may want to create it on its own layer so that you can center it. Once it's centered correctly, turn off visibility to the Background layer with the visibility toggle while you merge the two line drawing layers into one (Layers|Merge|Merge Visible).

If you have some clip art on hand, you can resize it and use it as a centerpiece image—stained glass is a great way to liven up those drab black-and-white clip art images.

10.

To give the lead lines some dimension, you will use the Inner Bevel effect (Image|Effects| Inner Bevel). You can use the Auto Proof option to play around with the settings until you are happy with the look of your lead. I've chosen to apply Metallic, one of the many bevel Presets.

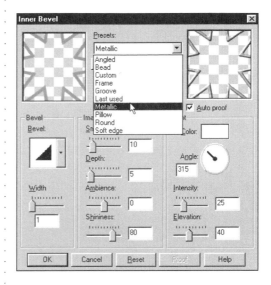

11.

The bevel really makes the lines stand out and also gives a realistic appearance to the areas where the lines are "joined."

12.

Now that the lead is finished, you can begin adding some color to the image. First, make a duplicate of the Lead layer (Layers|Duplicate). Name the duplicate layer Color (Layers| Properties), click on the layer title, and drag this new layer to just below the Lead layer. Leave the Color layer as the active layer.

13.

You'll want to select the panes of glass one by one to fill with different colors. To select a pane, choose the Magic Wand selection tool and click in one of the pane areas.

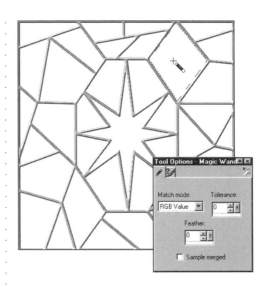

14.

The selection area will need to be expanded so that the color fills you are about to perform on the Color layer will extend all the way up underneath the lead lines on the Lead layer. Go to Selections|Modify|Expand and choose to expand by 3 pixels or so. After doing so, notice how the selection marquee is running right along the center of the lead lines, as in this zoomed-in portion of the image.

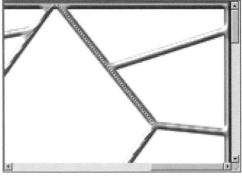

15.

Pick a color as the foreground color in the Color palette, and then use the Flood Fill tool with the Solid Color fill style setting to fill the selected area.

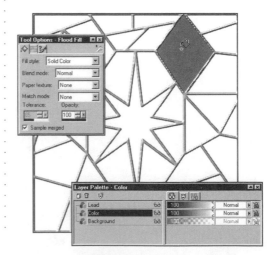

16.

Keep repeating the same process to fill the other panes one by one:

1. Select a pane with the Magic Wand tool.

2. Choose Selections|Modify|Expand (expand by 3 pixels).

3. Choose a new color.

4. Use the Flood Fill tool to fill the selected area.

You may choose to fill each pane with a different color, or you may want to pick a theme of just a few colors.

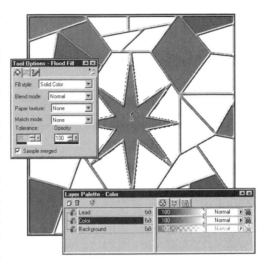

17.

Continue the filling process until each pane has a color fill.

18.

Although some stained glass is smooth, most that I've seen has been created from glass with some form of texture to it, so that will be the next step—adding texture to the digital glass. First, add a new layer. By default, the new layer will be created directly above the active layer (which is the Color layer you were just working with). Name the new layer Texture. The Texture layer is now the active layer.

19.

A quick and easy way to form the texture is to use one of the available painting textures that comes with the Paint Shop Pro 6 program. To view the numerous available textures, just use the Browse function (File|Browse) to navigate to the Textures folder located in the Paint Shop Pro 6 directory.

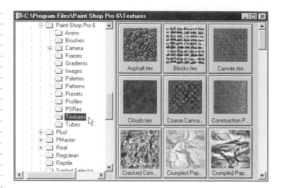

20.

There are several good textures that will serve the purpose of creating the glass surface texture. I've chosen to use the one called Parchment, which will result in a rather course surface texture. To apply the texture to the active Texture layer, begin by choosing a dark neutral color, such as black or a dark gray, as the foreground color in the Color palette. Because a texture is basically simulated on a flat image surface by the use of shading, a dark "shadowy" color will create a realistic texture effect. Set the options for the Flood Fill tool to Solid Color and use the drop-down Paper Texture menu to choose Parchment or a texture of your own choice. Fill the Texture layer.

21.

With the addition of the texture, you will notice that your image has suddenly taken on a much more realistic appearance.

22.

If you feel that perhaps the texture is too dark or harsh and you would like to tone it down a little, the task can be accomplished with ease. The application of the blend mode called Soft Light to the Texture layer can reduce the rough texture to a much softer, lighter version—seemingly like magic—by blending the pixels with the underlying Color layer. Apply the Soft Light blend mode to the Texture layer now via the drop-down Layer Blend Mode menu in the Layer palette.

23.

The texture effect has now become much more subdued. One of the advantages of working with layers is the total versatility and control you have over the individual layers, and the blending capabilities offer even greater variations with layering.

24.

The stained glass needs just one more thing to give it that "special" touch, and a light source is just the item to fill the bill. This is where the Background layer will be put to use. Activate the Background layer now by clicking on the layer title.

25.

The creation of the light will require the use of the Flood Fill tool (what would we do without that great tool?) and a simple gradient effect. The first step is to choose the colors for the gradient. In the Color palette, set the foreground color to white and the background color to black.

26.

Activate the Flood Fill tool and choose Rectangular Gradient for the fill style. Make sure the Paper Texture option is set back to None.

27.

Click on the center tab of the Tool Options dialog box and set the following parameters:

- *Gradient*—Foreground-Background

- *Repeats*—0

- *Horizontal*—50

- *Vertical*—50

The thumbnail image in the lower-right corner of the dialog box gives an example of the chosen gradient effect.

28.

Click in the image to fill the Background layer with the gradient. At this point, you will not be able to see the effect of the gradient because the upper layers are blocking the view of the Background layer. However, you can hover your cursor over the Background layer title in the Layer palette, and you will see that the layer did indeed get filled with the gradient.

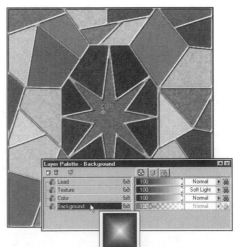

29.

Once again, this is a situation where the fabulous functionality of layer blend modes will prove to be handy. Notice on the Layer palette that the layer blend mode and also the opacity slider are grayed out on the Background layer. This means they are nonfunctional for that layer because there are no underlying layers to which the effects could be applied.

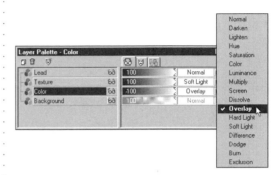

30.

Because it is the Color layer that stands to gain the benefit of the lighting effect, switch over and make the Color layer active. Change the blend mode on the Color layer to Overlay. If you recall from Chapter 3, this mode will basically make the dark areas darker and the light areas lighter, which is perfect for the light source effect.

31.

The result is a *shining* example to the usefulness and flexibility of layers in the image-creation process.

32.

The Overlay blend mode gave the colors a dark, rich, jewel-toned appearance by darkening the colors in the areas where they blended with the dark portions of the Background layer. If you wish to lighten the image, you can simply lighten the Background layer. Jobs like this are where adjustment layers can pitch in and help. Activate the Background layer now and add a new adjustment layer. Choose the adjustment called Hue/Saturation.

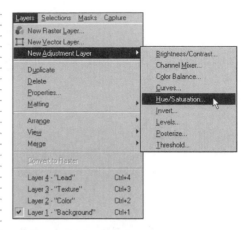

33.

For this type of adjustment, you will notice that, on the Adjustment tab of the Layer Properties dialog box, there are three control sliders: Hue, Saturation, and Luminance. Because the desired result in this case is just a lightened layer, slide the Luminance (or lightness) slider slowly up. Make sure the Auto Proof option is checked so that you can see the changes in your image as you drag the slider to a new position. Set it around 20 and click on OK.

34.

With the luminance change in place, the colors in the image are back to a brighter look, whereas the other effects have remained unchanged. Choose Layers|Merge|Merge All to complete the project.

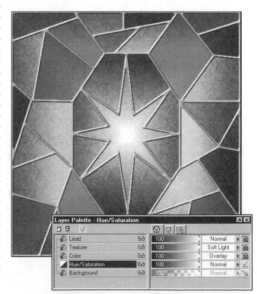

Project 3: Matted And Framed

In this project, you will create a mat as an enhancement to a picture frame.

1.

As illustrated in the zoomed-in corner shot here, a mat, in the nondigital realm of the art world, is a border that serves as a sort of inner frame for a framed image or painting. Real mats are usually made from a type of cardboard known as matboard and often have a decorative texture similar to linen or canvas.

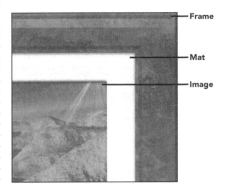

2.

Open or create an image that you would like to see matted and framed. For this project's illustrations, I will use a digital "painting" of a landscape.

The Picture Frame Wizard was enhanced in a Paint Shop Pro update and in version 6.01 of the program. You can choose to add a new frame either inside or outside the borders of an image.

3.

As you may recall from Chapter 8, when you add a frame, it automatically sizes to fit within the borders of the image, therefore you will need to increase the canvas size first so that the frame does not cover important image areas. How much to increase? That will be a matter of trial and error because it depends on the size of your image and the width of the frame and mat. I like to play it safe and add plenty of room to work with because the frame layer can always be resized later if necessary. To increase the canvas, choose Image|Canvas Size.

4.

The landscape image used in this project is 700 by 525 pixels, so I will increase both the height and width by 400 pixels, making the new canvas size equal 1100 by 925. While in the Change Canvas Size dialog box, make sure the options to center the image both horizontally and vertically are checked.

When you use the Canvas Size function on a background layer, the added area will be the same as the current background color in the Color palette. When it's used on a layer, the added area will be transparent.

5.

Your image will now have a nice wide border area large enough to hold a frame and mat. If you feel it needs to be larger or smaller, simply undo the settings (Edit|Undo Canvas Size) and try again with new canvas size settings.

6.

Use the Image menu to open the Picture Frame Wizard (Image|Picture Frame). Choose one of the rectangular picture frames that will complement your image.

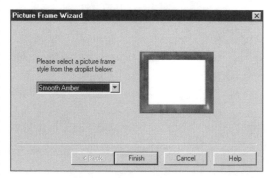

7.

You will notice in the Layer palette that the Picture Frame Wizard has automatically added a new layer for the frame, and the new layer has become the active layer. In the sample image here, the frame was not wide enough to meet the edges of the original image, resulting in some free space between the frame and image. The free space will be perfect for the addition of a mat.

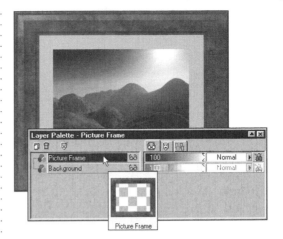

8.

Use the Magic Wand selection tool and click on the area in the center of the frame layer to select it. Use the Zoom tool to zoom in on one of the selection edge areas to see if it is selected all the way to the edge of the frame. If not, expand the selection by a pixel or two (Selections|Modify|Expand) to get it all the way to the edge.

9.

Invert the selection (Selections|Invert) so that the frame, rather than the inner transparent area, is selected. The addition of a drop shadow to the frame will give an appearance of depth that you would see in a real frame. Go to Image|Effects|Drop Shadow to bring up the Drop Shadow dialog box. Choose the following settings:

- *Color*—Black
- *Opacity*—100
- *Blur*—15 or so
- *Offsets*—3

Click on OK to apply.

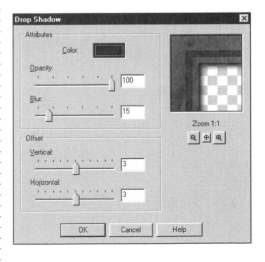

10.

Eliminate the selection (Selections|Select None) and add a new layer (Layers|New Raster Layer). Name the new layer Mat and move it so that it is located just below the Picture Frame layer (Layers|Arrange|Move Down).

11.

Activate the Background layer and use the Magic Wand tool to select the area surrounding the original image.

12.

Leaving the selection intact, switch over to the Mat layer as the active layer. Use the Flood Fill tool with the Solid Color fill type to fill the selected area with a color that is neutral, such as white or off-white, or choose a color that is complementary to both your image and your frame.

13.

To add the texture, go to Image|Effects|Texture. You can choose to use one of the preset textures or choose a particular texture from the Texture drop-down menu. I've chosen to use texture #60, which looks like woven cloth. Adjust the texture options until you are satisfied with the look and click on OK to apply.

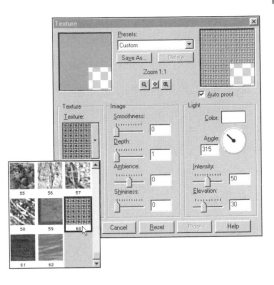

14.

Add a drop shadow to the selection using the same settings used for the drop shadow that was added to the frame (see Step 9) to make the mat "stand out" from the image.

15.

The last couple of steps, although subtle, will add just a tad more authenticity to the realism of the mat. These last steps will use the Cutout effect. To apply this effect and still keep the color and texture of the mat intact, you must first float the selection. Do this via the Selections menu (Selections|Float).

16.

Now move on to Image|Effects|Cutout. This is really just another way to add a bit of shading, just as you did to the puzzle pieces in this chapter's first project. Set the options as follows:

- *Fill Interior With Color*—Unchecked
- *Shadow Color*—Black
- *Opacity*—80
- *Blur*—14
- *Offset (both Vertical and Horizontal)*—Minus (-) 2

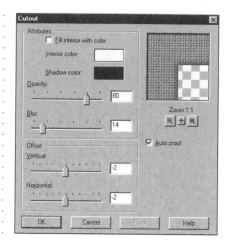

Click on OK to apply.

17.

One more time, pull up Image|Effects|Cutout to apply a lighter shading in the opposite direction:

- *Fill Interior With Color*—Unchecked
- *Shadow Color*—Black
- *Opacity*—40
- *Blur*—14
- *Offset (both Vertical and Horizontal)*—2

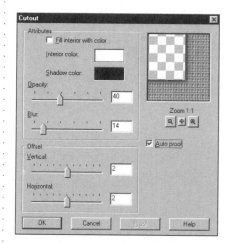

Again, click on OK to apply.

18.

And, there you have it. Just merge the layers (Layers|Merge|Merge All) and your image is framed, matted, and ready to save and hang in your virtual gallery.

Chapter 10
Photo Restoration And Enhancement

Project 1: Bring new life to old or damaged photos by using the Clone brush

Project 2: Utilize the color tools to repair red-eye, a commonly needed correction

Project 3: Revamp a photo by replacing the background that surrounds an object

Project 4: Experiment with a quick and easy collage method to combine images

Project 5: Learn the most efficient ways to catalog and print your photos and images

By Ramona Pruitt

Working With Photos

Working successfully with photos used to be strictly for the pros. Luckily, that's no longer true. Whether you want to repair cherished family photos or just add a touch of interest or a special effect to newer images, the tools in Paint Shop Pro 6 can work virtual wonders and achieve stunning results in photo enhancement. This chapter is dedicated to exploring the ins and outs of photo manipulation.

In this chapter, you'll also learn that by using the Browser as a thumbnail image catalog, you can create handy reference (or *contact*) sheets by printing the labeled thumbnails. Additionally, you will discover how you can instantly arrange images in the best possible ways for multiple image printing.

Project 1: Repairing Damaged Images

In this project, you will be introduced to the tools and processes used to restore an extremely damaged photo to a much more pleasing state.

1.

Okay, it's time to dig that old box of family photos out of the closet. To follow along with the first project, find a photo that's in really bad shape. Scan it in at a size large enough to work with comfortably. As you can see, the photo here has really been through the wringer. It has been bent, scratched, torn, and is terribly discolored.

*If you don't have a scanner, contact local print shops and photo-developing facilities, most of which have scanners you can use for a small fee. For online scanning tips and advice, check out **www.scantips.com**.*

2.

When you're working on a photo as damaged as this one is, you'll need to zoom in on specific areas. By making a new window of the image, you can see the zoomed-in area and also a copy of the image as it appears in normal size as the changes take place. That way, you don't have to keep zooming in and out to view the changes as you work. Choose Window|New Window.

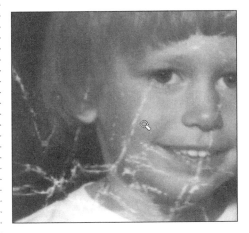

Choosing Duplicate also opens another image window, but changes will affect only the active window.

3.

Choose one of the most damaged portions of the image and zoom in closely to get a starting point. You'll be amazed at how easily and quickly the damage will disappear when you simply repair one small area at a time.

4.

The damage here can be easily repaired with the use of just one amazing tool, the Clone brush. This brush works by picking up a duplicate of a specified image area (called the source area) and using it to paint over damaged areas (called target areas). You have the same basic brush options to choose from here as with the paintbrush, such as Shape, Size, Hardness, Opacity, Step, and Density. For now, choose a medium to large brush size setting.

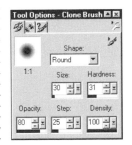

If you don't see the Tool Options window, you can bring it up by clicking on the Toggle Tool Options window icon on the toolbar.

5.

Click on the center tab for more specialized brush options. Here, you have two clone modes to choose from: Aligned and Non-Aligned. The next order of business will be to take a brief break from photo repair and spend some time learning how these modes function. First, choose the Aligned mode.

6.

Use your mouse to right-click anywhere in the photo image. A right-click is the method used to pick up a clone source. Then open a new blank image to use for a testing ground. The blank window will be used in this experiment as the target, in which you'll place the source you just picked up from the photo. Left-click once in the blank image to place it, and then release the mouse button.

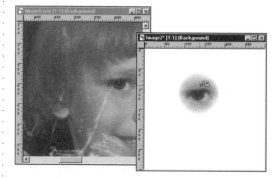

7.

Click once again at another spot in the blank image and drag the cursor around a bit to paint. Notice that when you stop painting and then start again, the surrounding area is filled in exactly as it is in the source area, relative to the distance from the original target area.

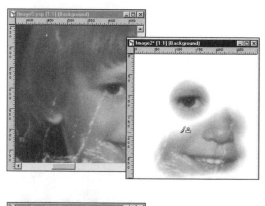

8.

Next, switch over to Non-Aligned clone mode. Once again, right-click in your photo to pick up the clone source. Open another blank image window and left-click to place the source to the target. Release the mouse and click again. You'll quickly see the difference made by switching to Non-Aligned mode. In this mode, when you stop painting and begin again, it starts over with the clone source.

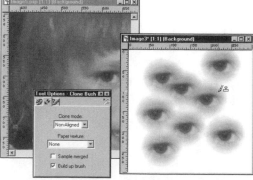

9.

If you choose a paper texture in the Tool Options window, the source area is painted into the target with the texture built in. In addition to being virtually indispensable for detailed photo repair work, the Clone brush is definitely worth playing around with in your spare time to get some cool effects.

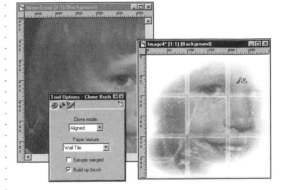

10.

Now you have the general idea of how the Clone brush works. To get back to the original project, close those blank test windows, put the Clone brush in Aligned mode, and set Paper Texture to None. Choose a small soft brush size (7 or so). Begin by right-clicking in an area directly beside a scratch or smudge and then left-clicking to fill in the scratch with the clone. Keep up this right-click, left-click technique until the scratch begins to blend in with the surrounding area.

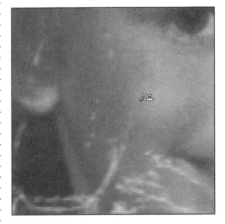

11.

Work through your entire image and get rid of all the scratches and smudges in the same manner. Reduce the brush size if needed for tiny pixel-by-pixel editing. It will probably seem tedious at first, but after you practice for a while and get the hang of it, you'll be clicking your way right through those damaged areas. Remember to keep your New Window view open while you're working. Sometimes when you work on a zoomed-in portion of an image, it's hard to tell just how much progress you're making.

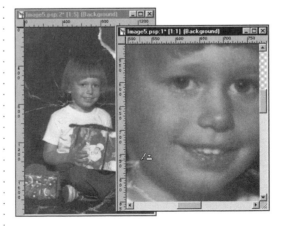

12.

This image still needs some work, but the scratch and smudge removal with the Clone brush already has it looking a lot better than it did in the beginning.

13.

Most of the finely detailed cloning work is finished, but because the image here has such a large missing piece torn from the corner, the Clone brush size can be increased to clone large background areas and fill in the damage quickly.

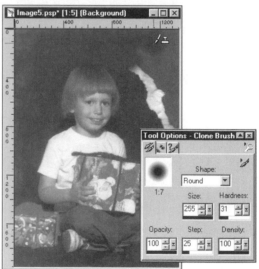

14.

Once you're finished touching up with the Clone brush, it's time to start on necessary color repairs.

See this book's color section for a better look at the effects of the restoration and colorization process.

15.

The color adjustments will vary with each picture you work on. The image here has acquired a reddish tone throughout, so there are a couple of things that could be done. You can use the Gamma Correction dialog box (Colors|Adjust| Gamma Correction) to adjust the balance of color in an image. Because this image has a red cast to it, moving the Red slider to the left reduces the red, and slightly increasing the blue and green improves the color even more.

If the Link button is checked, the sliders will all move in unison. Uncheck it to move the color adjustment sliders one at a time.

16.

For an image as color-damaged as this one, another option would be to turn the saturation all the way down to eliminate the color altogether, and color it back in yourself. To do so, go to Colors|Adjust|Hue/Saturation/Lightness.

Reducing saturation works wonders with older black-and-white images that have yellowed with age.

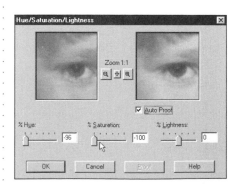

17.

To add some color back in, first add a new layer (Layers|New Raster Layer), and name it Color. In the Layer palette, set the blend mode on the Color layer to Color. This way, anything you paint on this layer will add only color; the saturation and luminance of the underlying layer will show through.

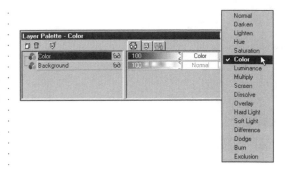

18.

Choose a starting point and set your foreground color in the Color palette to the color you wish to add. You may want to zoom in to the area you have chosen to work on. Use the paintbrush and start with a small to medium brush size. Continue the process of filling in areas of color until the picture is completely recolorized, or you may want to colorize just a portion of it to achieve a different look. If the colors are too vivid, just reduce the opacity in the Color layer.

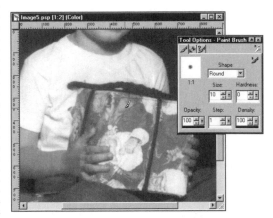

Project 2: Red-Eye

Red-eye is one of the most common problems in the area of photo restoration.

1.

When the light from a camera flash hits the eye of a subject at a particular angle, the flash can reflect off the eye and cause an unattractive (and sometimes downright eerie) glow in the eye in the final picture. On people, it is marked by an orangish red tint (hence the name red-eye), and in animals, it is sometimes a bright yellow or green.

2.

Fixing red-eye is easy with the tools at hand in Paint Shop Pro. First, isolate the problem area so that any changes applied to the eye area will not affect the rest of the image. Zoom in and use one of the selection tools to select the affected eye. The Circle selection type usually works fairly well in these situations. Keep Antialias checked in the Tool Options window to help ensure that the necessary adjacent pixels are included and to prevent jagged edges.

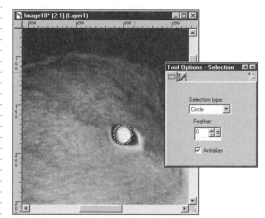

3.

To get rid of the bright glare emanating from the eye, use the Hue/Saturation/Lightness adjustment found in the Colors|Adjust menu option. With this tool, you can not only reduce the lightness, you can also lower the color saturation so that you can colorize it yourself.

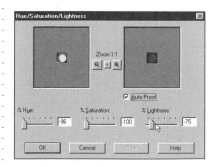

Desaturating and colorizing a selected eye area is not only a great way to get rid of red-eye, it's also an easy way to change normal eye color. Who needs colored contact lenses?

4.

Now, all you need to do is select the correct eye color. Sometimes there are surrounding pixels of the eye color that have not been affected by the flash, in which case you can use the eyedropper to just pick one up. Otherwise, it's a matter of trial and error. For brown eyes, the darkest brown in the basic color chart of the color picker usually works pretty well.

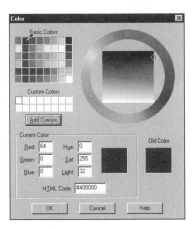

5.

Choose the Retouch tool on the toolbar and set the brush settings to a medium-sized soft brush tip. Reduce the brush opacity to about 50 so that you can start lightly and build up the color as needed each time you click. Use the center tab in the Tool Options window to access the retouch modes, and choose the Color To Target mode. Retouch modes work much like layer blend modes, but they're applied with a brush directly to the image layer you are working with.

6.

Paint in the color to bring the eyes back to a natural state. If there are stray pixels around the edge that don't seem to be getting enough color, just feather the selection by a pixel or two (Selections|Modify|Feather) and paint again around the edges.

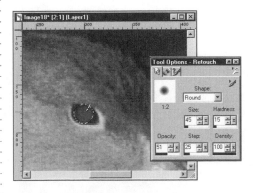

7.

Deselect the area (Selections|Select None). If the eye looks too bland, use the paintbrush set to a small size at reduced opacity with white or a light shade of the eye color to add a little specular highlight.

Project 3: A Change Of Scenery

Sometimes you may have a good picture that just needs a little enhancement. Try a new background to add a completely different feel to an image.

1.

Find a photo with a good main subject but an uninteresting background. For the example here, I'll use a photo of a nice muscle car I saw in the park one fine day.

2.

Begin the process by promoting the image to a layer (right-click on the layer titled Background and choose Promote To Layer). By doing this, you will be able to eliminate the area surrounding the car (or your subject) to a transparency.

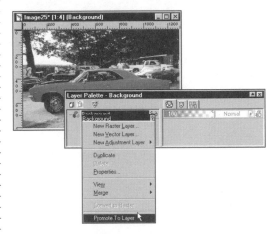

3.

Use a selection tool to select the subject. If the color of your subject is in high contrast to the background, you can use the Magic Wand, but with most images, you won't be that lucky. In the image here, I used the Freehand selection tool with the Point To Point setting to click all the way around the car to select it. If you use this method, remember to double-click to set the selection once you get all the way back to your starting point.

4.

Because the background is the area you want to replace, invert the selection so that it becomes the selected area (Selections|Invert). Now you can eliminate the background by either pressing the Delete key on your keyboard or choosing Edit|Cut.

5.

To make sure your image will have a nice smooth edge that will blend into any background, feather the selected area (Selections| Modify|Feather) by one or two pixels and press the Delete key again.

6.

Check your image to see if it has any other inside areas to eliminate. For example, in the image here, the car windows allowed part of the old background to show through. Select those areas and delete them.

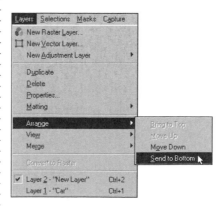

7.

Add a new layer (Layers|New Raster Layer) and place it as the bottom layer (Layers|Arrange| Send To Bottom).

8.

Whatever you decide to use to fill this layer
will become your new background. Use the
Flood Fill tool to fill the layer with a solid color
or gradient to make your subject really stand
out.

9.

On the other hand, place another image or
pattern in the new background layer to really
add some interest. Once you have your subject on a transparent layer of its own, the
possibilities for switching backgrounds are limited only by your imagination.

Project 4: A Quick Collage

By utilizing the power of the Feather option, you can create simple photo collages practically effortlessly.

1.

A photo collage (also called a montage) is an arrangement of several different photos placed together into one image. Gather together three or four pictures to experiment with.

2.

Open a new image window that will be large enough to hold your assortment of photos. It's better to make it too large than too small; you can always easily crop the size once you're done. Use the Flood Fill tool to fill the window with a color or pattern of your choice. For this example, the Sculpture filter (Image|Effects| Sculpture) was used with sculpture pattern #29 to create a grassy background.

3.

Choose the selection tool and set the Feather value to around 50 or so. You can use any of the selection shapes. A Circle shape will be used for the example.

4.

Choose one of the photos to begin with and drag the selection tool to enclose a portion of the main subject of the photo.

5.

As you release the mouse button, you will see that the selected area becomes much larger because of the large amount of feathering chosen. Copy the selection to the clipboard via Edit|Copy.

6.

Activate the pattern image and choose Edit|Paste As New Layer. Because each subject will be placed on its own layer, you can resize the layer if needed or use the Mover to drag the layer into the desired position. Notice how the feathering allows the image to blend in with the surroundings of the layer below.

7.

Move the rest of the photo subjects to the collage image with the same Copy|Paste As New Layer technique. You can then use the Eraser tool with a medium-sized soft brush and reduced opacity to clean up any areas of overlap and fine-tune each layer.

Project 5: Printing

The printing options in Paint Shop Pro 6 include single-image printing, thumbnail printing, and multiple-image printing.

1.

Printing a single image is pretty straightforward. Open an image and choose File|Page Setup. You'll see that the Page Setup dialog box includes settings such as Paper Size and Orientation. You can center your image, set margins, and even scale your image by percentage or to fit the paper to the fullest extent while still maintaining aspect ratios.

2.

Once you have your image set up the way you like, go to File|Print Preview for a close-up view of how it will appear on paper. If you want to change the settings, you can get back to the Page Setup dialog box from this window. When you're ready, simply click on the Print button.

3.

You can use the Browser not only to view thumbnails of your images, but also to print them. Use the Browser to browse to a folder containing images. Go to File|Print.

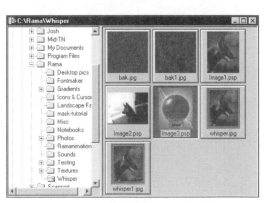

4.

In the Print dialog box, you can select the print range—whether to print all the pages, a range of pages, or just a selection of thumbnails you've chosen (through File|Select). By clicking on Properties, you can set paper options such as Portrait or Landscape.

5.

To arrange and print multiple images other than thumbnails on a single sheet of paper, first open all of the images and then choose File|Print Multiple Images. This will open a new window with your chosen images lined up on the left and the paper in the center.

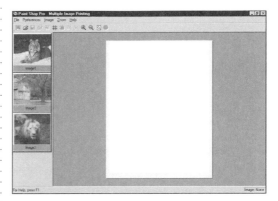

6.

You can simply click and drag the images to place them on the paper. Once the images are on the paper, you can resize them by first hovering the cursor over an image corner until the double-sided arrow appears, and then pulling on the corner. You can arrange the images either with the Image menu (Image|Placement) or by clicking and dragging with the mouse. Right-click on the page to bring up a list of often used commands, such as Zoom and Rotate.

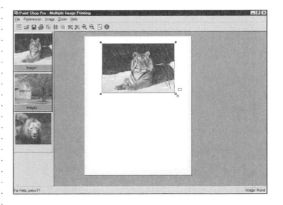

7.

The Image grid can help you get your images aligned correctly on the page. To bring the grid into view, either click on the Show Grid icon or choose Preferences|Show Grid.

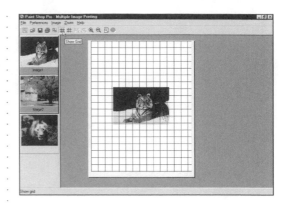

8.

The Snap To Grid function will automatically place an image along the grid lines. When this function is activated, images you move and then release will snap into position along the nearest grid line. The grid must be showing to use Snap To Grid. To activate Snap To Grid, use the Snap To Grid icon or choose Preferences|Snap To Grid.

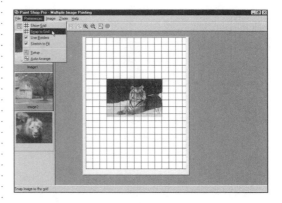

9.

Choose the Auto Arrange feature (Preferences| Auto Arrange), and the program will arrange your images for you. It works by dividing the paper into equal-sized sections and placing one image in each section. For this option to work, images must first be placed on the paper.

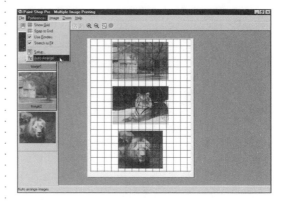

10.

When you use the Auto Arrange feature, you can choose to leave a specified amount of space between the images (border) and to enlarge (stretch) the images to fill their respective sections of the page. Use the Preferences|Setup dialog box to configure the Auto Arrange options, access printer settings, and change the grid preferences.

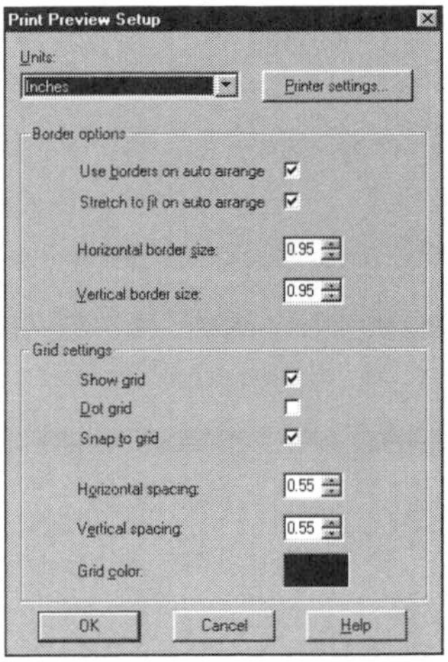

Print Preview Setup

Units:
Inches ▼   Printer settings...

Border options
Use borders on auto arrange ☑
Stretch to fit on auto arrange ☑
Horizontal border size: 0.95
Vertical border size: 0.95

Grid settings
Show grid ☑
Dot grid ☐
Snap to grid ☑
Horizontal spacing: 0.55
Vertical spacing: 0.55
Grid color:

OK   Cancel   Help

Print range
⊙ All
○ Pages from
○ Selection

Chapter 11
Projects Using Masks

 Project 1: Learn to use a mask to form a single image out of two separate ones

 Project 2: Enhance your images with great edge effects using masks

 Project 3: Add a message to a photo with a text mask

By Ramona Pruitt

Masking 101: The Hands-On Approach

In Chapter 4, you learned the fundamentals of masking and the tools used to create, edit, and save masks. By performing a simple gradient masking task, you learned that you have the ability to gradually fade an image in any number of ways—you can fade an image into a background color or pattern, or use the technique to fade one image seamlessly into another.

In this chapter, you will delve into several more ways that these amazing and mysterious masks can be put to use. The flexibility and special effects capabilities they offer can open the doors to virtually endless creative adventures. Let's have some fun.

Project 1: Masking And Composites

One of the easiest and most effective ways to create realistic-looking composite images is with the use of masks. For the first project, you'll learn how to combine two separate images into one, by applying the techniques demonstrated here to images of your own.

1.

The first image is a tiger relaxing in the snow. This photo stands on its own, but it could be spiced up a bit.

2.

The second image is a mere kitten, but he has a few tiger stripes himself (and possibly some tiger-like aspirations). The kitten and tiger images will fit together nicely and show the similarities between the two cats.

3.

To begin the process, copy the kitten image into the clipboard (Edit|Copy) and paste it into the tiger image as a new layer.

4.

Although I'm not planning to make the cats proportionately correct according to their true sizes, the kitten image is still a little too large for the project and needs to be reduced in size before you go any further. To reduce the image, choose Image|Resize from the menu bar and set a resize percentage of the original. By making sure that Resize All Layers is *unchecked* in the resize options, the kitten is the only layer affected by the operation.

5.

Next, to place the kitten layer in the correct position, use the opacity slider in the Layer palette to reduce the opacity of the kitten layer so that the tiger layer is visible through it. Being able to see both images while using the Move tool to move the kitten layer helps to ensure that the layer is placed in a suitable spot.

6.

Once the kitten is in position, the opacity can be turned back up to 100 on that layer. Now you'll add the mask and begin the blending process. Choose Masks|New|Show All to add a solid transparent mask to the kitten layer. The thumb-nail view of the mask in the Layer palette shows it as a solid white mask when the cursor is held over the mask symbol beside the layer title.

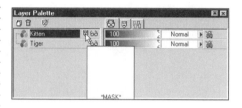

7.

Choose Edit from the Masks menu; the mask is now ready for changes to be implemented. Remember that a transparent mask is edited by painting with black in the portions you want masked. You'll start by using black to mask off the visible photo edge lines. With the foreground color set to black, choose a medium-sized soft brush from the brush options to accomplish this task.

8.

Start the blending process by brushing in black along the outside edges of the cat layer. Notice how those areas are now masked off, allowing the tiger layer to show through.

9.

You could just mask off the entire area surrounding the cat with the black brush, but what you really want is a gradual blending so that there are no harsh lines to differentiate where one image begins and the other ends. Gradually reduce the opacity in the brush settings by increments of 10 to 20 each time as you paint in closer and closer to the cat. Continue until you have created a smooth transition between images.

10.

Once the editing is completed, the mask and layers are merged using Layers|Merge|Merge All (flatten).

The final result—these two felines look as if they don't mind at all sharing the same snowy bank!

Project 2: Photo Edge Masks

An easy, albeit excellent, way to dress up photos is with the addition of cool edge effects. Masks can provide limitless possibilities in the area of photo edge creation.

1.

Our first edge project will be to give this peaceful swan image a somewhat softer look to her surroundings. Grab an image of your own and work along.

2.

To create a soft foggy edge effect, the first step is to add a new raster layer, using the default settings in the Layer dialog box. Use the Flood Fill tool with Solid Color chosen as the fill style to fill this new layer with solid white (or color of your choice).

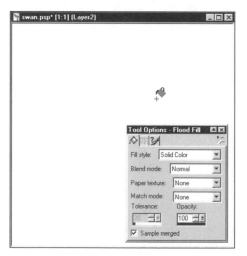

3.

This time, click on Masks|New|Hide All to add a solid opaque mask to the layer. The thumbnail view of the mask in the Layer palette shows it as a solid black mask. The top layer will no longer be visible to the eye until the mask is edited. Choose Masks|Edit so that the editing can take place.

4.

In the color palette, set the foreground color to black and the background color to white. Activate the Flood Fill tool and choose the fill style called Sunburst Gradient.

5.

Click on the middle tab in the gradient tool, which will bring up the Flood Fill Options, and use the Gradient drop-down menu to set the gradient to Foreground To Background. Set Repeats to 0, and under Gradient Center, set both Vertical and Horizontal to 50.

6.

Once you have the gradient settings, use the Flood Fill tool to fill the mask. You've just created a vignette effect.

7.

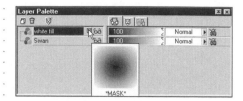

Take another look at the thumbnail view of the mask in the Layer palette to understand how the applied changes affected the mask and the image. The center portion of the mask is still masked in black, gradating to the outer edges, now unmasked (white), allowing the top white layer to show through.

8.

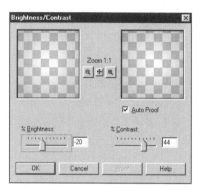

An easy way to bring the center of the vignette into better focus while still keeping the effect intact is to use the brightness/contrast adjustment on the mask itself. Make sure the mask is still in Edit mode and pull up the Colors menu (Colors|Adjust|Brightness/Contrast). Try setting the brightness down and the contrast up. Use the Auto Proof option to see what happens in your image while you make the adjustments.

9.

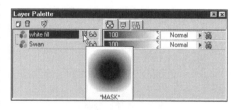

Check the mask thumbnail in the Layer palette to really see how the changes in the brightness/contrast adjustments have affected the mask.

10.

Tinker a bit with the brightness/contrast controls until you're satisfied with the result. Then merge the mask with the layer.

Remember that to merge the mask, choose Delete from the Masks menu. This will bring up a dialog box giving you the option to merge or not. Click Yes to merge.

11.

Once you have merged the mask with the layer, use the Layer Visibility Toggle tool to turn off visibility to the bottom layer so you can see what merging the mask has done to the white layer. The center portion, where the layer was masked off, is now transparent, gradating to white around the edge. Toggle the visibility back on again.

12.

Now that the mask is merged into the layer and the edge effect is firmly in place, there are some cool things you can do to the layer to enhance the edge effect even more before merging the layers into the final product. You can use the deformation and effects tools.

With the white layer active, go to the Image menu to pull up the wide array of deformations and effects.

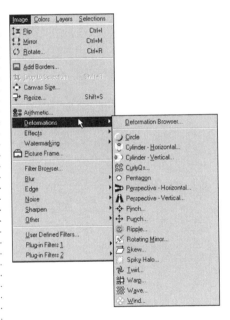

13.

For starters, try out the Ripple effect on the layer (Image|Deformations|Ripple). Check the Auto Proof option, so that you can see the effect it has on your image, and play with the various settings. Click OK when you are happy with it, or click Cancel to try another deformation or effect.

14.

Perhaps a Spiky Halo deformation edge would be more to your liking (Image|Deformations| Spiky Halo).

15.

A Wave deformation (Image|Deformations| Wave) on a gradient layer makes an interesting effect.

16.

Not finding what you want in the deformations? Move on to the Effects menu. Shown here is a Weave effect (Image|Effects|Weave) applied to the layer.

Experiment with the other effects in the menu to see how many unusual edges you can create.

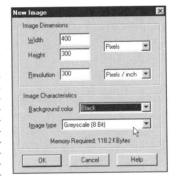

17.

The look of a roughly painted edge is a popular edge effect that can be accomplished easily with a mask. For this effect, make a separate mask image that can be applied to any photo. Open a new blank greyscale image in black. Size doesn't matter because the mask will later conform to any size image you choose to place it in.

18.

With the background color in the color palette set to white, go to the Image menu and choose Add Borders. Check the Symmetric checkbox and choose the number of pixels that you wish the border width to be. For this image, I've chosen a 50 pixel border.

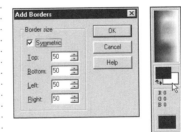

19.

Apply a Gaussian Blur (Image|Blur|Gaussian Blur) with the blur radius set to around 5 or so. You should have an image that now looks basically like the one shown here.

20.

The rough painted edges can be quickly achieved by using the Airbrush tool. Activate the Airbrush and choose a medium-sized soft brush.

21.

Click on the center tab in the Tool Options box to bring up the drop-down menu of available paper textures. I've chosen one called Asphalt. You can experiment to find one that's right for your project.

22.

Use the airbrush to lightly spray all around the edges, where the white meets the black, to create the roughness. This image will be your mask. If you want to save your new mask to use with other images, go to Masks|Save To Disk, give it an appropriate name, and choose the location on your hard drive where you wish to store it. Remember that masks are saved using the .msk extension.

23.

To apply the mask, first open an image, add a new layer to it, and fill the layer with a color or pattern of your choice. The example shown here will use an image of a lion and a second layer filled with a wood pattern.

You can use one of Paint Shop Pro's built-in patterns and textures, which are located in the program folders. Use the browser to find one you like, open it, and colorize it. The Flood Fill tool can use any open image as a pattern fill by choosing it as the pattern source in the Flood Fill Options.

24.

Activate the wood pattern (or top) layer by clicking on it in the Layer palette. This is the layer to which the mask will be attached.

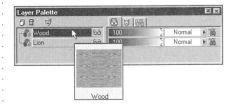

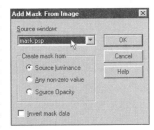

25.

Choose Masks|New|From Image. In the Add Mask From Image dialog box, use the drop-down menu to select the mask image as the source (the mask image must be open to be chosen as the source). Click OK.

26.

The image, with the mask in place performing its magic, will miraculously appear—rough edges and all.

Project 3: Text Mask

By using a text selection to create a mask, you can create some interesting combinations of words and images.

1.

To demonstrate a text mask, I'll use the image of the two cats from the first project in the chapter. You can use an image of your choice to learn this technique.

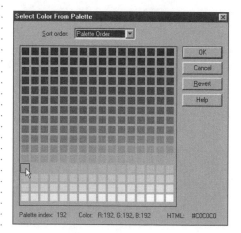

2.

First, add a new layer to the image and use the Flood Fill tool to fill the layer with a color that will complement your image. For the cat picture, I've chosen to use white.

3.

Now the image is ready and waiting. You just need to make the mask. Open a new blank greyscale image with the same dimensions as the original image. Use the Flood Fill tool to fill this blank image with a light shade of gray.

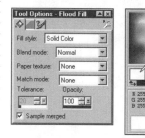

4.

Next you'll add the text. Activate the Text tool by clicking on the text icon in the toolbar and then clicking once in the gray image. In the Text Entry dialog box, choose a font that will go along with your image, and type in the word or words of your choice. Set the text color to black and choose to create the text as vector with the Antialias option enabled.

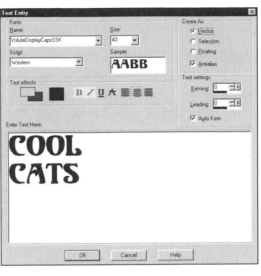

5.

When the text is placed, you'll notice that, because it was created as vector, you have access to the manipulating handles so that you can resize it, stretch it, or do whatever you choose.

6.

In this case, I've used the handles to enlarge the text and place it at an angle similar to the angle of the snowbank in the cat picture. Once you have your text the way you like it, just right-click anywhere in the image to deactivate the handles. This is your text mask. Leave it open.

7.

To apply the text mask, first go back to the original image—remember, we left it ready and waiting. All you need to do is choose Masks|New|From Image. In the Add Mask From Image dialog box, use the drop-down menu to choose the open text mask image as the source window.

8.

With the text mask in place, the image has an entirely new look. The text appears to be see-through, and the rest of the image has transformed into a lighter-colored version, serving as a backdrop to the text.

9.

To make the text really stand out and have more definition, use a drop shadow to finish off the task. To easily reselect the text, first choose Masks|Edit. Use the Magic Wand tool and click inside one of the letters to select it. Press Shift on your keyboard and click on each of the other letters in turn to add them to the selection.

10.

With the letters still selected, go back to the Masks menu and uncheck the Edit function by clicking on it once. Open the Image menu and choose Effects|Drop Shadow. Set the shadow color to black, the opacity to 100, the blur to around 20 or so, and the horizontal and vertical offsets each to 3. Click OK.

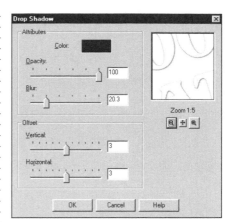

11.

With the addition of the drop shadow, the job is complete. Merge the mask into the layer and enjoy your new text effect!

Chapter 12
Cool Text Effects

 Project 1: Create stunning effects using common filters

 Project 2: Achieve even more dazzling results with text using the Gradient Editor

 Project 3: Use vector capabilities to create interesting effects

 Project 4: Manipulate text in dynamic ways, such as text on a path

By Joshua Pruitt

Project 1: Creating Cool Text Effects

Using art to enhance and embellish text is one of the most effective ways to draw attention to your message. Text logos and headers tend to be the first thing people see when they read a brochure, open a business letter, look at a business card, or visit a Web site. So when dealing with an important word or group of words, you want something that catches the eye and leaves a positive impression on the reader—first impressions are important, after all. Fortunately, creating good text effects in Paint Shop Pro happens to be a fairly simple task once you get the hang of it.

The Drop Shadow

One of the *easiest* effects to achieve with text is the drop shadow. Despite the ease with which they are created, drop shadows are attractive and effective, which is probably the very reason they are so popular.

1.

To begin, create a new blank image—big enough to play with—and then create a new transparent raster layer (Layers|New Raster Layer).

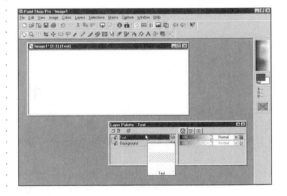

2.

Activate the Text tool, choose the Floating radio button in the Create As section, type in your text, and click on the OK button when the font, size, and so forth are set to your satisfaction.

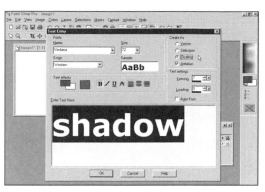

In most circumstances, you will want to use the Antialias option to create text effects. This ensures that your text will be legible, smooth, and pleasant to look at.

3.

Next, you need to *contract the selection* by 1 pixel (Selections|Modify|Contract). You don't have to perform this step to create drop shadows, but it does reduce the possibility of off-color pixel anomalies popping up, and in general, it tends to create a smoother effect (if you do happen to be a perfectionist).

4.

The next step is to apply the drop shadow effect. To do this, simply use the Paint Shop Pro Drop Shadow filter. You can get to it from the Image|Effects|Drop Shadow menu item. Once the dialog box pops up, use the preview window in the upper-right corner as a gauge while you adjust the various settings. My settings are as follows:

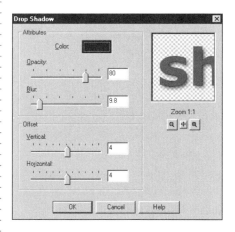

- *Color*—Black
- *Opacity*—80
- *Blur*—9.8
- *Vertical Offset*—4
- *Horizontal Offset*—4

5.

Choose OK on the Drop Shadow dialog box, and the effect will be applied. Your text will still be selected; simply right-click on it to de-select it. And there you have it—an effect that's simple, attractive, and classic. You can now merge your layers, reduce color depth if you need to, and save your image.

Cutout Text

Cutout text is another effect that is simple and clean and yet never fails to impress.

1.

Create a new transparent raster layer to work with. Then use the Text tool to select your font, size, and so on, and create your floating text. For this effect, it is a good idea to use a relatively thick, heavy font face, as well as a relatively medium to light color, so the effect will show up well.

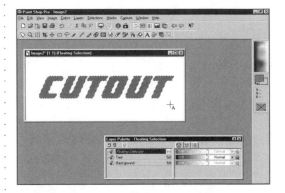

2.

Creating a cutout effect is as easy as applying a drop shadow—first, use the Image|Effects| Cutout menu option to bring up the Cutout dialog box. Uncheck the Fill Interior With Color option (you'll use your existing text color), and then, as you did in the Drop Shadow dialog box, adjust your settings and use the preview window until you achieve the effect you want. Click on OK to apply the effect. Your settings will depend on the size and shape of your text, but in this example, my settings are:

- *Opacity*—100

- *Blur*—9.8

- *Vertical Offset*—4

- *Horizontal Offset*—4

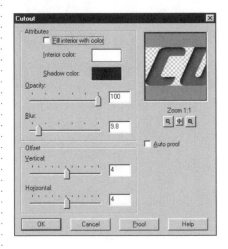

3.

Afterward, right-click on the text to deselect it and view your handiwork. The final effect is something that looks like it is cut out of your background, so to speak. It's a nice look, and one that can come in handy when you're trying to find a way to fill in blank space on a Web page, for example, with a quick and easy effect.

Beveled Text

Until the release of Paint Shop Pro 6, creating beveled text was a process that, without the aid of third-party plug-ins, was somewhat involved and time-consuming. This is no longer true.

1.

Again, start with a new, blank image, create a transparent raster layer, and use the Text tool to create your new floating text. Use a color for your text that is neither too dark nor too light.

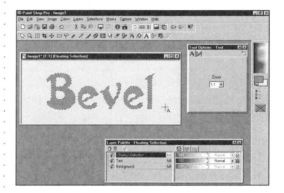

2.

With the text still selected, choose Image| Effects|Inner Bevel. Once the Inner Bevel dialog box is open, you can use the settings to add lighting and 3D texture to your text. Try a rounded bevel from the Bevel drop-down menu for a nice, rounded look, and put the Smoothness option to about 45 or so for a clean, realistic bevel. The Shininess adjustment can drastically change the look and feel of your text. A higher Shininess value (around 30 or greater, depending on the color) will make the text object appear harder and more metallic, whereas a lower Shininess level will create text with a look that's softer, with more of a plastic appearance.

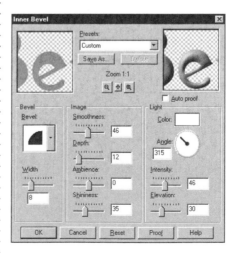

3.

Click on OK and your bevel will be rendered.

4.

Before deselecting your text, you can also combine some steps from this chapter's drop-shadow project to augment this effect. Follow Steps 3 through 5 in the first project to contract the selection by 1 pixel and then add a drop shadow. This will add even more depth to your beveled text. Once complete, right-click on the image to deselect the text, merge your layers, and save the image as usual.

Sculptured Text

Like the Inner Bevel filter, the Sculpture filter creates a three-dimensional lighted and shadowed effect—but the sculpture filter also automatically adds a pattern to create an extra level of depth and texture.

1.

Create your new layer and add your text. For this filter, it doesn't really matter what color you choose for your text.

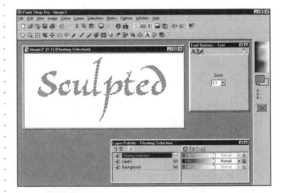

2.

Select the Image|Effects|Sculpture menu item. The Sculpture dialog box that appears works much the same as the Inner Bevel filter. The main difference is that you can choose a pattern from the drop-down menu instead of a bevel type. Any pattern you choose here will do—I chose #27 because I like the way it looks—as long as the text is still legible. Adjust the settings according to the size and shape of the text, until the image shown in the preview window to the right is to your satisfaction.

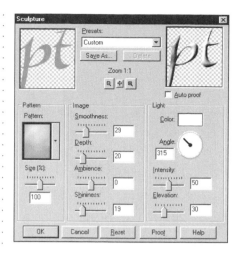

Many of the presets emulate real textures and can make for some interesting effects as well.

3.

And after you're finished, you can either merge and save the text as is or, again, contract the selection by 1 and add a drop shadow for that extra touch. In truth, I can think of only a few situations in which a drop shadow simply doesn't look right on text atop a relatively light background. Of course, that all depends on your composition in general.

Glowing Text

Glowing text is an effect that is fairly easy to achieve, and yet it's definitely hard to miss.

1.

First, create a new image, this time with a background color of black, and create a new text layer to work with. Obviously, this glow effect works best with dark backgrounds.

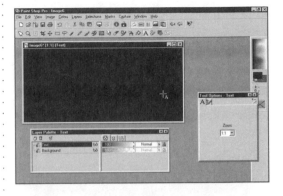

2.

Next, use the Text tool to create your text. Make sure the color of your text is set at very dark or black—the outline of the marquee will make it possible to still see the outline of the text. Rounded fonts tend to look a bit better for glow effects, but there are always exceptions.

3.

Once your text is in place, go to Image|Effects| Drop Shadow. Choose white as the shadow color, set Opacity to the full amount, and set both your Vertical and Horizontal Offset values to 0. This makes the drop shadow function serve as more of a "glow" function when used on dark backgrounds. You may not want to set Blur too high. For me, a value of 16 through 20 is a good place to start.

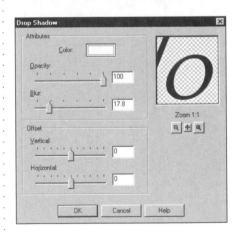

4.

Once you've added your drop shadow (by selecting OK from the dialog box), you should see a slight glow surrounding your text (because this is hard to preview in the Drop Shadow dialog box at times, you can use the Undo function to go back if you need to). Now, use the Image|Effects|Glowing Edges filter to add a thin, bright border around your text. To do so, set the Intensity value to 1 and the Sharpness value to 0.

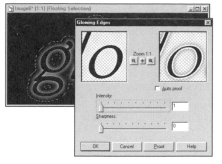

5.

Once the border is in place, you'll intensify the glow effect. This is done simply by reapplying the Drop Shadow filter with all the exact same settings. Each time you do this, the glow effect becomes more pronounced.

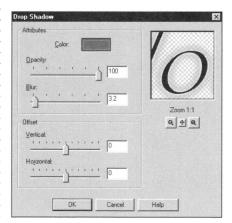

6.

The final step is to give the glow effect a bit of depth by adding just a touch of color. Open up the Drop Shadow filter again, this time choose a nice bright color as the shadow color (I chose a neon blue), and then set the Blur value down a bit from the previous Blur setting. You'll want to go with at least half the original value here.

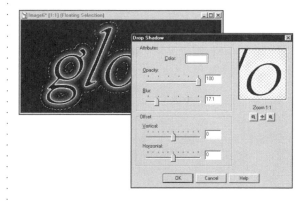

7.

Once the effect is complete, it's merely a matter of merging and saving the image.

You can also use the Brightness/Contrast dialog box (Colors|Adjust|Brightness/Contrast) to manipulate this effect by either toning it down or making it a bit brighter.

Project 2: Utilizing Gradients

Besides simple colors and patterns, gradients too can make for some pretty interesting text effects. They can add an appearance of depth and texture, as well as create the illusion of sheen, luster, and other properties dealing with light and color.

Simple Metallic

This effect simulates the appearance of brushed or polished metal. It is attractive and detailed, but probably best reserved for use in a situation most appropriate for such a look.

1.

To create a simple metallic texture, first create the text on its own layer. Then activate the Flood Fill tool.

2.

To give text a metallic look, you really only need a two-color gradient using black and white. Select black as your background color and white as your foreground color. Activate the Flood Fill tool, and in the Tool Options dialog box, choose Linear Gradient. Use the Flood Fill options (second tab in the dialog box) and choose Foreground-Background as your gradient type, position the gradient at any angle you wish, and then set the Repeats value to 2. Fill in the selected text with the Flood Fill tool when the options are set. This will fill one letter at a time with color. Set your Match Mode Option to None in order to fill in all the letters at once.

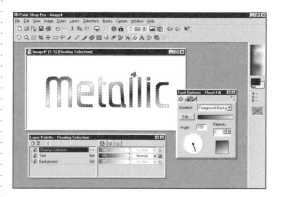

3.

Contract the selection by 1 (Selections|Modify|
Contract), add a good drop shadow (Image|
Effects|Drop Shadow), and you have eye-catch-
ing text that takes less than a minute to make.

---

*The Gradient Editor has some nice built-in metallic
gradients. If you want to change the color of your
metal (that is, to gold or copper), just use
Colors|Colorize to adjust the hue.*

Project 3: Using Vector Text

Vector capabilities in Paint Shop Pro not only help you create shapes, curves, and objects, they can also be used to edit and manipulate text. The advantages are numerous—you can edit, resize, deform, respace, and reshape text without affecting its quality or legibility. This is yet another reason why vectors are such a valuable tool for aiding in the creative process.

Glassy Shine Effects

This effect—which uses various filters, gradients, and vectors—is detailed, complex, a bit tricky, but pretty slick when all's said and done.

1.

For this project, you'll use both vectors and gradients. Create a new image, as usual. There is no need to worry about creating a new transparent layer here because you'll be creating vector layers as you go. Activate the Text tool and create your new text as a black vector object by selecting the Vector option in the text dialog box.

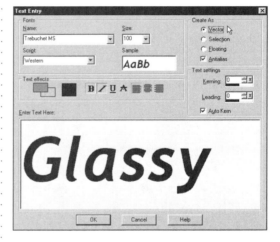

2.

Activate the Vector Object selection tool and then move, resize, and reshape the text as you see fit using the resize tabs.

At this point, you can also edit the content of the text (font, size, and so on) by right-clicking and selecting Properties.

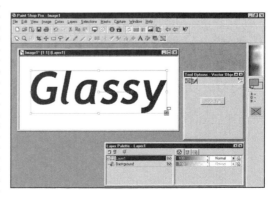

3.

Once you get the text just the way you want it, you'll create an exact duplicate. Do this by right-clicking on the vector layer in the Layer palette and selecting the Duplicate option. This will create an exact copy of the object on its own layer.

4.

Repeat Step 3 and create another duplicate layer. You'll now have three layers with exactly the same content—feel free to rename them however you wish, or you can keep the default names.

5.

Click on the original text layer in the Layer palette. Then click on the plus sign next to the layer name to bring up the text object sublayer and click on it once to activate it. Enable the Vector Object selection tool, right-click on the text object, and choose the Convert Text To Curves|As Single Shape. (This lets you manipulate the text as one vector object—as opposed to Character Shapes, which treats each individual letter as a separate shape and vector object.) Doing this allows you to apply the many vector functions to text, such as node editing, caps and joins editing, and so forth (of course, converting to curves also means that you can *no longer edit* the *content* of the text itself).

6.

Right-click on the text object again and choose Properties. Instead of bringing up the Text Tool dialog box as before, this will bring up the Vector Properties dialog box (because you've converted it to curves—that is, you added the editing nodes). In this dialog box, go ahead and change the draw style from Filled to Stroked And Filled. Keep the Line Style and Fill Style colors the same, but increase the Line Style Width value until the text looks good and thick (but still readable). Then set the Join option to Rounded to make a cleaner, more polished effect.

7.

Convert the three text layers to raster format for color and effects editing. Use the Layer palette to right-click on each vector layer in turn and choose Convert To Raster.

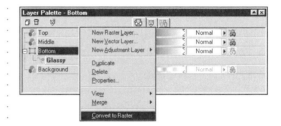

8.

Now you'll add color to your original element. To do so, you'll create a custom gradient. First, make sure that the original text layer (the one you made wide and thick) is active (highlighted) in the Layer palette. Toggle the layer visibility for the two duplicate layers *off* for the time being (via the glasses icons in the Layer palette). Go to Selections|Select All, activate the selection tool, and click once on the image to snap the selection directly to your text. Activate the Flood Fill tool, select Linear Gradient from the Tool Options dialog box, and then click on the second tab to bring up the Flood Fill options. Click on the Edit button to open the Gradient Editor to create a new gradient.

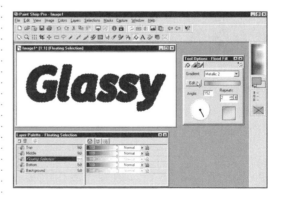

9.

In the Gradient Editor, click on the New button to give the gradient you're creating a new name (so that none of the original gradients will be changed). In this example, I'm trying to replicate a bronze effect, so I've chosen the name Old Bronze and will be creating the gradient from mostly darkish oranges and yellows.

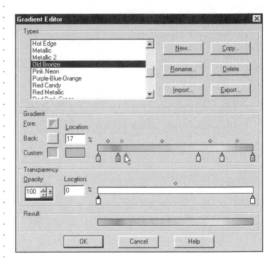

10.

Use the markers (the little hanging bucket icons) to select and edit the colors. Click once on a marker to select it, then click on the color picker box next to Custom to select the desired color (selecting the Fore and Back options will set the color to your current foreground or background colors, respectively). You can stretch the gradient simply by clicking and dragging any one of these marker points to the left or right. Use the diamonds above the gradient preview bar to adjust the midpoint between any two gradient colors. To add more colors to your gradient, simply click on a blank space directly below the gradient preview bar to add a marker. Deleting a marker is simply a matter of dragging it back to the gradient edit window. Leave the Opacity setting for this gradient at 100. When you're finished editing your gradient, click on OK.

11.

Set the Repeats value to 2, set the angle at whatever value looks right to you and fill in your text selection.

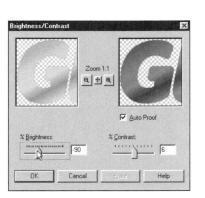

12.

Because this portion of text is the backdrop for the rest of the effect, you'll want to tone it down and darken it a bit. You can easily do this from Colors|Adjust|Brightness/Contrast. This layer should be darkened quite considerably—but you should still be able to make out the gradient. The amount of proper brightness reduction will vary depending on the colors in your gradient. Just eyeball it here, then click on OK.

13.

Choose Selections|Modify|Contract (by 1), and then choose Image|Effects|Drop Shadow and set the options as follows:

- *Color*—Black
- *Opacity*—100
- *Blur*—8
- *Offsets*—3

Choose Selections|Select None to deselect the text.

14.

Toggle the layer visibility back on for the middle text layer. As you can see, this in and of itself is a pretty neat-looking effect. You can merge and save your image right here if you're completely satisfied with the effect. There is, however, even more you can do to this effect.

15.

Make sure the middle text copy layer is active, then select the text (Selections|Select All) creating a floating selection. Activate the selection tool and click once on the image to snap the selection to your text. Go to Colors|Adjust| Brightness/Contrast to lighten it up from black to a dark gray—a Brightness value of about 60 should do the trick.

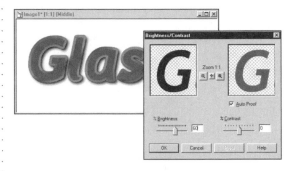

16.

The next step is to add an inner bevel (Image| Effects|Inner Bevel) to this layer to give it a bright reflective shine. The shine should be prominent, so you'll be setting the Shininess and Intensity values higher than you may be used to. Use the round bevel shape and the following approximate values:

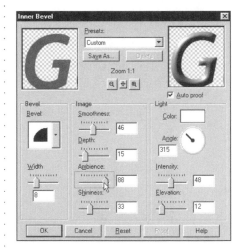

- *Width*—8
- *Smoothness*—46
- *Depth*—15
- *Ambience*—88
- *Shininess*—33
- *Intensity*—48
- *Elevation*—12

17.

Choose Selections|Select None to deselect the text. Now set the blend mode for this layer to Overlay in the Layer palette.

18.

Toggle the layer visibility for the background layer off so that only these two text layers (the middle and the bottom) are visible. Then use Layers|Merge|Merge Visible to merge these two layers, and at the same time, leave the top and bottom two layers intact. Afterward, you may bring the background back into view. Once again, this is a pretty cool look, but there's even more that can be done.

19.

Now you will edit the remaining text layer. Toggle the layer visibility to bring it into view and make sure it's the active layer in the Layer palette. Select the text (Selections|Select All), activate the selection tool and click once on the image to snap the selection to your text.

20.

Activate the Flood Fill tool and select the same gradient as before (see Step 9). This time, however, apply it in the opposite direction (angle). The gradient should be a lot brighter than the one on the background text layer—use Colors| Adjust|Brightness/Contrast if you need to.

21.

With the text still selected, choose the Image|Effects|Cutout menu item to bring up the Cutout dialog box. Make sure the Fill Interior With Color Option is *unchecked* and that the shadow color is set to *white*. This will be a refined, subtle effect, so make sure your Offset values are at no more than 3 and your Blur option is set fairly low (less than 5 in most cases). You'll want a thin, bright, slightly soft edge here. Click on OK to apply.

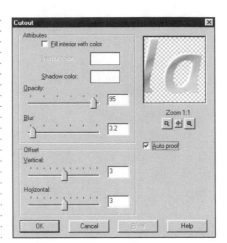

22.

And finally, set the blend mode for the top layer to Screen and adjust the opacity down a bit if you need to (to let the lighting specular shine through). And there you have it. Once you're satisfied with the effect, merging and saving your image is all that is left.

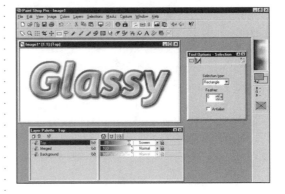

For some interesting color effects, experiment by applying different blend modes on either of the two text layers before merging. Altering the colors (Colors|Colorize) can also produce some interesting results.

Skewed And Bold

This project illustrates how you can use vector capabilities to edit and manipulate each individual letter of text to create a bold, eye-catching effect.

1.

Open a new image and create your text as a vector object. Then activate the Vector Object selection tool, right-click on the text object, and choose Convert Text To Curves|As Character Shapes.

2.

Click on the plus sign in the Layer palette. You can see by looking that converting to curves as character shapes produced each letter as a separate vector object. You can manipulate, size, skew, and rotate each individual letter separately.

Using shaped curves on text also allows you to use Node Edit to manipulate each individual letter just as you would any other vector shape—in essence, you can create your own custom fonts this way!

3.

One-by-one, select each individual letter, either with the Vector Object selection tool or by clicking on the object in the Layer palette. Rotate and skew each letter until the word (or words) as a whole is sufficiently jumbled and disarrayed to illustrate an intense dazed and confused mood.

4.

After your letters are sufficiently confusing, select all the letters on the Vector Text layer by using the Vector Object selection tool to draw a selection box around the entire phrase. Select Edit|Copy. You now have a copy of this layer on the clipboard.

5.

Right-click on the image and select Properties to bring up the Vector Properties dialog box. As in the last tutorial, you'll use the Stroked And Filled style in the same foreground and background colors. Increase the line width for a bold look. Rounded joins might be a good idea as well, if you like the look of rounded edges rather than sharp corners.

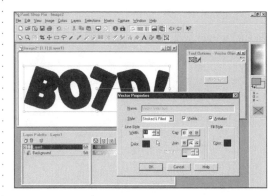

6.

Create a new vector layer (right-click on the Layer palette and choose New Vector Layer). From the Edit menu, choose Paste As New Vector Selection. Position the text so that it appears directly in the center of the text underneath and then click to place it there.

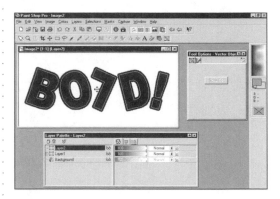

7.

Now convert your layers to raster format (in the Layer palette, right-click and choose Convert To Raster), and you're ready to add your colors and effects.

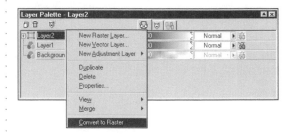

8.

Activate the top text layer, choose Selections|
Select All, and then click once in the image to
snap the selection, fitting it around the text so
that it alone is selected. What you do from here
is really up to you—here I chose to use the
Flood Fill tool to add a simple sunburst gradient (a multicolored gradient will add even
more of the feeling of chaos to the image).

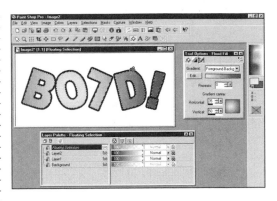

9.

And then, for an added touch, I used the Weave
filter (Image|Effects|Weave) to throw in some
more confusion. Ah, it looks like a migraine
ready to happen!

Project 4: Manipulating Text On A Path

Another function of vector capabilities is the creation and use of *paths* and *contours*. Not only can you use paths and contours to create lines and shapes, you can map text along the lines and shapes. This way, text can be manipulated into many strange shapes and directions.

Circular Text

Before Paint Shop Pro added vector functionality, good circular text was one of the most complicated things to accomplish with precision. Now it's one of the easiest.

1.

Open a new image window, and begin by activating the Preset Shapes tool. Choose Circle as the shape type, Stroked as the style, and 1 as the line width. Check the Create As Vector checkbox.

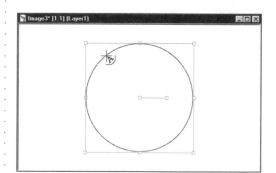

2.

Activate the Text tool and place your cursor over the image. Hover the cursor directly over the outline of the vector shape. When positioned directly over the vector, the font cursor will appear to be curved (called a "rocking A"), indicating that it will place the text around the other objects path. When you see this, click to bring up the Text Entry dialog box.

3.

Create your text as you want it to appear around the circumference of your circle. Select the Vector radio button under Create As and click on OK when you're ready to proceed.

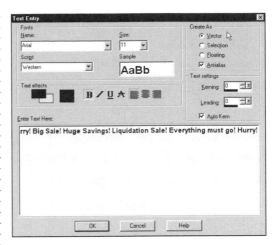

4.

Your text will now be created along the path of the vector circle. You can rotate the circle as you normally would to get the text right side up.

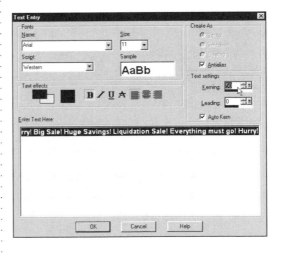

5.

If the text is not perfectly spaced on the first try, it's easy to fix. First, make sure your text object is the selected, active object in the Layer palette. Then, right-click on the text with the Vector Object selection tool and choose Properties. This will bring up the standard Text Entry dialog box again, except that all the settings are reapplied to the selected text. You can adjust font, size, message, and so on, as many times as you see fit. A useful text function to use here is the Kerning function. Without getting too technical, kerning simply refers to the ability to space text—that is, to adjust the amount of space between words and letters. So go ahead and increase the Kerning value to some degree, then click on OK.

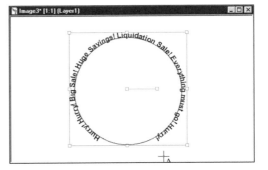

6.

As you can see, the letters are farther apart, and the gap left at the bottom of the circle is closer to being filled in. The process behind getting text kerned just right for a perfect shape match is nothing more than trial and error—adjust kerning, and preview the changes, then repeat the process until the text looks good (it took me four times to get it set just right).

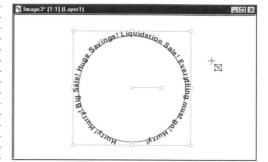

7.

Now your text looks great, but you have that pesky circle in the way. You needed the circle as a path to map the text to, but now you can easily hide it from view by using the Object Visibility toggle in the Layer palette (next to the object itself within the vector layer, not just the layer itself). Now you can edit the text as desired, but the circle is hidden from view.

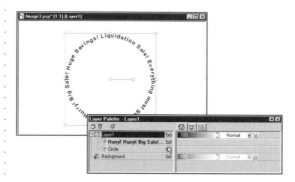

8.

At this point, simply right-click on your vector layer and choose Convert To Raster. As you can see, as long as the Object Visibility toggle is toggled off for the circle itself, when you convert to a raster object, the circle is gone, leaving only the text.

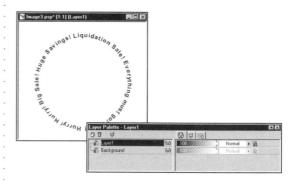

Text On A Curve

Text on a curve (line) works in pretty much the same way as text on a shape. To begin with, you can either create a simple curve, such as a wavy line, or you can do something a bit more complex, like draw a vector shape around the circumference of an object and map text around it.

1.

First, create a new image. Activate the Draw tool, and choose a stroked Bezier line with a width of 1 (check Create As Vector). Draw your object as a wavy line; first click and drag to form a straight line, then create the curve by clicking anywhere in the image and dragging to shape the curve (with a Bezier line, you only get two clicks to shape your line—if your line needs further shaping, activate the Vector Object selection tool, right-click on the line, and choose Node Edit).

2.

Once your wavy line is set, activate the Text tool and position your cursor over the line object until you see the rocking A cursor. Add your text, click on OK, and you'll see that your text is perfectly mapped in the direction of the curve.

3.

As you did in the preceding project, use the Object Visibility toggle in the Layer palette to hide the wavy line so you can concentrate on the text itself—size, kerning, and so on.

4.

If you want to flip the text in the other direction, first click on the plus sign next to the vector layer containing the Bezier line (in the Layer palette) and click on the Bezier object layer to select it. Enable the Vector Object selection tool, right-click on the image, and choose Node Edit. Once in Node Edit mode, right-click again and select Edit|Reverse Path.

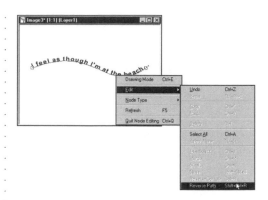

5.

The result is that now the text runs in the opposite direction.

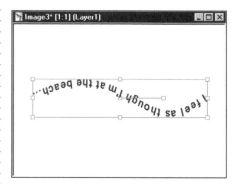

Text Around An Object

You can place text around an object in the same way—by drawing your lines or curves and then mapping the text to that curve.

1.

Open an image with an object around which you wish to place some text. Preferably, there should be high contrast between the object and the background for text readability.

2.

Activate the Draw tool, and choose a stroked, point-to-point vector line with a width of 1 from the Tool Options dialog box. Begin drawing your points around the circumference of the object, dragging slightly to create curves around the round parts. It's not essential that you get it perfect here—you'll be able to use node editing later—but try to get it mapped as closely as you can.

3.

Once you get down to the last node in the drawing process, click and, holding down the Ctrl key, drag that node directly over the first node. You should see the word "JOIN" hovering next to your cursor—when you do, release the mouse button to join the two nodes.

4.

Once you've created your shape, chances are it may not be exactly perfect. To tweak it a bit, activate the Vector Object selection tool, right-click on the active vector shape, and choose Node Edit.

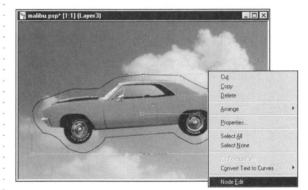

5.

Go through and smooth out the outline of your curve by adjusting and arranging the nodes. You'll want to be especially careful not to have any really tight curves or angles that will degrade text legibility.

6.

Once you're satisfied with the nodes and curves, activate the Text tool. Click on the curve outline (with the rocking A) and create your text—make sure that it is created as vector object as well. Now you will have text that maps around the contour of the shape.

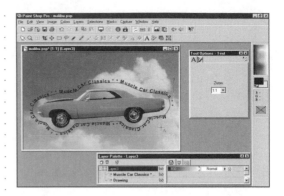

7.

Activate the Vector Object selection tool again, and make sure the text vector object—as represented in the Layer palette—is the only active vector object. Then, right-click, choose Properties, and adjust your text kerning until it lines up evenly around the outline of your object.

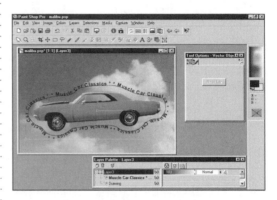

8.

Finally, use the Object Visibility toggle to hide the curve from view, convert the vector layer to raster, and merge and save your image. As you can see, this process is not too difficult for such a complex text effect.

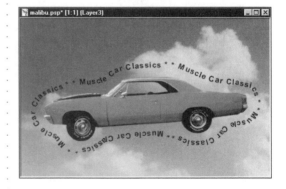

Chapter 13
Creating Web Graphics And Animations

 Project 1: Create a matching theme set for Web use

 Project 2: Make seamless tiling backgrounds

 Project 3: Create an animated banner ad

 Project 4: Find out how to embed a digital watermark to protect your images

By Joshua Pruitt

Web Graphics Fundamentals

Creating Web graphics entails more than simply creating images and surrounding them with text. You want the images you put online to serve a specific purpose, which more often than not is simply to convey your message clearly and easily. And to do that, they not only have to look good, but they should be utilitarian if at all possible (which doesn't exclude them from being fun, too).

Web designers traditionally use any number and combination of *web elements*, or graphical components that make a Web site more navigable, illustrative, easier to read, interesting, or just visually pleasing. In this chapter, you'll explore some of these concepts and learn how to create basic Web-site graphics in practical applications.

Project 1: Create A Matching Web Theme

In this first project, you'll go through the steps of creating a simple Web site using many common graphical elements. The first elements you'll play with embody the most basic elements that most Web sites use to give a site some measure of personality and uniqueness.

The first step in beginning any Web-site design venture is to determine the kind of audience your site will attract and then create your graphics accordingly. For example, if your site is a research resource—a copy of the United States Constitution, for example—the only kinds of graphics you may want to concentrate on, if any, are simple navigational aids to facilitate finding information more easily (a very minimalist approach). Anything else will detract from the information you're presenting. On the other hand, if your site is intended to be a rich multimedia experience for the masses, perhaps for an online toy reseller or movie studio Web site, then obviously your needs are going to be very different.

But the most important thing to keep in mind (and one of the main points I want to make in this chapter) is that no matter what a Web site looks like, it should be consistent; that is, pages with similar topics should have a similar look and feel. Visitors go to your Web site to retrieve information of some sort, so navigating your pages should not be a disconcerting experience. A consistent look and feel makes it much easier to navigate.

The First Element: The H-Rule

In this project, you'll create a simple Web site dedicated to a specific topic and geared toward a specific type of audience. As such, you'll need to use a set of common elements and navigational aids that reflect the nature and tone of the audience and content matter and at the same time look clean and utilitarian.

1.

In this example, I chose to go with a smooth beveled-wood-grain appearance for most of the site and to match all my elements to that standard look and feel.

Choose a pattern that you like for your project and open it. Incidentally, the one I chose is in Paint Shop Pro 6's Patterns directory; it's called Finished Wood.pat. Any pattern that is seamless and not too "busy" or distracting will do.

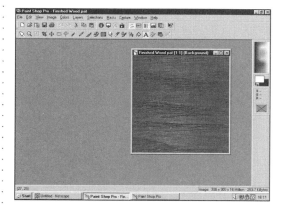

2.

Once you have a color or pattern in mind, you can start making your elements. First, make a simple *h-rule*, which is actually a page separator. Create a new image, and then a new layer, and then make a thin rectangular selection, no longer than, say, 500 pixels (with antialiasing and feathering off) on this new transparent layer (you can view the dimensions of your rectangle in the status bar, in the lower-left corner).

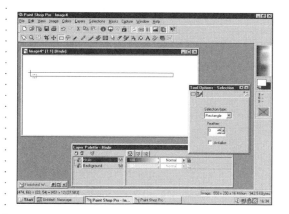

Remember that people with monitors set to the lowest standard screen resolution can't see elements any wider than 640 pixels (even less, actually, after accounting for application border, scrollbars, and so on). So, with the exception of background images, it is not a good idea to create elements any longer than about 600 pixels wide at most.

3.

To fill the selection using the Flood Fill tool and the chosen pattern, the pattern image must be open in Paint Shop Pro along with the image you're working on. Select the Flood Fill tool, and choose Pattern from the Fill Style drop-down menu in the Tool Options dialog box.

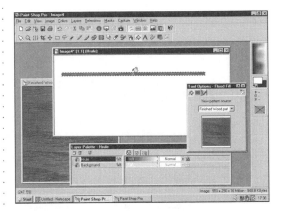

4.

Click on the second tab in the Tool Options dialog box (Flood Fill options), choose the pattern image from the New Pattern Source drop-down menu, and click on the selection with your Flood Fill tool to fill the selection with the pattern in a repetitive, seamless manner.

5.

Once you've done this, you have at your disposal a number of filters or effects that can be applied to the selection for a certain look. I chose to use the Inner Bevel filter to give the h-rule a nice polished and lacquered look (Image| Effects|Inner Bevel). You can make it look more polished by adding just the right amount of Shininess factor. This filter works very well on a number of patterns. My settings for this example are as follows:

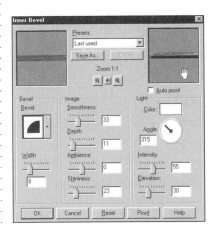

- *Width*—8

- *Smoothness*—33

- *Depth*—11

- *Shininess*—23

- *Angle*—315

- *Intensity*—55

- *Elevation*—30

Contact Us

Guestbook

6.

Now the object looks like a solid piece of beveled and polished wood. You can create a bit more realism by adding a drop shadow (Image|Effects|Drop Shadow) with the following settings:

- *Color*—Black

- *Opacity*—88

- *Blur*—7.2

- *Vertical Offset*—3

- *Horizontal Offset*—3

7.

Click on OK, and there you have it. A nice-looking page divider that simulates a real 3D object. Now you just need to get it Web-ready.

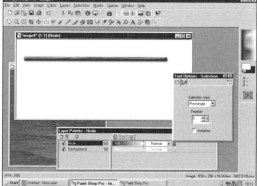

8.

Creating this image on a transparent layer gives you flexibility in making this graphic compatible with any type of background color or texture. If you plan to make your Web-site background blue, for example, you can use the Flood Fill tool to fill in the background layer with the appropriate shade before merging layers—for a perfect match with the rest of your site. Because the background in my sample Web site will be mostly white, I'll merge my layers with no changes (Layers|Merge|Merge All).

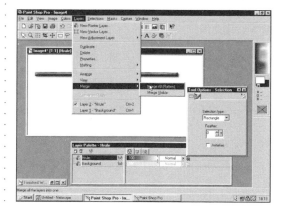

You may want to keep a backup, in layered PSP format with transparent layers intact, of all your Web elements handy just in case you decide to change the background color or pattern on your Web site. This will make such a change more bearable and less time-consuming.

9.

Use the Crop tool to crop the image. Just adjust the borders of the crop frame to include the image area and then click on Crop Image in the Tool Options dialog box. Be careful not to chop off any of your drop shadow here. (You may want to zoom in and make sure you get a clean crop.)

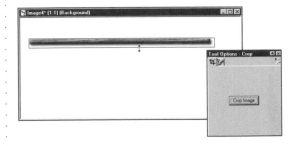

10.

Because this image doesn't have many different colors to begin with (mine is mostly browns, blacks, and white), it can be saved as an 8-bit GIF. To do this, reduce the color depth to 256 colors or less (Colors|Decrease Color Depth|256 Colors).

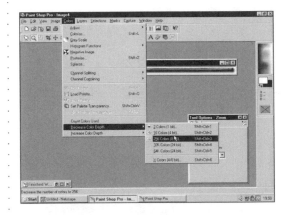

11.

Additionally, for a clean match with your site, you may want to choose the background color as transparent before you save it (Colors|View Palette Transparency, Colors|Set Palette Transparency). For this example, the background will be almost completely solid white, so setting a transparency for this image is really an unnecessary step. However, if I were to use a light or grayish-white pattern for a background, for example, then a transparency here would provide a smooth blending of color. I'll go ahead

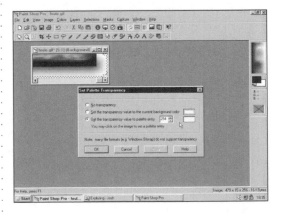

and apply a transparency anyway, just in case
I change my mind about the background later.
(Chapter 6 has more information about choosing transparent colors.)

12.

Save the image as a GIF (File|Save As). You
can, of course, run the Transparent GIF Saver
here if you prefer (File|Export|Transparent GIF).

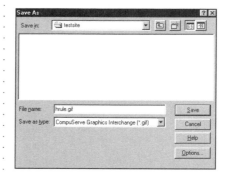

13.

Here's what my first Web element looks like
on a blank white page so far—not too shabby,
and a lot more interesting than the standard
<**HR**> HTML tag.

The Second Element: Standard Navigational Buttons

Because the pattern fill/bevel/drop shadow
technique was applied to one element, you'll
do pretty much the same thing to all the elements for a matching set. The next phase of
the project is to create standard navigational
buttons.

14.

The process for creating the navigational buttons is exactly the same as the process for creating the h-rule, with a few modifications. First, create a new image (200 by 200 pixels is a good place to start) and then a new transparent layer. Name this layer Button or something similar (it's named Layer1 by default, as shown in this figure).

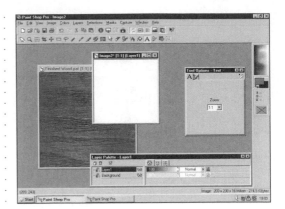

15.

Now you'll use the Preset Shapes tool to create the form you want your button to take. In this example, I'll make a button that's mostly rectangular, but with soft, rounded edges.

To make a rectangular button, first select the Preset Shapes tool, and make sure that both your Foreground Color and Background Color values are exactly the same (black will work just fine). Then, select the Tool Options window and use the following settings:

- *Shape Type*—Rectangle
- *Style*—Stroked And Filled
- *Line Width*—25
- *Antialias*—Enabled

16.

Now, use the tool to select and fill an area on your new transparent layer as shown. You will probably want to make your navigation buttons long and slender.

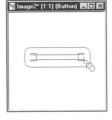

17.

Upon releasing the mouse button, you will have a solid black shape.

Next, you need to get this shape perfectly selected for applying effects. Paint Shop Pro has an ingenious method for doing this. First, select everything in the layer by choosing Selections|Select All. The marquee will surround the border of the frame.

18.

Choose the selection tool and click *once* anywhere on the image; the program will snap the selection to your object for a perfect fit—semi-transparent pixels and all!

Keep in mind that this trick only works with objects on their own transparent layer. Otherwise, you may have to use one of the other selection methods discussed in Chapter 3.

19.

With the shape selected, you're now ready to apply your pattern. First, make sure your pattern source image is still open, and then select the Flood Fill tool. In the Tool Options window, set Fill Style to Pattern, Match Mode to None, and Pattern Source in the second tab to your source image. Fill in your selected object.

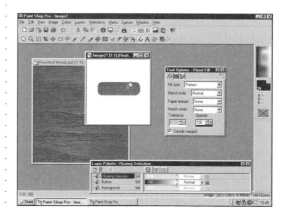

20.

With the object still selected, you can use the Inner Bevel effect as you did in Step 5 (Image|Effects|Inner Bevel). Try it with these settings, then modify to suit your tastes:

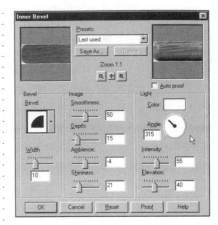

- *Width*—10
- *Smoothness*—50
- *Depth*—15
- *Shininess*—21
- *Angle*—315
- *Intensity*—55
- *Elevation*—40

You may want to set some of the settings higher here than you did with the h-rule object because this one is larger.

21.

Before you add a drop shadow, contract the selection by 1 pixel. Doing so prevents any edge and corner anomalies from cropping up (such as a non-antialiased edge over a contrasting background). It makes for a cleaner effect. It's easy to do—simply go to Selections|Modify|Contract and enter a value of 1.

22.

To add your drop shadow, use the Drop Shadow filter (Image|Effects|Drop Shadow) and apply settings similar to these:

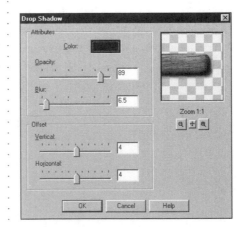

- *Opacity*—89
- *Blur*—6.5
- *Vertical*—4
- *Horizontal*—4

23.

You've now created the button base image. Cropping it and saving it as a layered PSP file will enable you to add text and create multiple matching button images quickly and easily.

First, zoom in and use the Crop tool to make a clean crop around the image, being careful not to cut off any drop shadow, of course!

24.

Save it as a PSP file somewhere safe, with layers intact. Now you have a template file with which to create all your navigation buttons.

25.

The last thing you need to do is add some text to your buttons. Make sure your layered template image is open, then create a new transparent layer and name it Text or something similar.

Zoom in a bit and turn on your grid lines via View|Grid. This will help you accurately position your text so your images line up well together. (Remember, you can change the grid settings by going to File|Preferences|General Program Preferences|Rulers and Units.)

26.

Activate the Text tool and click on your new layer. Choose the font, size, and color you want your text to have and then type your message. Keep in mind that you will want your text to be in high contrast with your button image (hence, use patterns that are more subdued than busy). For my text, sitting atop a wood texture, I chose white.

27.

After setting your text properties, click on OK and position it on your image. Use the grid lines to get it lined up to your satisfaction. You'll want to make sure the text lines up in the same vertical position on every button, so take note of where the text is in relation to the grid line (I put the top of my uppercase letters exactly three pixels from the nearest horizontal line, for example, so from now on, I will position the other text buttons in exactly the same way).

28.

After positioning the text, merge your layers, reduce to 256 colors, and save your image as a GIF. Again, you may want to run the GIF Saver here, as well as set any transparent colors if necessary.

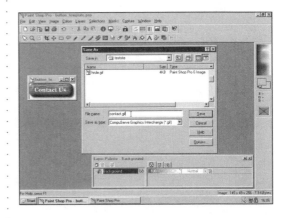

29.

To create the rest of your navigation buttons, simply open up your template image and repeat Steps 25 through 28, making sure to line up your text vertically at the exact same location and to center it horizontally as best you can.

The Third Element: Matching Background Image

Now you'll create the background image. In many situations, you may want to use a background that's interesting to look at but still unobtrusive to make sure the text remains easy to read. Here, you'll make such a background using the same pattern you used for the buttons.

30.

Create a new image with a width of at least 1,800 pixels. Yes, this is big, but it will keep the backdrop from retiling itself sideways at higher resolutions.

31.

Select an area to the left starting at the corner that's about 30 to 40 pixels wide (you may need to use the Normal Viewing button to get a good, close look). Fill it with the same pattern using the Flood Fill tool (making sure your source pattern is open in Paint Shop Pro, of course). Then, apply the same filter you've been using on your other elements (Image|Effects|Inner Bevel), with the same settings as before (Step 20). Right-click to deselect when you're finished (Selections|Select None will also work).

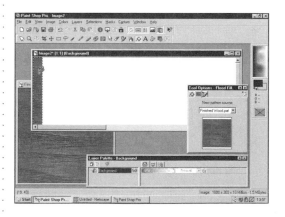

32.

Zoom in a bit, and make a thin, 3- to 4-pixel vertical selection directly to the right of the object, all the way down the edge as shown. Here, providing a simple, smooth gradient will make a clean transition to the background.

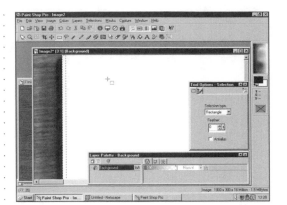

33.

Activate the Flood Fill tool again, and make sure your foreground and background colors are set to black and white, respectively. Change the Fill Style setting for Flood Fill to Linear Gradient in the Tool Options dialog box.

Go to the second tab, choose the Foreground-Background Gradient, and choose a 90-degree angle and 0 repeats as shown. Then fill the selection to create the gradient.

34.

Now you'll make the image slightly smaller. Using the Crop tool, start at the left and select an area about 40 pixels tall and the full 1800 pixels wide (you may need to drag the right-side resizer to the right edge of the image window until the scrollbar scrolls to the complete edge). Crop the image when your area is satisfactory to make a good, small background suitable for seamless tiling.

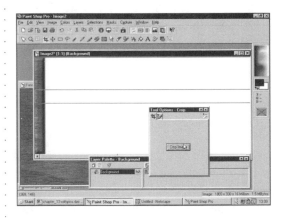

35.

Save the background as a GIF. GIF is well suited for this type of compressed image—mine, for example, weighs in at a whopping 2K, despite being 1800 pixels wide!

36.

You may need a couple more elements to complete your site, elements such as a header logo and some little buttons, bullets, and so on.

Creating small round bullets is easy using the techniques in this tutorial. Simply select (in this case, a small, antialiased circular selection), use the Flood Fill tool to fill the element with pattern, bevel, add a drop shadow, decrease to 256 colors, select transparency if need be, and save.

Make sure you turn selection antialiasing on when working with roundish objects and off when working with rectangular ones.

37.

To create a text logo, you can use the techniques you learned in Chapter 12 and combine them with the same look and feel you've created for this project.

Text, as a floating selection, should be treated simply just like the other objects have been treated (you can see the drop shadow being applied in this figure).

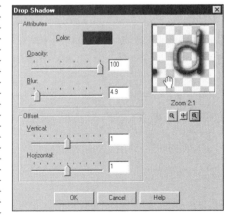

38.

And now, the final step in creating a matching Web-theme set is simply to put it all together (using a plain text editor or an HTML editor, whatever you wish). Here, for this example, you can see the original geeky and very dull site.

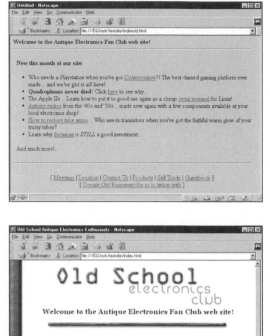

Putting It Together

And after adding my matching set of elements, the same geeky and dull site is, well, no less geeky, but at least much more interesting to look at. This goes to show that many kinds of content can be presented in such a way that can make it more appealing to the audience (and now it's apparent why I chose this particular pattern for this page—the wood grain emulates the old wood cabinets of older '70s-style electronic equipment).

Of course, creativity permits us to take this example alone into many other possible directions (perhaps a darker, more solid background, buttons on the side, a general metal texture instead of wood, cut-outs instead of beveling, and so on). Nevertheless, in each possible case the use of a consistent Web theme can provide a clean and easy-to-navigate look for your Web site.

Project 2: Make Generic Tilable Backgrounds

Web site designers use a general method to create background images. For the most part, they don't use full-page images for backdrops (unless the file size is *extremely* small), but instead take advantage of a Web-browser feature called *tiling*.

Tiling is a method by which a Web browser takes an image and displays it repeatedly, side-by-side, to create a textured background. This makes it easy to create backgrounds with images that aren't really that big (such as the background image in this chapter's first project) but fill up an entire page width and length.

1.

As an example, the image displayed here is shown in a Web browser, but in this case, it's not being used as a tiled background.

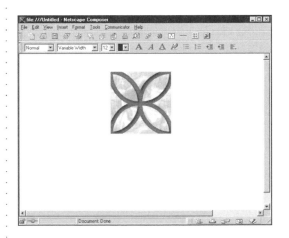

2.

Here, the same image is used as a tiled image. It has the appearance of being one big image but is in fact a smaller one repeating itself.

To use an image as a tiled background, simply add the following modifier to the <BODY> tag in your HTML as follows:

```
<BODY BACKGROUND="file.gif">
```

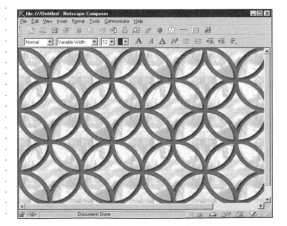

3.

Background images for the Web can really be any dimension (such as the really long and slender one from this chapter's first project), but there is one thing to always take into consideration—*seamlessness*. Seamlessness refers to a state in which an image, repeating itself side-by-side and top-to-bottom, has no visible boundaries between where the left and right sides meet and the top and bottom meet. In this illustration, you can see that this image is badly seamed, thereby creating a distracting effect.

Two things—the distracting seams and the fact that the image has high contrast that makes it hard to read any text placed on it—show why it is a bad choice as a background image.

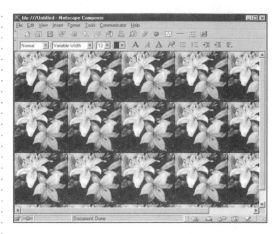

4.

By contrast, this background image made from the same source, albeit still a bit too busy for text, has no seams and is, therefore, not as distracting in that regard. It is difficult to tell where the image ends and begins (or repeats) on any side, and that makes it a better choice for a background pattern.

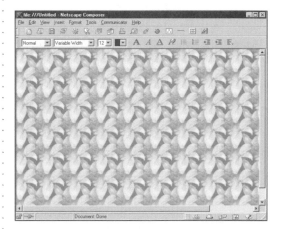

5.

Fortunately, creating seamless tiles with Paint Shop Pro is pretty easy. In fact, you can use virtually any pattern you want as a background as long as you end up with no seams and text is still legible on top of it. If your texture meets these two requirements, chances are it's a pretty good one.

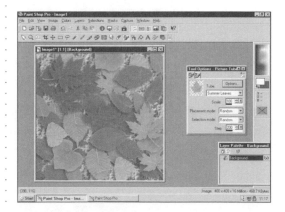

To create a simple tile, first find or create an image without too many high-contrast colors and with a fairly uniform color scheme—nothing too detailed and object-specific. You can even make one yourself using patterns, brushes, tubes...you can experiment with many different things here.

6.

To make the image tilable, make a rectangular selection within the image, with enough buffer space on all sides for PSP to use for calculating a seamless tile.

7.

Then use Selections|Convert To Seamless Pattern to crop and calculate a seamless tile based upon your selected area.

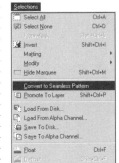

8.

If the area you selected happens to be a bit too close to the edges of the image, a dialog box will pop up to tell you so. If this happens, simply make a new selection and try again.

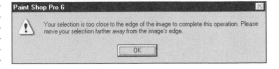

9.

After Paint Shop Pro calculates the seamless tile, you should have an image that's suitable as a background texture.

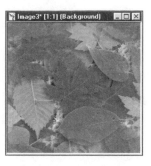

10.

If you plan to display text on top of your tiled texture, as is the case in most Web pages, it is a good idea to make sure the text is in high contrast to the image. This means that, for a light background, dark text is optimal, and for dark backgrounds, bright text is more suitable. Medium-luminance backgrounds are seldom great for text, so if you have a texture that is neither very light nor dark, use the Brightness/Contrast dialog box (Colors|Adjust| Brightness/Contrast) to brighten or darken it a bit.

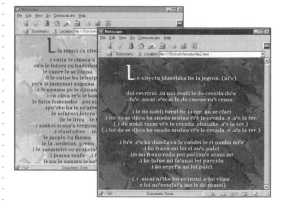

Project 3: Use The Animated Banner Wizard

One of the most popular things posted on Web sites in general are banner animations and ads. Frequently, heavy animation with text is used to catch the viewers' eyes and get the message across quickly and effectively. Paint Shop Pro's Animation Shop has a tool that lets you create simple yet effective text banners with ease—the Banner Wizard.

1.

Open Animation Shop, then click on the Banner Wizard button in the Tool Bar, or use the File|Banner Wizard menu item.

2.

In the first step in the Banner Wizard, you're asked what kind of background you would like to use—transparent, an opaque color, or a background texture. Click on the color box to choose a color if you want an opaque background. Click on Next when you're ready to continue.

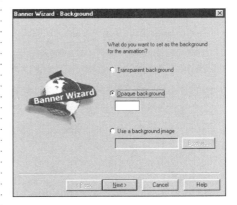

3.

In the next screen, you can choose the dimensions you want your animated text banner to take. There are a few dimensions that are pretty much standard for banners and such on the Web, but there is no rule that says your banners must be a predetermined size. You can use the As defined here option to set any image dimensions you wish.

4.

In the next step, set your animation options as usual. I personally find that a frame rate of 15 frames per second is good for a high-quality image, but of course, your experiences may be different. In any case, any values lower than the default usually aren't good for animations in most situations. Remember, the more frames, the larger the image will be. Sometimes this takes a bit of experimentation to gauge properly.

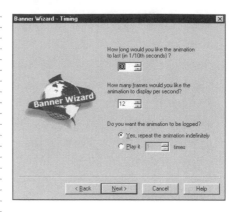

5.

The next step lets you choose your text message and your font. Click on the Set Font button to bring up the Text dialog box.

6.

From within this step, you'll choose the color or texture of your text. Using texture on your text can make it look really sharp, but make sure you account for legibility.

7.

And from the final step you can choose your effect. There are many to choose from, but they all add tremendous eye-catching value to plain ole text.

Once you choose an effect, click on the Customize button to set various options for the effect. When you've chosen all your options, click on the Finish button to create your animation (you can then use View|Animation to see your banner in action).

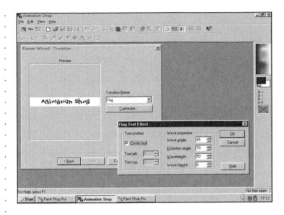

8.

In less than a few minutes, you can create a banner with dazzling effects and a professional look and feel. And with Animation Shop's other effects filters and tools, it is not a difficult task to take other graphical elements and combine them within your banner to create a sophisticated graphic that can carry your message with style.

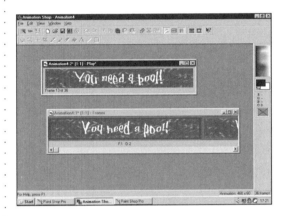

When you're ready to save your Web banner, I strongly recommend that you run the Optimization Wizard—as great as it may look, you don't want your Web banner taking up too much file space (compare it to other non-animated images on your site). This is doubly true with advertising banners—if a client has to wait for the graphic to download, he or she may become frustrated and move on.

Project 4: Watermarking

The Internet is a relatively new medium, enabling people to easily post and retrieve massive amounts of data with just the click of a mouse. And with this new terrain comes a completely new set of issues—and sometimes a new approach to some old ones, one of which is the issue of intellectual property. Not everyone has the same ideas about how they want their work displayed and used in other mediums, repackaged, redistributed, sold, or used in other artistic works online. Some people post their works online to be distributed in the public domain or under the Open Content or Artistic licenses. Others, however, do wish to further protect their claim on their work, and U.S. copyright law does support their right to do so. Many works are copyrighted—syndicated cartoons are but one important example of how popular images can be restricted in their use.

If you wish to create copyrighted and protected works for others to enjoy under *your conditions*, Paint Shop Pro does supply you with tools to help you enforce them.

1.

A watermark is a digital cryptographic code that you can embed into your images to create proof of authenticity (author, date, copyright, and so on). Watermarks are invisible to the viewer, but they're embedded in such a way that certain applications (such as Paint Shop Pro) can retrieve this information and display it.

If the image you have opened has a digital watermark embedded already, you can tell by looking at the title bar—there should be a small copyright symbol next to the name of the image.

2.

Select the Image|Watermarking|Embed Water- mark menu item to bring up the Embed Watermark dialog box. From here, you can add your watermarks and adjust various options. For example, the Image Attributes checkboxes allow you to set various conditions for your im- age—restrictions on copying, protected usage, and adult content. The Watermark Durability setting refers to the strength of the encryption— a durability of 8 or below usually results in no visible artifacts (distortions), but a stronger wa- termark, although some visible degradation may occur, creates a watermark that is much more difficult for someone to get rid of through tinkering. Once you're satisfied with your set- tings, click on the OK button to create the watermark in your image.

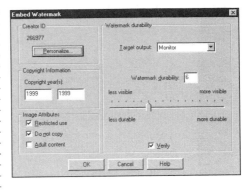

Digital watermarks are not compatible with indexed images of 256 colors or less—so you cannot use them with GIFs. However, they are handy with the JPEG format for Web use. Do make sure, however, that embedding a watermark is the last step you do before saving your image—otherwise, some editing procedures could damage the watermark.

3.

To embed a watermark, you need to obtain a Basic Digimarc ID. You can obtain one free from Digimarc (a digital authentication service). To enter your own Digimarc ID, click on the Per- sonalize button in the Embed Watermark dialog box. If you don't yet have a Digimarc ID, you can use the demo ID that comes with Paint Shop Pro to experiment with, or you can go ahead and register to receive one of your own. Regis- tering for a personal ID is easy. Click on the Register button, which will open your favorite Web browser and take you to the Digimarc Web site where you can sign up for one.

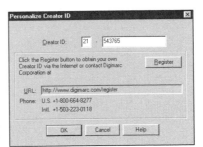

4.

Choose Image|Watermarking|Read Watermark to bring up the Watermark Information dialog box and view your (or someone else's) watermarking info. To verify the watermark, click on the Web Lookup button to view the Web site at Digimarc containing the registered and authenticated author's information.

Chapter 14
Creating Vector Graphics

 Project 1: Build a vector-based character from the ground up

 Project 2: Learn the secrets of combining vector shapes to create a cutout effect

 Project 3: Use vector objects to create a unique shape for a logo or interface template

By Ramona Pruitt

Perspective On Vectors

You've learned quite a bit about the fundamental operations of vector graphics in earlier chapters. Chapter 7 focused on the basics of vectors, and Chapter 12 included some pretty cool ways to put vector capabilities to work with text.

Now that you are armed with that base of knowledge about vectors, it's time to really get down and systematically practice techniques to gain an even better understanding and create some interesting pieces of vector art in the process.

Project 1: Rudimentary Vector Drawing

In the first chapter project, you'll experiment with vector shapes by creating a simple cartoon-like teddy bear.

1.

To prepare yourself for the creation of vector "beings," try to imagine how people and animals would appear if they were made from nothing but ovals (think of wooden puppets, for example). Learning to picture things in this way will give you a great start at the vector drawing process.

2.

Open a new image window (450 by 450 pixels will do) with a white background. In the Color palette, set the foreground color to black and the background color to a color of your choice, which will be the basic color of your character. Activate the Preset Shapes tool and set Shape Type to Ellipse, Style to Stroked And Filled, and Line Width to 1. Check both Antialias and Create As Vector.

3.

Begin by forming a medium-sized ellipse shape about half the height of the image window. Don't worry too much about size at this point. After all, one of the marvelous things about vectors is the ease with which you can resize objects.

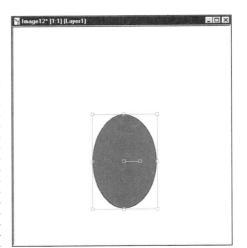

4.

Place your cursor at the lower-right corner of the Vector Object selection box. Hold down the Ctrl key and drag to the right just a little to turn the oval into an egg shape. This shape will serve as the body of the bear.

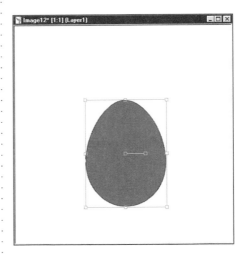

5.

Draw another, rounder ellipse just above the first shape. This is going to be the head.

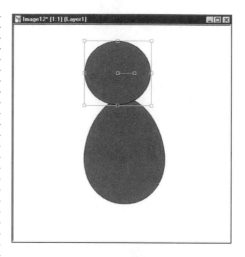

6.

To form the ears, switch the Shape Type option in the Tool Options dialog box to Circle and form a round ear on each side of the top of the head. If you want the ears to be exactly the same, you can copy the first one (Edit|Copy) and paste it as a duplicate in the same object layer (Edit|Paste As New Vector Selection).

7.

To place the ears so they will appear to be coming up from behind the head, go to the Layer palette and click on the plus sign beside the vector layer. One by one, drag the object layers (or layer, if you copied the ear) containing the ears (which will be labeled as Circle in the Layer palette) under the Ellipse object layer used as the head.

You can only drag an object layer in the stack while the object is selected with the Vector Object selection box. With the Vector Object selection tool active, a left-click on either the actual object or on the object title in the Layer palette will select it.

8.

To the left of the body shape, form another ellipse, this time in an elongated vertical manner, to use as the arm. Use the Vector Object selection box to rotate the arm and place it touching the body in the area where the shoulder would begin. Repeat on the other side to form the other arm.

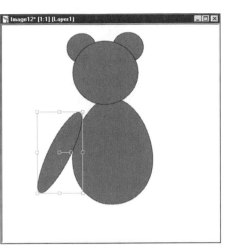

9.

Form an ellipse for each leg and foot. In the example here, the legs are attached in a sitting position.

10.

To form the muzzle, you can either keep working with the same color or switch the background color in the Color palette to a lighter or darker one for contrast. I've switched to a lighter color here. Form an ellipse for the muzzle just as you did for the body parts. Use the Ctrl key while you drag with the cursor at the upper-right corner of the Vector Object selection box to shape the ellipse so that it is just a little wider at the top.

11.

You may want to zoom in to complete the rest of the face. To form the nose, set the Preset Shapes tool to a Triangle shape type and a Filled style. Place the triangle in position and use the Vector Object selection box handles to flip the triangle over so that it is pointing down.

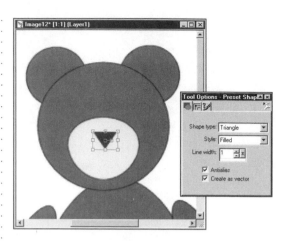

12.

Switch over to the Draw tool and set the following options:

- *Type*—Freehand Line
- *Style*—Stroked
- *Width*—1
- *Antialias*—Checked

Start at the bottom of the triangle and draw in the mouth (smiling, of course). As long as you have the Draw tool out, you may want to add a little line shaping to define the inside of the ears.

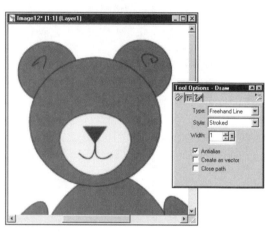

13.

For the eyes, use the Preset Shapes tool set to the Circle shape type with the Filled style (check both Antialias and Create As Vector). To make sure the eyes are the same size, draw one eye, choose Edit|Copy, and then choose Edit|Paste As New Vector Selection to get the other one.

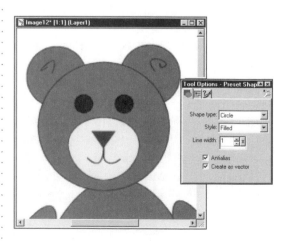

14.

To put just a little gleam on those plain black button eyes, set the foreground color to white and use the Preset Shapes tool again with the same settings used in the previous step to draw in a small white circle in each eye. Then set the foreground color back to black, draw a small black circle in each eye over the white circles, and use the center controller of the Vector Object selection box to move the black circles so they're offset just a little to the right and down from the white.

15.

Now you have your basic bear shape, but it could use some node editing and tweaking of individual characteristics to give it some personality, and maybe some fur! Activate the Vector Object selection tool and click on one of the vector components of the bear to select it. As shown in the example, I'll begin with the head.

16.

Right-click on the selection and choose Node Edit. You only have four editing nodes on a circular or elliptical shape, so you'll want to add more (a lot more!). Add nodes all along the path by holding down the Ctrl key and positioning the cursor over the path until you see the +ADD option, and then click. Repeat the process until the entire path is full of nodes.

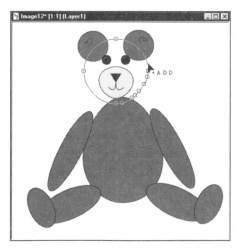

17.

Once the path has many nodes all along it, go through and pull every other node out just a little. When you're in Node Edit mode, sometimes it's hard to really know when you have done enough node editing, so you can right-click and choose Quit Node Editing at any time along the way to check your progress.

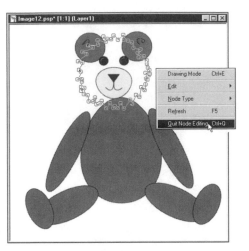

18.

Adding and pulling nodes will result in the bear having a fuzzy look (or shaggy, depending on how far out you pulled the nodes). Once you begin editing the nodes in this manner, you can go back and forth between Node Edit mode and the Quit Node Editing option to adjust the nodes to your satisfaction.

19.

Repeat the node-editing process on the other components of the image. At the points where the arms and legs meet the body, use the nodes to shape the connections to the body.

20.

An easy way to add more texture to the fur is with the texture effect. To use filters and effects, first you will need to convert the active vector layer with all its objects to raster (Layers|Convert To Raster). Go to Image|Effects| Textures and experiment with the different textures. In the example here, I've chosen texture pattern #36 from the Texture menu in the Texture dialog box, but there are several textures there that give a good "fuzzy" look.

If you don't want the texture on the muzzle, use the Magic Wand tool to select the muzzle, and then choose Selections|Invert before applying the effect.

21.

Congratulations! You have created a bear. Now you can add some finishing touches if you like. Try adding more vector ellipse shapes to form the pads on the bottom of the feet. Maybe you will want to use the Draw tool with the Freehand Line option to draw a bright bow around your bear's neck, or maybe...well, you get the idea. I'll leave the embellishments up to you and your imagination.

Project 2: Creative Cutting

In this project, you'll learn how to perform cutouts to enhance your vector shapes. Vector cutouts can be a little tricky, so follow the instructions closely.

1.

Open a new square image window with a white background. Set the foreground color in the Color palette to a dark color to contrast with the light background. Activate the Preset Shapes tool and choose the Star 2 shape. Set Style to Filled and make sure the Antialias and Create As Vector options are checked.

2.

Place your cursor near the upper-left corner inside the image window. Hold down the Shift key to maintain the aspect ratio of the star shape and drag toward the lower-right corner until the star points are fairly close to the edges, but still within the image, and release the mouse button.

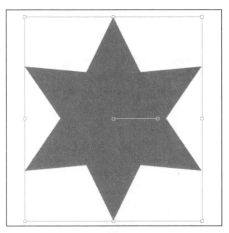

3.

Use the Preset Shapes tool with the settings you used in Step 1 to form a smaller star shape in one of the corners of the image. Once again, use the Shift key to retain the aspect ratio. The Vector Object selection box will now be present on the new shape only. As you may remember, a new shape is automatically created on its own object layer.

4.

Activate the Vector Object selection tool. In the Tool Options dialog box, click on Node Edit. The Vector Object selection box around the small star will change to nodes at each corner of the star.

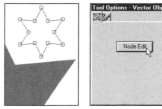

Remember that if you click anywhere outside the image window when you're in Node Edit mode, the nodes will change back into the selection box.

5.

Vector paths (including shape paths) are created by default in a clockwise manner from the start to close points. During node editing, the path can be reversed to go counterclockwise. Reverse the small star to a counterclockwise path now by right-clicking and choosing Edit|Reverse Path (you'll understand the reason for this change of direction when you get to Step 14).

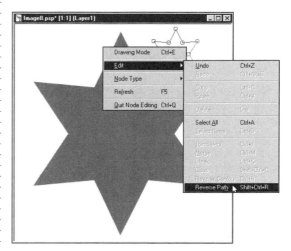

6.

Right-click in the small star to bring up the menu again and choose Edit|Select All. This will turn all nodes black, meaning that they are selected as a unit.

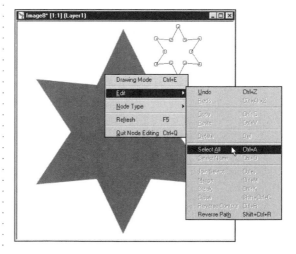

7.

Next you'll copy the selected unit to the clipboard in preparation to add it to the larger one. Right-click in the star again and choose Edit|Copy.

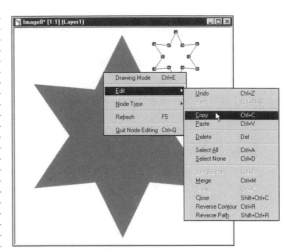

8.

Now that the small star selection is copied into the clipboard in Node Edit mode, you can eliminate the original small star and the object layer on which it was formed by first right-clicking once more on the small star and choosing Quit Node Editing, and then right-clicking and choosing Delete.

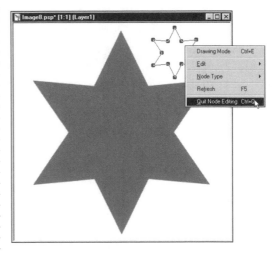

9.

Now you need to get your large star into Node Edit mode so that the smaller one in your clipboard can be pasted into it. Right-click on the large star and choose Select All, which will surround your star with the Vector Object selection box, then right-click again and Node Edit. Your image will look like the one in the example here, with nodes now at each corner point of the large star.

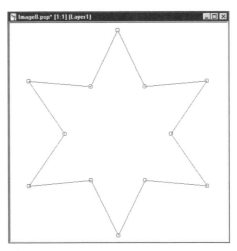

10.

Right-click in the large star and choose Edit|Paste to place the smaller star back into the image on the same object layer as the large star. Position the small star by placing the cursor directly on one of the black nodes and dragging the unit to the center of the large star.

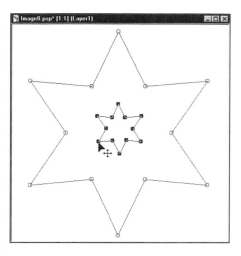

11.

Once you have the small star centered within the larger one to your satisfaction, left-click once in the center of the small star to return the nodes that were selected as a unit to normal Node Edit mode.

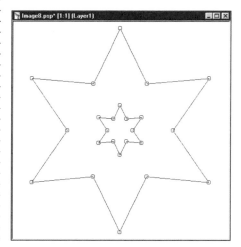

12.

One by one, pull the nodes at the outer points of the small star and place them directly on the corresponding nodes of the large star.

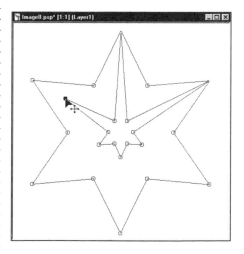

13.

Once you have the points arranged, right-click in the image and choose Quit Node Editing, and then left-click in the image to eliminate the control box.

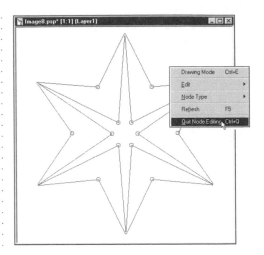

14.

When a shape with a counterclockwise path is pasted into a shape with a clockwise path (or vice versa), the result is that the contents of the pasted shape act to "cut out" any areas of the first shape where the two overlap. Hold your cursor over the star layer in the Layer palette and you'll see that the area of the small star has indeed been cut to transparency, leaving you with a much more interesting large star shape to work with than the original.

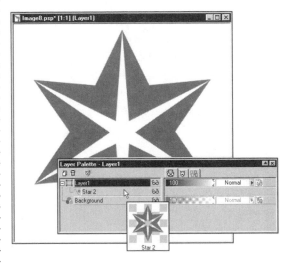

15.

Convert the layer to raster by either using the Layers menu (Layers|Convert To Raster) or right-clicking on the vector layer in the Layer palette to access the menu there.

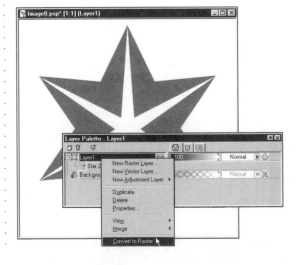

16.

Now that you have the completed shape converted to a raster layer, you can use the effects, deformations, gradients, and so on to transform and decorate your star shape in any number of ways. Use your imagination and experiment with different looks. How about a simple woodcut star? Choose Image|Effects| Sculpture (pattern #13 in the sculpture options is a nice wood look), then Image|Effects|Drop Shadow to set it off.

17.

Woodcut too conservative for you? Click on the old Undo button a couple of times to get back to the basic shape and try something else. This time, select the star by using the Rectangle selection tool to draw a rectangle surrounding the shape and then click on the image to snap the selection to the star. Use the Flood Fill tool set to the Sunburst Gradient fill style and go through the Gradient menu to find one you like.

18.

Okay, just one more, and then you're on your own with your star shape: Choose Image| Deformations|Twirl and set the twirl to 240 degrees or so to take your star to an entirely new dimension. Additionally, because the star is on its own layer, don't forget that you can change the color or pattern on the background layer for a different look altogether.

Project 3: Shape Combinations

In the final project, you'll create a combination shape that you can use for just about anything—a logo background, a Web interface, or even just a cool doodad.

1.

Open a new image window with a white background. Set the foreground color in the Color palette to black. Activate the Preset Shapes tool and set the following options:

- *Shape Type*—Rounded Rectangle

- *Style*—Filled

- *Line Width*—Any (doesn't matter)

- *Antialias And Create As Vector*—Checked.

2.

In this project, you'll be lining things up, so you may want to activate the grid lines to help you with precision (View|Grid).

3.

Place the cursor at or near the center of the image and drag to the right almost all the way to the edge of the image to form an elongated, rounded rectangle.

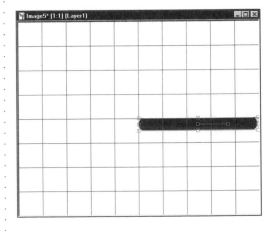

4.

Use the rotation controller of the Vector Object selection box surrounding the shape to position it so that it begins in the center of the image and points upward at an angle toward the upper-right corner. Line up the left edge of the control box with the grid line closest to the center of the image.

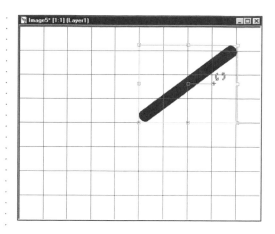

5.

Make a copy of the shape by choosing Edit|Copy and then Edit|Paste As New Vector Selection.

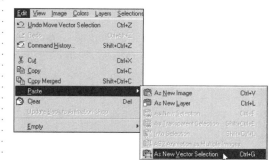

6.

Line up the pasted selection so that the shape is directly below the first shape. Use the grid line to help by once again lining up the left edge of the control box with the center grid. Repeat the copy-and-paste process until you have several of the bar shapes aligned, as shown in the example.

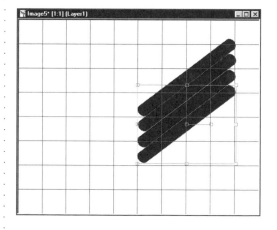

7.

Left-click once in the image area to eliminate the Vector Object selection box (or right-click and Select None). Click and drag the cursor to enclose all of the objects in a new Vector Object selection box so they're one selection.

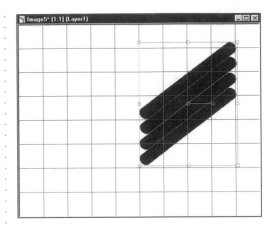

8.

Choose Edit|Copy and Edit|Paste As New Vector Selection. Click and drag the controller located in the middle of the left side of the Vector Object selection box to drag the selection to the right, until it has reversed "inside out," so to speak, so that it's an opposite of the original shape. Line up this copy with the center grid line alongside the first shape.

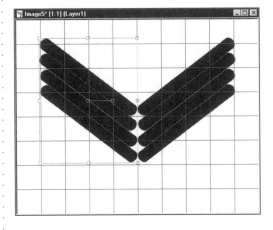

9.

Convert this layer to raster (Layers|Convert To Raster) in order to add special effects. Once it's converted, use the Rectangle selection tool to surround the shape, then left-click once on the shape to select it. Using the Flood Fill tool set to a Linear Gradient fill style, set the following Flood Fill options and fill the selected area:

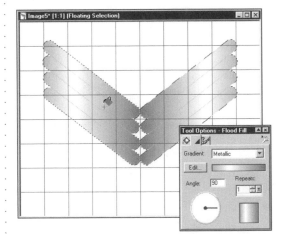

- *Gradient*—Metallic

- *Angle*—90

- *Repeats*—1

If desired, add a drop shadow (Image|Effects| Drop Shadow) to set it off and then deselect it (Selections|Select None).

10.

Activate the Preset Shapes tool once again and choose Ellipse as the shape type and Filled as the style. Check Antialias and Create As Vector. Place the cursor in the center of your image and drag outward to form a large ellipse.

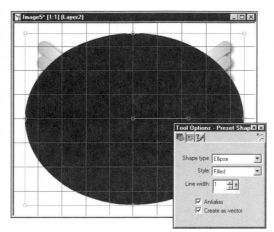

11.

Activate the Vector Object selection tool and go into Node Edit mode. You will have four nodes by default, one each at the left, right, top, and bottom.

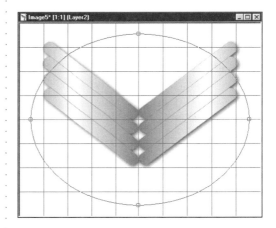

12.

Grab the bottom node with the cursor and drag it up past the center of the image, forming a sort of boomerang shape. Pull each of the side nodes downward to adjust the shape to your liking. If you end up with a shape that is different from the one shown here, but pleasing to you, then by all means keep it; the following steps will translate to any shape.

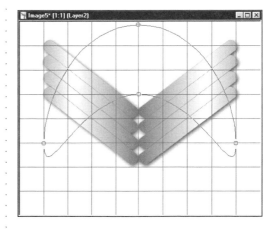

13.

Right-click on the image and choose Quit Node Editing. Use the center controller of the Vector Object selection box to move the shape down toward the bottom of the image. Line up the controllers at the top and bottom of the Vector Object selection box with the center grid line, so the shape will be centered well from left to right. You won't be needing the grid after this, so disable it via View|Grid.

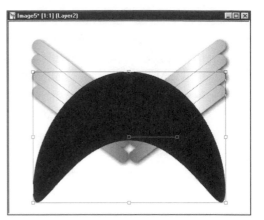

14.

Now this shape is ready for some special effects. Convert to raster (Layers|Convert To Raster). Just as you did on the last shape, use the Rectangle selection tool to surround the shape, and left-click once on the shape to select it. Use the Flood Fill tool to fill with the same metallic linear gradient, but this time, change Repeats to 0 in the Flood Fill options.

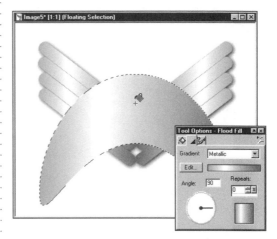

15.

What the heck, it's the last project in the book, so let's go ahead and do a couple more effects on the shape and give the edge a brushed-metal look. First, defloat the selection (Selections|Defloat) and add a drop shadow.

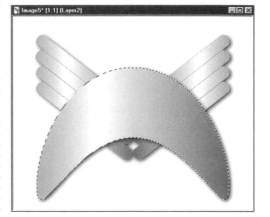

When you add a drop shadow to a floating selection, the marquee surrounds the entire area, including the shadow. If you defloat the selection before adding the drop shadow, the selection marquee will stay intact for other effects.

16.

Use the Image menu to add some noise to the selection. Go to Image|Noise|Add, set the noise percentage to 50, and choose Uniform as the type. Click on OK. This will create colored noise in your selection—pretty, but to make it look more metallic, you need to desaturate the colors. Go to Colors|Adjust|Hue/Saturation/ Lightness. Turn the saturation control all the way to the left and keep the hue and lightness controls at 0.

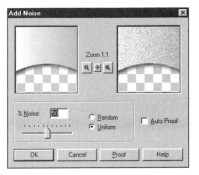

17.

Add a motion blur (Image|Blur|Motion Blur) to give the brushed-metal look. Set the angle to 315 and the blur intensity to 5 pixels or so. To sharpen the lines a little, choose Image| Sharpen|Sharpen.

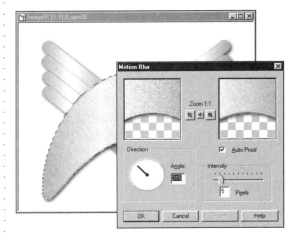

18.

Contract the selection by 10 pixels (Selections| Modify|Contract). Use the Flood Fill tool to fill the selection with (you guessed it) the metallic linear gradient. Change the gradient angle to 270 this time. Choose Selections|Select None or right-click on the image to deselect.

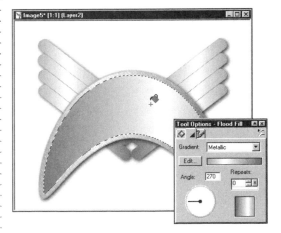

19.

Activate the layer on which the first shape was created (by default, it will be named Layer1). Use the Eraser tool to erase any area that extends below the image on the most recently created layer. When the erasing is complete, click on the top layer in the Layer palette to make it the active layer once again.

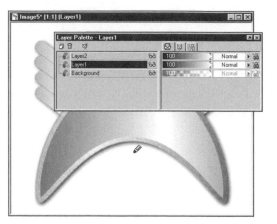

20.

Now you have your template, and you can decorate it in any number of ways. To get your creative juices flowing, I'll show you one way to add a finishing touch to the template. Using the Preset Shapes tool, change the shape style to Circle and draw a circular object. Position it in the center of the metallic plate and choose Selections|Select None.

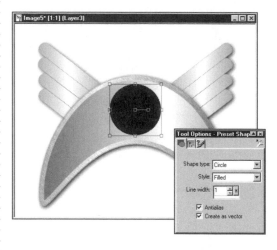

21.

Change the foreground color to white and use the Preset Shapes tool again, this time to draw a smaller white circle. Center it inside the black circle.

22.

Activate the Text tool and hold the cursor over the white circle until you see the Rocking A, indicating that the text will be placed on the path of the circle. Click to bring up the Text Entry dialog box.

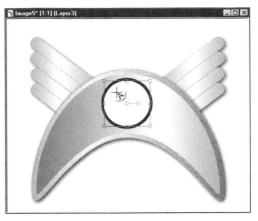

23.

Select Vector in the Create As section and check Antialias. Type in some text. Because there are so many factors involved, such as image size and which font you choose to use, it may take some experimentation to get the text size and kerning the way you want them. I want to spread the letters out some, so I've set Kerning to 350. It sounds like a lot, but if you want to spread out the letters, you have to be generous with the kerning numbers. Click on OK to apply.

24.

Now your text will be along the outside of the circle. What you are going to do next is a neat little reversal trick to get the text moved to the inside of the circle.

25.

Activate the Vector Object selection tool, right-click on the text circle, and choose Node Edit. Once your nodes are visible, right-click again and choose Edit|Reverse Path.

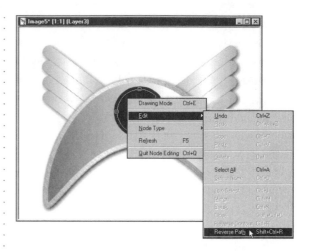

26.

Right-click one more time and choose Quit Node Editing. Your text will now be showing (seemingly miraculously) on the inside of the circle.

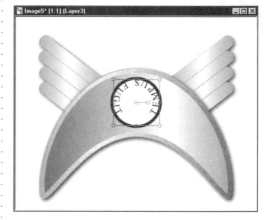

27.

Use the Vector Object selection box rotation controller to turn the text around so that it appears right-side up. Then choose Selections|Select None or click in the image to deselect it. Convert the layer to raster (Layers|Convert To Raster). Use the Rectangle selection tool to surround the circle and left-click once on the image to select it. Apply a cutout effect (Image|Effects|Cutout) with 0 offset values to give the white circle just a slight inner shading.

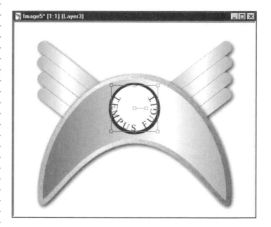

28.

Because my text had a "timely" message, I've used the Draw tool to simply place a couple of clock hands in the middle of the circle. And the message is one that holds especially true when you are doing something you love, like creating graphics. Time absolutely flies! Enjoy.

Index

Z